THE
FLOWER OF
ALL CITIES

THE
FLOWER OF
ALL CITIES

THE HISTORY OF LONDON FROM
EARLIEST TIMES TO THE GREAT FIRE

Dr Robert Wynn Jones

AMBERLEY

First published 2019

Amberley Publishing
The Hill, Stroud
Gloucestershire, GL5 4EP

www.amberley-books.com

British Library Cataloguing in Publication Data.
A catalogue record for this book is available from the British Library.

ISBN 978 1 4456 9135 0 (hardback)
ISBN 978 1 4456 9136 7 (ebook)

Typesetting by Aura Technology and Software Services, India.
Printed in the UK.

Contents

Preface		7
Acknowledgements and Dedication		8
Chapter One	Bedrock and Foundation	9
Chapter Two	Ancient British or Celtic London	11
Chapter Three	Roman London (*c.* 47/8–410)	15
	Social History	16
	Building Works	19
	Archaeological Finds	22
Chapter Four	Dark Age (Saxon and Viking) London (*c.* 410–1066)	25
	Social History	27
	Building Works	30
	Archaeological Finds	33
Chapter Five	Medieval London (1066–1485)	35
	Norman History	37
	Plantagenet History	38
	Lancastrian and Yorkist History, and the Wars of the Roses	47
	Social History	53
	Building Works	76
	Archaeological Finds	92

Chapter Six   Post-Medieval (Tudor and Stuart)
                     London (1485–1666)   93
                 Tudor History   97
                 Stuart History   116
                 Social History   132
                 Building Works   164
                 Archaeological Finds   180
Chapter Seven   The Great Fire   181
Chapter Eight   Aftermath   188
Appendices   194
   Appendix One   Roman Londinium Walk   194
   Appendix Two   Saxon Lundenburg Walk   202
   Appendix Three Medieval City of London Walk   207
   Appendix Four   Tudor and Stuart City of London Walk   225

Bibliography and References   240
   Other Resources   269
Index   271

Preface

A large part of London, and almost all of the old walled City that lay at its heart, was burned down over the space of a few short days during the Great Fire of 2–6 September 1666. This book attempts as it were to unearth from the ashes something of the already age-old and burnished City that had gone before. The City founded by the Romans in the middle of the first century AD, on the damp maritime frontier of their vast continental empire, and named by them Londinium. The City abandoned by the Romans at the beginning of what some still think of as the 'Dark Ages' of the seaborne Saxons and Vikings, and known by the former in turn as Lundenwic and Lundenburg. And the City of the – later – Middle Ages or Medieval period, and the post-Medieval or early Modern, one of the first true world-cities, called by some Londinopolis. A City of bustling waterfronts and imposing walls, of praying spires and nodding masts, of plunging shadow and abiding light. That which the poet William Dunbar in 1501 described as 'sovereign of Cities' and 'the flower of Cities all'.

The City of London as presently defined incorporates some areas that lie a little outside the original walls (including Southwark, south of the river). Pre-Great Fire Greater London, that is to say the more-or-less continuously built-up area, extended even farther out, especially along the Thames: on the north side of the river, as far west as the West End and Westminster, as far north as Spitalfields and Shoreditch and as far east as Stepney, Wapping, Shadwell, Ratcliff, Limehouse, Poplar and Blackwall; and on the south side, as far west as Lambeth and Vauxhall, as far south as Borough and Newington, and as far east as Bermondsey and Rotherhithe, but not as far as Deptford, Greenwich, and Woolwich, which remained isolated settlements. The Great Fire was substantially confined to the old walled city.

Acknowledgements and Dedication

I wish to acknowledge the great help given by the Guildhall Library and by the Museum of London, and Jon Jackson, Nikki Embery and Shaun Barrington of Amberley in seeing the project through to publication. I would also like to thank my wife, Heather, and my younger son Gethin, for their forbearance, and for their assistance in the production of the maps.

This book is dedicated to the memory of my father, Emrys, who died while I was writing it. Goodbye, lovely man.

CHAPTER ONE

Bedrock and Foundation

The bedrock on which London is built is arranged in the form of a basin, with its base buried beneath the city, and its rim exposed at the surface in the Chilterns to the north and in the North Downs to the south. The basin is filled with, in ascending order, chalk, London Clay, and Thames alluvium. Chalk is composed of the skeletal remains of innumerable individually microscopic algae and associated organisms that once flourished in an ancient ocean around 100 million years ago. It is a porous rock and contains an abundant underground water supply, capable of being tapped into through so-called Artesian wells. London Clay, in contrast, is non-porous, impervious to the flow of water, and poorly drained, and often associated with presently or formerly marshy areas. It is constituted of detrital clay, silt and sand as well as abundant plant and primitive animal fossils, for which latter the site of Abbey Wood in south-east London is famous, accumulated on the strandline of a sub-tropical sea some 50 million years ago. Thames alluvium is formed of material deposited along the watercourse of the city's river, past and present. The Thames assumed its present course when it was diverted during the Ice Age a few hundred thousand years ago. During glacial periods of the Ice Age, woolly mammoths roamed the then tundra around what is now Canary Wharf, and reindeer around Royal Oak. During the last inter-glacial, elephants and hippopotamuses wallowed in water-holes in what is now Trafalgar Square.

The human occupation of Britain began during the Ice Age. Footprints have been found in inter-glacial deposits at Happisburgh in Norfolk that date back around 750,000 years, and actual human remains in inter-glacial deposits at Boxgrove in West Sussex that date back around half a million years. It appears, though, that humans were essentially unable to live in Britain during glacial periods, and only really became established here in the post-glacial period, during the thaw, and the regrowth of the wildwood, commencing some fifteen thousand or so years ago.

There is – albeit sparse – archaeological evidence from Stratford to the east of London, Southwark to the south, Hounslow and Uxbridge to the west, and Hampstead to the north, for hunting and gathering activity in the Late Palaeolithic (Old Stone Age); and for woodland clearance and farming in the Mesolithic (Middle Stone Age) and Neolithic (New Stone Age), between the eighth and fourth centuries BCE (Merriman, 1990; see also, for example, Bishop *et al.,* 2017). There are also the remains of a Mesolithic flint-tool manufactory at North Woolwich, a Mesolithic timber structure of as yet undetermined function at Vauxhall, a Neolithic henge at Hackney Wells, and a reportedly Neolithic barrow-burial at what is now known as 'King Henry's Mound' in Richmond Park.

Further Reading
Bishop et al., 2017; Clements, 2010; Merriman, 1990; Sidell et al., 2000.

CHAPTER TWO

Ancient British or Celtic London

There is archaeological evidence from a number of localities around London for at least transient settlement and associated activity, by Ancient Britons or Celts, in the Bronze Age, in the third and second millennia BC/BCE, and in the Iron Age, in the first millennium BC/BCE. Bronze Age timbers still survive at Plumstead, together with a number of Bronze Age burial mounds, including the so-called 'Boudicca's Grave' on Parliament Hill, and the 'Shrewsbury Tumulus' on Shooters Hill (*Figures 1, 2*). And a number of hill-forts or

1. Bronze Age Boudicca's Grave, Parliament Hill.

2. Bronze Age Shrewsbury Tumulus, Shooters Hill.

enclosures survive from the Iron Age, including 'Caesar's Camp' on Wimbledon Common, and Ambresbury Banks and Loughton Camp, both in the timeless wilds of Epping Forest (*Figures 3, 1c, colour plates*). 'Grim's Dyke', an intermittently preserved bank-and-ditch earthwork running for some miles through North-West London, from Pinner Green, or possibly Ruislip, to Harrow Weald Common, or possibly Stanmore, also survives from the Iron Age (*Figure 2c*). It is thought to have marked the boundary of the territory occupied by a tribe of Ancient Britons or Celts known as the Catuvellauni, which had its heartland on the north side of the Thames, in and around London and the northern Home Counties, and its capital at Verlamion (modern St Albans in Hertfordshire). The Catuvellaunian tribal territory was bordered to the north and east by those of the Corieltauvi, Iceni and Trinovantes, to the south by those of the Cantiaci and Atrebates, and to the west by that of the Dobunii. Incidentally, it is not known for certain what the Ancient Britons called London. Coates (1998) has suggested *Lowonidonjon*, meaning something like 'settlement on the Thames', and deriving in part from a pre-Celtic name for the London section of the Thames, *Plowonida*

3. Iron Age hill-fort, 'Caesar's Camp', Wimbledon Common.

('river too wide to ford'). According to the antiquarian John Stow, in his magisterial *Survay of London, written in the Year 1598*:

> Geoffrey of Monmouth ... reporteth that Brute [Brutus of Troy], lineally descended from the demi-god Aeneas, the son of Venus, daughter of Jupiter, about the year of the world 2855, and 1108 before the nativity of Christ, built this city near unto the river now called Thames, and named it Troynovant [New Troy] ... King Lud ... afterwards ... increased the same with fair buildings, towers and walls, and after his own name called it Caire-Lud ... This Lud has issue two sons, Androgeus and Theomantius, who being not of an age to govern at the death of their father, their uncle Cassibelan took upon him the crown: about the eighth year of whose reign, Julius Caesar arrived in this land with a great power of Romans to conquer it.

Geoffrey of Monmouth has since been thoroughly discredited, not least for 'interlacing divine matters with human, to make the first foundation ... more ... sacred'. Though some historians have recently attempted to defend his *Historium Regum Britanniae* as being, at the very least, not a complete fantasy. Cassibelan, or Cassivelaunus, for example, was an actual historical figure, and most likely belonged to the Catuvellauni (see above). The Catuvellauni are documented as having resisted the Roman invasion under Caesar in 55-4BCE, and it is speculated that they engaged the Romans in battle at Brentford as they attempted to cross the Thames from south to north.

The only actual archaeological features from the Bronze or Iron Ages still surviving in Central London are some enigmatic pits and post-holes interpreted as representing the sites of former homesteads or farmsteads, in Leicester Square in the West End, near the Houses of Parliament in Westminster, and south of the Thames in Southwark, and the remains of a bridge or jetty at Vauxhall. There are no features at all in the City of London, perhaps at least in part because, again as Stow put it, '... the Britons call that a town ... when they have fortified a cumbersome wood with a ditch and rampart.' This period of the city's history remains opaque.

Important archaeological finds from the Bronze or Iron Ages include much equipment associated with horses and chariots, a horned helmet recovered from the Thames at Waterloo, and an ornate shield recovered from the Thames at Battersea (possibly offered as a plea to the gods of the river at the time of the Roman invasion), as well as more everyday items such as worked flints, pot-sherds, and coins, some of them from Cannon Street in the City (Elsden, 2002).

Further Reading
Cotton, 2017; Elsden, 2002; Gordon, 1932; Merriman, 1990; Parsons, 1927; Taylor, 2018.

CHAPTER THREE

Roman London (*c.* 47/8-410)

Rome under Claudius invaded Britain in 43CE, and Roman London, or Londinium, was founded in c. 47-8, as evidenced by dendrochronological or tree-ring dating of timbers from a Roman drain uncovered during archaeological excavations at No. 1 Poultry (see Further Reading). The city was sited in a strategic position on high ground overlooking the Thames, at the lowest crossing-point on the river, and at a point at which it was also still tidal, enabling easy access to the open sea, and the empire beyond the sea. (There is some evidence that the tidal head moved downstream in the later Roman period, and that some port facilities followed it, from the City eastward toward Shadwell and Ratcliff.) If Rome was built on seven hills, Roman London was built on two, Ludgate Hill to the west, and Cornhill to the east, with the valley of one of the 'lost' Thames tributaries – the Walbrook – in between.

The early Roman city was razed by revolting ancient Britons under Boudica or Boudicca (Boadicea of the Victorian re-imagining), the Queen of the Iceni, in 60 or 61, while the legions under the Governor Suetonius Paulinus were away attacking the druid stronghold on Anglesey. Tacitus wrote: 'The inhabitants ... who stayed because they were women, or old, or attached to the place, were slaughtered ... For the British ... could not wait to cut throats, hang, burn and crucify – as though avenging, in advance, the retribution that was on its way.' This was the so-called Battle of Watling Street, one of the many purported locations for which is the aforementioned Ambresbury Banks.

After the Boudiccan revolt, the city was rebuilt, initially by the Procurator Julius Alpinus Classicianus under the Emperor Nero, and subsequently under the Flavian, Trajanic and Hadrianic emperorships, in the late first to early second centuries, only to be partially destroyed again by the so-called 'Hadrianic fire', *c.* 125 (Dunning, 1945). The enclosing wall was built at the turn of the second and third centuries.

The city then declined through the 'crisis' of the third century, and into the fourth, during which time the Roman Empire as a whole came under increasing attack from within as well as without – Britain was ruled by its own rival Emperors Clodius Albinus in the late second century, and Carausius and Allectus in the 'Carausian Revolt' of the third, after which it was retaken by the Emperor Constantius Chlorus in 296. It appears that many of Roman London's public buildings, including the 'Governor's Palace', the Basilica and the Forum, were more or less demolished at the turn of the third and fourth centuries – perhaps as punishment for perceived British support of the Carausian Revolt. 'Barbarian' raids – by Picts and Gaels, and by Saxons and other Germanic tribes – began in the fourth century. The city finally fell and was essentially abandoned in the early fifth, around 410, after the occupying army and the civilian administration, the instruments of Empire, were recalled to Rome to assist in its defence against the encroaching Barbarians (on the orders of the Emperor Honorius).

Social History
The social history of Roman London is discussed by, among others, Porter (2000) (see Further Reading). Everyday London life in Roman – as indeed in all other – times would have revolved around the search for sustenance for body and soul.

Religion
The predominant religion during the early part of the Roman occupation was pantheistic paganism, which perceived deities in all things, abstract as well as tangible; and during the later part, Christianity. The principal funerary rite was cremation, although this later gave way to inhumation. Remains were typically buried outside the city limits, for example, just outside Aldgate, Bishopsgate, or Newgate, or beside the Walbrook in Moorfields, or on the south side of the Thames in Southwark. One particular fourth-century Roman woman was buried in Spitalfields, just outside Bishopsgate, in a decorated lead coffin inside a plain stone sarcophagus, resting on a bed of laurel leaves, shrouded in damask silk interwoven with gold thread, covered in an

Imperial Purple robe and accompanied by further high-status grave goods, including delicately wrought glass vials that once contained oil, perfume, and possibly wine, and a carved jet box and hair-pins. Isotopic evidence from her teeth indicates that she may actually have come from Rome itself. A facial reconstruction of her can be seen in the Roman gallery in the Museum of London. Interestingly, at least one woman buried in the southern cemetery in Southwark has been determined on morphometric and isotopic evidence to have been of Black African origin (Ridgeway *et al.*, 2013). And a further two individuals buried in Southwark have been determined to have come from the Han Empire in what is now China (Redfern *et al.*, 2016).

Mithraism, the cult of the god Mithras, was one of the many forms of paganism evidently in existence in Roman London, where there was a dedicated Temple of Mithras, or Mithraeum. It originated in Persia, where Mithras was one of many gods in the Zoroastrian pantheon, arriving in Rome in the first century BCE and spread throughout much of the Roman Empire by the first century CE and was at its zenith in the third. According to the Roman version of the Mithracan creation-myth, Mithras was ordered by the god of the Sun, Apollo, to slay the bull of the Moon to release its vital-force, in order to bring life to the Earth (carved reliefs of the bull-slaying – or 'tauroctony' – are characteristic features of Mithraean iconography). He eventually came to be identified with the *Sol Invictus*, or Unconquered Sun, and to epitomise the moral virtues of fidelity, loyalty and obedience (whence, presumably, his supposed popularity with Roman soldiers). Mithraism was practised in dedicated Mithraea, each representing the heavens, with stars and zodiacal symbols painted on the ceilings. Many Mithraea, including that in London, were at least partly underground, because Mithras slew the bull underground (in a cave).

Christianity arrived in the late Roman period, after the conversion of Emperor Constantine in 312, and the passage of the Edict of Milan, which ensured tolerance of Christianity, in 313 (at least one representative from Londinium, named Restitutus, attended the Christian Council of Arles in 314). There is little surviving evidence of Christian worship in Roman London, and hardly any of the existence of Christian places of worship (but see under 'Building Works' below). However, a metal bowl inscribed with the Christian 'Chi-Rho' symbol has been found in Copthall Close in the City, and in the River

Walbrook; and a number of ingots also inscribed with the symbol, together with the words *Spes in Deo* (Hope in God), in the River Thames near Battersea Bridge.

Food and Drink
The diet of the average citizen of Roman London would appear to have been a surprisingly healthy one. There were evidently numerous shops both within the Forum and lining the roads leading to and from it, where all manner of imported as well as locally produced foodstuffs could be bought, including olives, olive oil, wine, grape juice, dates, figs, salted fish and fish sauce, from all around the Empire. The remains of a bakery and hot food shop have been unearthed on Poultry, more bakeries on Pudding Lane and Fenchurch Street, and those of a mill on Princes Street. The remains of two 'water-lifting machines', one at 63 and the other at 110, have been unearthed on Gresham Street, and those of a system of water pipes on Poultry.

Sanitary conditions were also conducive to good public health. There were numerous bath-houses intended for daily use, for example, public ones on Cheapside and Huggin Hill, dating to the late first or early second century; and a private one in Billingsgate, dating to the late second to third. There was even a rudimentary drainage and sewerage system.

Administration and Governance
The population of Roman London is estimated to have been at most a few tens of thousands, essentially the same as that of Pompeii, a provincial town in Italy. In contrast, that of the coeval imperial capital, Rome itself, was of the order of one million.

The province of Britannia was governed centrally from Rome, and neither it nor its provincial capitals, including London, had much in the way of locally devolved power. Nonetheless, Londinium had become a comparatively important administrative centre by the turn of the first and second centuries. Its principal public building, possibly the largest north of the Alps, was the *Basilica*. Also here was the 'Governor's Palace'.

Trade and Commerce
Roman London was important as a commercial and trading centre, with the port at its heart (see Smither, 2017, on the trade crafts, and the systems of weights and measures used for the various commodities).

Tiles stamped *CLBR* have been found in London, suggesting at least some link between the port and the *Classis Britannica* or 'British fleet', which was the part of the Roman imperial navy responsible for supplying the province of Britannia with personnel and material. Foodstuffs were brought into the port-city by boat from all around the Empire, in amphorae. Pottery, notably Samian ware, was also brought in from Gaul; brooches from Belgium; amber from the Baltic; millstones from the Rhineland; decorative marble, bronze table-ware and lamps from Italy; marble from Greece and Turkey; glassware from Syria; and emeralds from Egypt. Slaves were also brought into London, to be sold at markets like those known to have existed on the waterfront, and then put to work (in the worst cases, as draught-animals, for example, turning water-wheels; or as concubines or prostitutes). A recently discovered writing tablet of *c.* 80 CE records the sale of a Gaulish slave-girl called Fortunata – 'warranted healthy and not liable to run away' – to a senior imperial slave called Vegetus for 600 *denarii*. This was a substantial sum, approximately equivalent to two year's wages for a skilled labourer.

Building Works

Restoring the mosaic of Roman London from the isolated *tesserae* that remain is a challenging task. The Roman London Bridge and embryonic Port of London was originally built *c.* 50. A recently discovered post-Boudiccan fort on Mincing Lane was built in *c.* 63, although it appears to have been out of use by *c.* 80 (Dunwoodie *et al.*, 2016). The Governor's Palace was built during the Flavian period of the late first century, *c.* 69-96, on the then waterfront, which was much farther north in Roman times than it is today. It remained in use throughout the second and third, before being substantially demolished at the turn of the third and fourth, the remains being discovered during the nineteenth. The first undoubted Basilica and Forum were built in *c.* 70 (there may have been earlier ones, destroyed during the Boudiccan Revolt of 60 or 61), and rebuilt and considerably extended *c.* 100-30, before being substantially demolished *c.* 300, the remains being discovered during excavations at 168 Fenchurch Street in 1995-2000. The Amphitheatre was originally built in timber in *c.* 75, rebuilt in stone in the second century, and renovated in the late second to early fourth, before falling into disuse, and eventually being substantially demolished in the late fourth, possibly around 365, the remains coming to light again during excavations on the site of the Medieval Guildhall in 1987.

The City wall, incorporating the early second-century fort at Cripplegate to the north-west, was originally built in the late second to early third century, from east to west; extended from the mid to late third onwards, when a river wall was added; and strengthened in the mid fourth, when bastions were added (the original wall cuts through and thus post-dates a deposit containing a coin of Commodus dating to 183-4, and is in part contemporary with a deposit containing a coin of Caracalla dating to 213-7) (Bell *et al.*, 1937). There being no local source of stone, the wall was constructed with an estimated 85,000 tons of Kentish ragstone, quarried near Maidstone and transported down the Medway and up the Thames to London on barges, the remains of one of which have been found at Blackfriars, with its 50-ton cargo intact.

The Temple of Mithras on the Walbrook was originally built in the early third century, *c.* 220-40, and abandoned in the fourth, when Christianity came to replace paganism throughout the Roman Empire, the remains being revealed during the Blitz. The Temple of Mithras was reconstructed on Queen Victoria Street in 1962, and reconstructed again – inside a specially designed space – in the Bloomberg Building on Walbrook in 2017. Some of the finds from the recent archaeological dig on and around the temple site may be viewed in the Bloomberg Space (other finds from the original post-war dig, including a marble bust of Mithras in his distinctive Phrygian cap, may be viewed in the Roman gallery in the Museum of London).

There was probably also a Temple of Isis on the Thames in the third century, as indicated by the finding of a re-used altar stone dedicated to the goddess in Blackfriars; and plausibly a Temple of Diana on Ludgate Hill, as indicated by the finding of a bronze statuette of the goddess to the south-west of St Paul's Cathedral, between the Deanery and Blackfriars (Schofield, 2011). (No Temple of Cybele has as yet been found, although the worship of that goddess was evidently practised in Roman London, as indicated by the finding in the Thames of a curious piece of liturgical equipment, interpreted by some as a 'castration clamp', featuring figures of her and of consort Atys, and also by the findings at various locations in the city of figurines of Atys.

An enigmatic, only partially excavated building, variously interpreted as a late Roman Basilica or – on the basis of similarity to the *Basilica di Santa Tecla* in Milan – a palaeo-Christian church or cathedral, was built in the south-east, between Pepys Street and Trinity Square, sometime in the fourth century. Note also that a late Roman, fourth-century origin has been postulated, although not proven, both for the church of St Peter-upon-Cornhill in the City and for St Pancras Old Church in Camden. Perhaps significantly in this context, the present church of St Peter-upon-Cornhill lies, and presumably the previous one(s) lay, within the footprint of the disused second- to third-century Basilica, possibly at least in part adopting its form, as was common practice in the early Christian church. In the case of St Pancras Old Church, there is clearly recognisable Roman tiling incorporated into the surviving Norman north wall, which could indeed have been robbed from a Christian church that once stood on the site – or perhaps from a pagan *compitum* or shrine (such as was often located on such prominent ground adjacent to a water-course). The local historian Charles Lee went so far – in other words possibly too far – as to suggest a date, 'possibly as early as 313 or 314' (313 was the year of the Edict of Milan, which ensured tolerance of Christianity; and 314 was the year of the Christian Council of Arles). The fourteen-year-old Roman citizen Pancras was martyred on the orders of the Emperor Diocletian in 304.

The Roman roads within and outwith the City radiate out from the Basilica and Forum toward and beyond the various City Gates, which were, anti-clockwise from the east, Aldgate, Bishopsgate, Cripplegate, Aldersgate, Newgate and Ludgate (Moorgate, between Bishopsgate and Cripplegate, was a later addition). Interestingly, the Romans do not appear to have had names for their roads. Ermine Street, which was the main south-to-north route of Roman Britain, linking London to Lincoln and York, takes its name from the Saxon Earninga straet, after one Earn(e). Watling Street, the main east-to-west route, linking Richborough on the Kent coast to London and London to Wroxeter, takes its name from the Saxon Waeclinga straet, after one Waecel.

Surviving Structures
Essentially the only structures that survive from Roman London are parts of the 'Governor's Palace', the Basilica and Forum, the Amphitheatre (*Figure 3c*), the City wall (*Figure 4c*) and the Temple

4. Temple of Mithras, Bloomberg Building, Walbrook (*c.* 220-40).

of Mithras (*Figure 4*). The Governor's Palace forms a Scheduled Ancient Monument substantially buried beneath Cannon Street Station (the so-called 'London Stone' that stands opposite the station is likely a relic of the palace). A pier base from the Basilica can be seen in the basement of No. 90 Gracechurch Street. The Amphitheatre and associated artefacts can be viewed in the basement of the Guildhall. The best-preserved sections of the City wall are near the Museum of London on London Wall to the west, and around Tower Hill to the east. As noted above, the recently reconstructed Temple of Mithras may be viewed inside the Bloomberg Building on Walbrook.

With the sole exception of the wall, all of these structures, are below – and indeed 20 ft or more below – modern street level. Over the two millennia of London's existence, street level has risen at an average rate of 1 ft per 100 years – simply through the accumulation of demolition rubble.

Archaeological Finds
The more important archaeological finds from Roman London are on exhibition in the City's principal museums, that is to say, the Museum

of London on London Wall, the British Museum in Bloomsbury in the West End, and the Victoria and Albert in South Kensington. There are also interesting displays of *in situ* Roman tessellated pavements and of associated finds in the crypts of the churches of All Hallows Barking, on Byward Street, and St Bride, off Fleet Street. All Hallows Barking also features a fine dioramic reconstruction of Roman London (made before the Amphitheatre was discoved). Part of a timber from one of the Roman wharves stands outside St Magnus the Martyr on Lower Thames Street. Another part of the same timber has recently been dendrochronologically dated to 62 or 63 (that is, immediately after the Boudiccan Revolt).

The Museum of London houses a particularly extensive collection of finds from Roman London in its Roman gallery, including an excellent display of those from the Temple of Mithras. It also features fine scale models of the Roman London Bridge and waterfront, the Basilica and Forum, and the Huggin Hill bath-house; and reconstructions of a kitchen from a high-status Roman house, and of two formal dining rooms, or *triclinia* (sing., *triclinium*), complete with mosaics.

A series of Museum of London and other publications describe in detail the findings of archaeological excavations on the Roman London Bridge and waterfront, Governor's Palace, Basilica and Forum, Amphitheatre, and Temple of Mithras. On Poultry, entire streets of Roman houses of various status have been described; and on Gresham Street, a number of Romano-British round-houses. Other pubications describe the findings from around the various gates to the Roman city, from the waterfront, and from Southwark, south of the river (see, for example, Killock *et al.*, 2015). One further publication worthy of mention describes the only Roman villa in a London Borough, in Orpington in Bromley (Philp, 1996).

Note here that recent excavations on the Bloomberg Building site to the west of the street of Walbrook have led to one of the most important archaeological discoveries ever made in London, that of the so-called Pompeii of the North (Hill & Rowsome, 2011). Here have been uncovered an entire Roman waterfront development, and many, many thousands of artefacts – including, importantly, many made of organic materials that would normally have perished but that were preserved in the abnormal anaerobic conditions of the waterlogged deposits of the river Walbrook (see, for example, Tomlin, 2016, on the writing tablets – 'Roman London's first voices').

Further Reading

Ackroyd, 2000, 2011; Aldhouse-Green, 2018; Anonymous, undated; Bateman, 2000, 2011; Bateman et al., 2008; Bell et al., 1937; Bird et al., 1996; Brigham & Woodger, 2001; Burford, 1973, 1990; Casson et al., 2014; Cotton et al., 2014; de la Bedoyere, 2013; Derwent, 1968; Dunning, 1945; Dunwoodie, 2004; Dunwoodie et al., 2016; Elliott, 2018; Elsden, 2002; Elsden & Howe, 1923; Grimes, 1968; Hall & Merrifield, 1986; Harris, 2009; Hibbert, 1969; Hill & Rowsome, 2011; Hingley, 2018; Home, 1948; Inwood, 1998, 2008; Killock et al., 2015; Lewis, 2008; Marsden, 1975, 1980, 1987, 1994, 2018; Matthews, 2008; Merrifield, 1969, 1983; Milne, 1985, 1992, 1995; Mitchell & Leys, 1958; Morris, 1982; Panton, 2005; Pearson, 2006; Perring, 1991; Redfern et al., 2016; Richardson, 1995, 2000; Ridgeway et al., 2013; Ross & Clark, 2008; Rowsome, 2000, 2018; Saint & Darley, 1994; Schofield, 2011; Shepherd, 1998; Stone, 2017; Thomas, 2004; Tomlin, 2016; Toynbee, 1986; Wallace, 2014; Walsh, 2018; Webb, 2011a; White, 2010; Wright, 2017.

CHAPTER FOUR

Dark Age (Saxon and Viking) London (*c.* 410-1066)

Considerably less is known about this period of history than either the succeeding or preceding one, such that it is often referred to as the 'Dark Ages'. One of the reasons we know so little is that the Saxons appear to have built almost exclusively using perishable materials such as timber, wattle-and-daub, and thatch, which typically leave very little archaeological record. What is known is that there was essentially a hiatus in the occupation of London between when the Romans left, in the fifth century, and when the Saxons arrived in numbers at the turn of the sixth and seventh (archaeological evidence points to a Saxon presence in the city, although not a full-scale occupation, from around 430-450).

When the Saxons did arrive, they chose for some reason to make their principal settlement about a mile to the west (upstream), and without the wall, of the old Roman City of Londinium, around what is now Aldwych in the City of Westminster, and they named it Lundenwic. Lundenwic became subject to increasingly frequent and savage raids by the Vikings in the ninth century. On the wings of dragons they came in 839, axes agleam, and according to the Old English *Anglo-Saxon Chronicle* went only after 'great slaughter'. And back they came in 851 and 'stormed ... London', and again in 872 'and there chose their winter-quarters'.

In 878, Alfred the Great emerged from the fastnesses of Athelney to defeat the Vikings at the Battle of Edington in Wiltshire, and subsequently to force them to withdraw into what became known as the Danelaw in the north and east of the country (east of the River Lea in London). Eight years later, in 886, according to Asser, a monk and later Bishop of Sherborne, in his *Life of King Alfred*, written in 893, he 'restored the [Roman] city of London [Londinium] ... splendidly ... and made it habitable again ...' and moved the Saxon settlement to within its perimeter and river walls, and renamed it Lundenburg. In the process, he set out the street plan that still in essence survives to this day. He then 'entrusted it [and command of its *burgwara* or militia] to the care of [his son-in-law] Ethe(l)red, ealdorman of the Mercians.'

The raids continued, though. In 994, again according to the *Chronicle*, 'Swein [Forkbeard, the Danish King] came into London ... with 94 ships, and they proceeded to attack the city stoutly and wished also to set it on fire... But the holy Mother of God showed her mercy to the citizens on that day and saved them from their enemies.'

In 1013, the city fell again to the Danish Vikings, albeit only temporarily, being retaken in 1014 by the English King Ethelred 'The Unready', in alliance with the Norwegian Viking Olaf, Olav or Olave Haraldsson. According to the Norse 'Olaf Sagas', Olaf destroyed the Saxon incarnation of London Bridge and the Danish Viking army assembled on it by pulling it down with ropes tied to his long-boats. The court poet Ottar Svarte wrote, in the eleventh century, and Snorri Sturluson rewrote, in the thirteenth: 'London Bridge is broken down./Gold is won, and bright renown./Shields resounding, war-horns sounding,/Hild is shouting in the din!/Arrows singing, mail-coats ringing – /Odin makes our Olaf win.' (Many believe this ode to be the origin of the nursery-rhyme 'London Bridge is Falling Down'.) Olaf later converted to Christianity, and, as King Olaf II, introduced the religion to Norway in 1015. He went on to be martyred fighting heathen Danish Vikings at the Battle of Stiklestad in 1030, and to be canonised by the English Bishop of Selsey, Grimkell or Grimketel, in 1031 (the local canonisation was later confirmed by Pope Alexander III in 1164). In the later Middle Ages, his tomb, in the most northerly cathedral in Christendom, in Nidaros (Trondheim), became an important pilgrimage site, and the centre of a widespread 'cult of Olav'. A number of churches in and around the City of London are or were dedicated to him, including St Nicholas Olave, St Olave Broad Street, St Olave Hart Street, St Olave Jewry and St Olave Silver Street in the City, St Olave in Southwark, and St Olave in Rotherhithe.

In 1016, the Viking Cnut, son of Swein Forkbeard, son of Harald Bluetooth, decisively defeated in battle the Saxon Edmund 'Ironside', son of Ethelred and Aelgifu of York, to become King of England as well as Denmark; and in 1017 he married Ethelred's widow, Emma of Normandy, one of the more remarkable women of the age, wife of two kings, mother of two more, and in her own right an influential political as well as important dynastic figure, as described in the *Encomium Emmae Reginae*. Cnut was in turn succeeded by Harold Harefoot, his son by Aelgifu of Northampton, in 1035, and Hardicanute, his son by Emma, in 1040.

Finally, the Saxon Edward the Confessor, son of Ethelred and Emma, became King when the Viking Hardicanute died, leaving no heir, in 1042; followed by the ill-fated Harold Godwinson, Harold II, in 1066.

Social History

The social history of Saxon London is discussed by, among others, Porter (2000) and Mount (2014) (see also 'Further Reading' section). The role of women in Saxon society – in London and elsewhere – is discussed by Leyser (1995). Saxon women were granted some not inconsiderable freedoms in law, and although their principal responsibilities were household, they also held the right to own land.

Religion

The early Saxons were pagan, but they later began to become Christianised from around the turn of the sixth and seventh centuries onwards. In 597, Pope Gregory I sent a mission from Rome to attempt their wholesale conversion, one of the members of which was Augustine, and another Mellitus, who later went on to become the first Bishop of London in 604 and the third Archbishop of Canterbury in 615. In 616, the previously converted East Saxons temporarily reverted to paganism after the death of their King. As the Venerable Bede put it in 731, in his *Historia Ecclesiastica Gentis Anglorum* (*Ecclesiastical History of the English People*):

> In the year of our Lord 616 ... the death of Sabert [Sebert], King of the East Saxons ... left three sons, still pagans, to inherit his ... crown. They immediately began openly to give themselves up to idolatry [and] granted free licence to their subjects to serve idols. And when they saw the bishop [Mellitus] ... celebrating Mass ... filled, as they were, with folly and ignorance, they said unto him ...

'We will not enter into that font, because we … do not stand in need of it, and yet we will be refreshed by that bread'. And being … earnestly admonished by him, that this could by no means be done, nor would any one be admitted to partake of the sacred Oblation without the holy cleansing, … they said, filled with rage, 'If you will not comply with us in so small a matter as that which we require, you shall not stay in our province.' And they drove him out … and his company … from their Kingdom [Essex].

The early Vikings were pagan, but they began to become Christianised from the ninth century onwards.

Food and Drink
Evidence from finds from Saxon rural occupation and riverside fish-trap sites in the Greater London region, within a 25-kilometre (16-mile) radius of the City indicates that the agricultural economy centred on the production of cereal crops, including wheat, barley, oats and rye, and of cattle, presumably for milk as well as meat. Pulses, nuts, fruit and berries were also consumed, some cultivated.

Plant- and animal-based remedies featured prominently in early Medieval medicine. The Old English text in the mid tenth-century *Bald's Leechbook* describes, among other things, how salves and potions were used to treat not only injuries and infections, but also, rather wonderfully, visitations from elves (*aelfcynne*), night goblins (*nihtgehgan*) and devils (*deofol*). The Old English and Latin text and accompanying illustrations in an anonymous early eleventh-century herbal indicate that both parsley (*peterslilie*) and sweet basil or 'snake plant' (*naedderwyrt*) were used to treat snake bites.

Administration and Governance
The population of Saxon London is estimated to have been at the most several thousand (that is, significantly less than that of Roman London). Saxon London was for the most part only a regional rather than a national administrative centre, as the 'Seven Kingdoms' only finally united to become England under Alfred's grandson Athelstan in 924 (the Seven Kingdoms, also known as the 'Heptarchy', comprised East Anglia, Essex, Kent, Mercia, Northumbria, Sussex and Wessex; of these, Essex, Mercia and Wessex in turn held sway over London). Nonetheless, it was the site of both the *folkmoot*, or outdoor assembly,

thought to have been on a site near the Medieval (St) Paul's Cross; and the *husting*, or indoor assembly, thought to have been on a site near the Medieval Guildhall. Saxon society was comparatively democratic, and any free man was entitled to voice his opinion at the *folkmoot* (and, as noted above, Saxon women were also granted some freedoms in law). However, only a noble *ealdorman*, or earl, appointed by the King could attend the husting, and only kings, greater nobles and bishops the peripatetic *Witanagemot* or *Witan*. Saxon society was also comparatively meritocratic, and permissive of a measure of mobility, albeit within an overall hierarchy (note that although kings were elected, they were elected from within the ranks of the nobility). The highest among the free men were the *thanes*, or knights, the lowest the various classes of *ceorls*, or peasants (whence *Cerle-ton* or Charlton in south-east London). Below them were the *theows*, or slaves.

The most famous law-giver of Saxon times was Alfred, who in the late 880s or early 890s established a new code of law, based on Christian principles, and enshrined in the so-called *Domboc*. The code established folk-rights and privileges. Judicial courts ruled on cases of alleged breaches, and meted out such fines or corporal or capital punishments as were deemed appropriate. Some of the punishments appear barbaric by modern standards, such as the possible judicial drowning of a Saxon woman whose skeleton has recently been excavated at Queenhithe (by the mid-tenth century, a woman could be punished by drowning either for theft, according to laws laid down between 924-39, or for witchcraft, as mentioned in a charter of 963-75). That is not to mention the 'oath-helping' Ordeals by Fire, Iron or Water! Athelstan passed laws relating specifically to the governance of London in the succeeding early tenth century (he reigned from 924-39). His *Judicia Civitatis Londoniae* makes explicit reference to a governance structure comprising a single governor, or in effect a mayor (in place of a bishop and port-reeve), 'eorlish' aldermen, and 'ceorlish' commons.

Trade and Commerce

Foodstuffs continued to be brought into Saxon London from the immediate hinterland and other goods brought in by boat from all around northern Europe, including the Low Countries and Scandinavia, and also, in the case of precious stones, gold, silk and other luxuries, from even farther afield.

Building Works
Within the walls of the City, the first St Paul's Cathedral was founded by Bishop Mellitus and the Kentish King Ethelburg in 604, a matter of a few short years after the arrival of the Gregorian mission in 597. The Venerable Bede:

> In the Year of our Lord 604, Augustine, Archbishop of Britain, ordained ... Mellitus to preach to the province of the East Saxons... [W]hen this province ... received the word of truth, by the preaching of Mellitus, King Ethelbert built the church of St Paul the Apostle, in the city of London, where he and his successors should have their episcopal see...

The first cathedral went on to be destroyed by fire in 675. The second, The Church of Paulesbyri, was built during the Bishopric of Erkenwald, between 675-85, and destroyed by the Vikings in 961. The third was built in 961 and destroyed by fire in 1087.

The church of All Hallows Barking was originally built in around 675. That of St Peter-upon-Cornhill was built at least as long ago as 1038, being mentioned in the will of Bishop Aelfric, who died in that year (Lethaby, 1902) and that of St Lawrence Jewry at least as long ago as 1046, wood from a coffin in the churchyard being dendrochronologically dated to that year. Many other churches are of probable or possible Saxon origin, the best substantiated being St Benet Fink, where a grave-slab tentatively dated on stylistic grounds to the late tenth or early eleventh century has been found (Schofield, 1994). The palace of the Mercian King Offa was originally built in the eighth century. What is now known as Queenhithe was first recorded, as "Ethered's Hithe', in 898; and it is evident, from dendrochronologically-dated timbers re-used in a revetment on the river-front, that an arcaded 'aisled hall' – in context most likely a royal palace or other high-status building – was built here between 956-79. Billingsgate was first recorded around 1000.

Without the walls, in Southwark, the nunnery of St Mary Overie (Southwark Cathedral) was founded in 606. In Westminster, the parish church of St Clement Danes on the Strand, 'so called because Harold (surnamed Harefoot) King of England of the Danish line and other Danes were here buried', was at least purportedly originally built in wood by Alfred in the late ninth century, and subsequently rebuilt in stone by Cnut in the early tenth (Cook, 1999); and in Camden, the church of St Andrew Holborn, in wood, at least as long ago as 951, being referred to as an 'old wooden church' in a Charter of that year. Also in Westminster, the Benedictine Monastery of St Peter was founded by Bishop Dunstan and King Edgar in 960, on what was then Thorney Island (and, according to legend, the site of a church founded by Sebert in 604) (Brooke-Hunt, 1902); and the Palace of Westminster, by Cnut, in 1016 (Thomas *et al.,* 2006). The Monastery was subsequently rebuilt, as Westminster Abbey, under Edward the Confessor, in the years up to 1065; and the Palace was also rebuilt at this time. A monk of St Bertin's Abbey wrote in 1065:

> Outside the walls of London ... stood a monastery [founded by Bishop Dunstan under King Edgar the Peaceable and] dedicated to St Peter, but insignificant in buildings... The King [Edward the Confessor], therefore ... gave his attention to that place, for it both lay hard by the famous and rich town and also was a delightful spot [and] decided to have his burial place there [he was to die in 1066]. Accordingly, he ordered that out of the tithes of all his revenues should be started the building of a noble edifice, worthy of the Prince of the Apostles.

The layout of the streets in the Saxon City of Lundenburg was essentially east-west, such as to allow easy access to Lundenwic. The principal streets were Eastcheap to the east and Cheapside to the west, with Leadenhall Street and Cornhill to the north, and Fenchurch Street and Lombard Street to the south, of the old Roman Basilica and Forum in the centre. The Saxons appear to have held Roman ruins in superstitious awe, a line in an Old English poem entitled 'The Ruin' referring to them as *enta geweorc* or 'labours of giants'. Saxon street names were characteristically blunt, often referring simply to available goods or services (*c(h)eap* meant 'market').

Surviving Structures
Structures that survive from Saxon and Viking London are extremely few and far between. Essentially nothing now remains of the original Saxon fabric in St Paul's Cathedral, St Mary Overie (Southwark Cathedral), or St Lawrence Jewry. Nothing remains either of the palace of the Mercian King Offa, incorporated into St Alban Wood

Street, in turn severely damaged during the Blitz and substantially demolished in the post-war period. There is nothing left of Queenhithe or Billingsgate, other than the names (and the aforementioned timbers from Queenhithe, now in the Museum of London), nor of the *folkmoot* or husting.

However, there are surviving – seventh-century and later – Saxon remains in the church of All Hallows Barking. These include a fine stone arch possibly as old as the late seventh century, *c.* 675, incorporating Roman tiles; and, in the crypt, two stone crosses, one of 900 and the other of 1000, the former plain and simple and bearing a Saxon Runic inscription, and the latter beautifully and intricately carved, and bearing a symbolic depiction of Christ over beasts, a characteristic of 'Dark Age' iconography (*Figure 5c*). There is also some surviving precisely dated eleventh-century and imprecisely dated pre-eleventh-century stonework fabric in the church of St Bride, off Fleet Street, the latter of which has been postulated, although not proven, to date to the late fifth or early sixth century, the church's purported founder Bride, or Bridget, the Abbess of Kildare in Ireland, living from 450-525. And in Westminster Abbey, there is a surviving eleventh-century shrine to Edward the Confessor (*Figure 6c*) and an eleventh-century crypt, containing the Chapel of the Pyx.

Further afield, there is a Saxon altar-stone in St Pancras Old Church in Camden, tentatively dated on stylistic grounds to the late sixth century, around the time of the conversion of the Saxons by St Augustine in 597, and the construction of the first incarnation of St Paul's Cathedral in 604 (interestingly, the land on which the church stands was granted to St Paul's in 604) (Anonymous, undated) (*Figure 7c*). The altar-stone, inlaid into a Georgian altar-table, depicts five crosses, whose unusual forms are remarkably reminiscent of that on the tomb on a small island in the Firth of Lorne believed to be of Columba's mother Eithne, who died in the late sixth century. There is also a Saxon rood in the church of St Dunstan and All Saints in Stepney, of the tenth (Cox & Chessun, 2002). Five miles east of Epping, in a dappled clearing in the dark heart of the ancient wild-wood that today bears its name, there is the extraordinary church of St Andrew in Greensted (*Figure 8c*). Greensted Church, as it is more commonly known, is purportedly the oldest wooden church in the world. The original church on the site was probably built at least as long ago as the middle of the seventh century, the time that St Cedd set about converting the East Saxons to Christianity from his base at Bradwell-on-Sea (incidentally, Cedd went on to attend the Synod of Whitby in 664, and to die of the plague in Northumbria later that same year). Sadly, though, the only remaining physical evidence as to the existence of this structure is in the form of post-holes discovered during an archaeological excavation in 1960. Work began on the present church in the middle of the eleventh century (dendrochronological evidence acquired in 1995 indicating that the trees used in its construction were felled between 1060-3). Nearly a thousand years later, much of the nave still stands, incorporated into later extensions. It was evidently originally windowless, aside from some small *eag-thyrels,* or eye-holes, and a single larger niche, known by many as a lepers' 'squint'. Rather wonderfully, scorch-marks can still be seen on some of the wall timbers, suggesting that the gloomy interior was once lit by wall-mounted lamps. Adze-marks can also still be seen on some timbers.

Archaeological Finds

The more important archaeological finds from Dark Age London are on exhibition in the City's principal museums. Hackney Museum features a reconstruction of a Saxon dugout canoe found in Clapton on the River Lea. The Museum of London houses an extensive collection of finds from Saxon and Viking London. The Saxon ones consist mainly of pottery, brooches and other items of personal adornment, locally-minted coins, and weapons. The Viking ones consist mainly of items of militaria or cavalry paraphernalia, but also include an eleventh-century grave-stone bearing 'Ringerike-style' decorations and Viking Runic inscriptions, which was found in St Paul's Churchyard. The museum also features a reconstruction of a typical Saxon dwelling of timber, wattle-and-daub, and thatch – it's really rather cosy inside!

A series of Museum of London and other publications deal with the finds from and reconstructions of Early Saxon sites in Lundenwic (Leary *et al.,* 2004; Cowie & Blackmore, 2012; Fowler & Taylor, 2013). Another describes the remains of a number of Late Saxon 'sunken-featured buildings', also known as 'grub-huts' (*Grubenhauser*) or 'pit-houses', in Lundenburg (Rowsome, 2000). Another deals with finds from Saxon rural occupation and riverside fish-trap sites in the Greater London region, within a 25-kilometre (16-mile) radius of the City (Cowie & Blackmore, 2008). As in preceding times, preferred sites for occupation were on well-drained land on gravel terraces close to rivers. Settlements consisted mainly of small isolated farms and hamlets, with only occasional larger and wealthier estates.

Further Reading

Ackroyd, 2000, 2011; Albert & Tucker, 2014; Ambler et al., 2015; Anonymous, undated; Ayre & Wroe-Bowsher, 2007; Breay & Story, 2018; Brechin, 1968; Brooke, 1975; Brooke-Hunt, 1902; Brown, 2015; Burford, 1973, 1990; Carpenter, 1966; Carruthers, 2013; Clark, 1989; Cook, 1999; Cotton et al., 2014; Cowie, 2018; Cowie & Blackmore, 2008; Cox & Chessun, 2002; Divers et al., 2008; Hibbert, 1969; Horsman et al., 1988; Houses of Parliament, 2012; Inwood, 1998, 2008; Jenkins & Trowles, 2018; Jenkyns, 2011; Keene et al., 2004; Lethaby, 1902; Lewis, 2008; Malcolm & Bowsher, 2003; Marsden, 1994; Matthews, 2008; Meara, 2004; Milne, 2003, 2014; Mitchell & Leys, 1958; Panton, 2005; Parrott, 2014; Richardson, 1995, 2000; Ross & Clark, 2008; Rowston, 2010; Saint & Darley, 1994; Saunders, 2012; Schofield, 2011b, 2016; Stone, 2017; Sullivan, 1994; Tames, 2012; Thomas et al., 2006; Thompson, 1904; Vince, 1990; Wheeler, 1935; White, 2010; Wilkinson, 2006; Wood, 1986.

CHAPTER FIVE

Medieval London (1066-1485)

The Medieval period was one of historical, political, religious and social transformation, not to say turmoil, over four hundred years and under four royal houses. It was a time of conquest and oppression; of crusade and pilgrimage; of pestilence and penitence; of fanfare and plainsong. It was also a time of rebellion and war, unending war: war between the English and the Scots, and the French, and the Welsh; and, when there was no-one else willing to fight, war among the English, in 'The Anarchy' of the twelfth century, the Barons' Wars of the thirteenth, and the Wars of the Roses of the fifteenth. The defining spirit of the age may be said to have been one of ebullient confidence, undercut in the dead of night by dread. The attitude toward death itself was less fearful than that of our own modern age; that toward an uncertain after-life, in Heaven, Hell or Purgatory, much more so. What perhaps most set the Medieval apart from our age was the nature and degree of religious observance: the Latin masses and sung chantries and the repeated summonings by bells. It would have felt utterly alien to us, to our more secular sensibilities.

There are sufficient surviving records of one kind or another to enable us to undertake a reasonably accurate reconstruction not only of the history of but also of the social history of Medieval London (see also 'Further Reading'). These include the *Chronicles of the Mayors and Sheriffs of London* of 1188-1274, deriving from the so-called *Liber de Antiquis Regibus*, produced for the Alderman Arnald Thedmar or FitzThedmar in the late thirteenth century (Riley, 1863); the *Letter-Books of the City of London* of 1275-1509, of which the most important are the *Liber Horn*, produced for the

City Chamberlain Andrew Horn between 1311 and sometime in the 1320s, and the *Liber Albus*, produced for the Common Clerk John Carpenter in the years up to 1419 (Riley, 1861; Sharpe, 1899-1912); and a multitude of other court, corporation, and ward records, many now in the Guildhall Library or London Metropolitan Archives. More personal contemporary eye-witness accounts include those of William FitzStephen, writing in the prologue of his *Vita Sancti Thomae* or *Life of St Thomas*, in 1183; Richard of Devizes, also writing in the late twelfth century; Jean Froissart, writing between 1377-1410; Wenzel Schaseck and Gabriel Tetzel, both writing in 1465; and the anonymous author of *A Chronicle of London*, writing around 1483. FitzStephen memorably, if gushingly, described London as

> ...the most noble city [that] pours out its fame more widely, sends to farther lands its wealth and trade, lifts its head higher than the rest ... happy in the healthiness of its air, in the Christian religion, in the strength of its defences, the nature of its site, the honour of its citizens, the modesty of its matrons [in which] the only pests ... are the immoderate drinking of foolish sorts and the frequency of fires.

Richard of Devizes wrote, at more or less the same time, although in a markedly different tone:

> Whatever evil or malicious thing that can be found in any part of the world, you will find ... in that one city... [D]ice and gambling; the theatre and the tavern... [M]ore braggarts ... than in all France... Acrobats, jesters, smooth-skinned lads, Moors, flatterers, pretty boys, effeminates, pederasts, singing and dancing girls, quacks, belly-dancers, sorceresses, extortioners, night-wanderers, magicians, mimes, beggars, buffoons: all this tribe fill all the houses.

Froissart was a French courtier from Valenciennes who made repeated visits to England between 1361, when he came to join the entourage of Edward III's Queen, Philippa of Hainault, and *c.* 1400. He wrote a series of *Chroniques* or Chronicles between 1377 and *c.* 1410, the first sometime after 1377; the second, in 1388; the third, in 1390; and the fourth, in *c.* 1410. The *Chroniques* cover, among other important events in the history of London, and indeed England, the Peasant's Revolt of 1381; Richard II's power struggles with Parliament, and with his uncle, Thomas of Woodstock, the Duke of Gloucester, and the other Lords Appellant, in 1386-8; and the King's eventual decline and deposition at the hands of Henry Bolingbroke, the Earl of Derby (and future Henry IV), in 1397-9. Schaseck, from Birkov in what is now the Czech Republic, visited London as part of the diplomatic delegation of Leo of Rozmital in 1465, and wrote:

> London is a grand and beautiful city and has two castles. In the first, located at the very end of the city surrounded by the ocean's gulf, lives the English King. He was present at the time of our arrival. Across the gulf there is a bridge made of stone and quite long, and houses have been built on both sides of it stretching its full length. I have never seen such a quantity of kite birds as I have here. Harming them is forbidden and is punishable by death.

Tetzel, from Grafenberg in what is now Germany, visited London as part of the same delegation in 1465, and wrote: 'We have passed through Canterbury through the English kingdom all the way to the capital, which is home to the English King. Its name is London and it is a very vigorous and busy city, conducting trade with all lands. In this city there are many craftsmen, and mainly goldsmiths and drapers, beautiful women and expensive food.'

Norman History

The first of the four Horsemen of the Apocalypse, Conquest, visited in 1066. The Norman William the Bastard, the Conqueror, was crowned King William I of England in Westminster Abbey in 1066. Orderic Vitalis wrote in his *Historia Ecclesiastica* of the occasion:

> So at last on Christmas Day ... the English assembled at London for the King's coronation, and a strong guard of Norman men-at-arms and knights was posted round the minster to prevent any treachery or disorder. And, in the presence of the bishops, abbots, and nobles of the whole realm of Albion, Archbishop Ealdred consecrated William duke of Normandy King of the English and placed the royal crown on his head. This was done in the abbey church of St Peter the chief of the apostles, called Westminster, where the body of King Edward [the Confessor] lies honourably buried. But at the prompting of the devil, who hates everything good, a sudden disaster and portent of

future catastrophes occurred. For when Archbishop Ealdred asked the English, and Geoffrey bishop of Coutances asked the Normans, if they would accept William as their King, all of them gladly shouted out with one voice if not one language that they would. The armed guard outside, hearing the tumult ... imagined that some treachery was afoot, and rashly set fire to some of the buildings. The fire spread rapidly ... the crowd who had been rejoicing ... took fright and throngs of men and women of every rank and condition ran out of the church in frantic haste. Only the bishop and a few clergy and monks remained ... and with difficulty completed the consecration of the King who was trembling from head to foot... The English, after hearing of the perpetration of such misdeeds, never again trusted the Normans who seemed to have betrayed them, but nursed their anger and bided their time to take revenge.

The following year, William granted the City of London a Charter, which read, in translation (from Old English rather than French): 'William King greets William the Bishop and Geoffrey the Portreeve and all the citizens in London, French and English, in friendly fashion; and I inform you that it is my will that your laws and customs be preserved as they were in King Edward's day, that every son shall be his father's heir after his father's death; and that I will not that any man do wrong to you. God yield you.' The so-called 'William Charter' is now in the London Metropolitan Archives. Two of William's sons went on to be crowned King: William II in 1087 and Henry I in 1100.

The second Horseman of the Apocalypse, War, visited during 'The Anarchy' of 1135-41, 'when Christ and his Saints slept', and there was prolonged and bloody fighting over the succession to the throne following the death of Henry I. Henry's only legitimate son had died earlier, aboard the 'White Ship'; his daughter, Empress Matilda, and his nephew, Stephen of Blois, laid rival claims. London lay under Stephen's control, and when Matilda attempted to seize control of the capital after he was captured at the Battle of Lincoln in 1141, it resisted, and she withdrew. London then turned its support to Stephen's wife Maud, and back to the man himself once he was released from captivity.

Plantagenet History
The Angevin or Plantagenet Henry, son of Geoffrey V of Anjou and Matilda, was crowned King Henry II when Stephen died in 1154. The

elder of Henry's surviving sons was crowned King Richard I in 1189. According to one account, which now resides in the Bodleian Library in Oxford, the coronation ceremony was accompanied by 'evil omens', including the presence of a bat fluttering around the King's head during the crowning, and the mysterious pealing of bells. Shortly afterwards, representatives of the Jewish community, who had been barred from the ceremony, arrived at the abbey to present gifts and their respects to the newly crowned King, only to beaten and stripped by the King's men and thrown out onto the street. Tragically, this came to be taken as a licence to attack the entire – sizeable – Jewish population of London. According to Roger of Howden, in his *Gesta Regis Ricardi*, the 'jealous and bigoted' citizens went on to kill many, including Jacob of Orleans, a respected scholar, to burn the houses of many others, and to force the remainder to seek sanctuary in the Tower of London, or to flee the city altogether until it was safe to return. According to Richard of Devizes, 'On the very day of the coronation, about that solemn hour in which the Son was immolated to the Father, a sacrifice of the Jews ... was commenced in the city of London, and so long was the duration ... that the holocaust [*holocaustum*] could scarcely be accomplished the ensuing day.' A horrified Richard was forced to issue a writ ordering the cessation of the persecution of the Jews (he also allowed those who had been forcibly converted to Christianity to revert to Judaism). He ordered the execution of those guilty of the most egregious offences against them. Later in 1189, Richard appointed the first (Lord) Mayor of London, Henry FitzAilwyn de Londonestone, in effect to run the City. Later in Richard's reign, in 1196, according to an account given by Roger of Wendover:

About this time there arose a dispute in the city of London between the poor and the rich on account of the tallage, which was exacted by the King's agents for the benefit of the exchequer: for the principal men of the city, whom we call mayors and aldermen, having held a deliberation at their hustings, wished to preserve themselves from the burden, and to oppress the poorer classes. Wherefore William FitzRobert [also rendered as FitzOsbert], surnamed 'with the beard' [William Longbeard] ... called the mayors of the city traitors to our lord the King for the cause above mentioned; and the disturbances were so great in the city that recourse was had to arms. [T]he King, his ministers, and the chief men of the city charged the whole crime on William. As the King's party were about to arrest him, he ...

escaped, defending himself with nothing but a knife, and flying into the church of St Mary of the Arches [St Mary-le-Bow], demanded the protection of our Lord, St Mary, and her church, saying that he had resisted an unjust decree for no other purpose than that all might bear an equal share of the public burden, and contribute according to their means. His expostulations, however, were not listened to ... and the archbishop [Walter] ... ordered that he should be dragged from the church to take a trial, because he had created a sedition ... among the people of the city. When this was told to William, he took refuge in the tower of the church, for he knew that the mayors ... sought to take away his life. In their obstinacy they applied fire, and sacrilegiously burned down a great part of the church. Thus William was forced to leave [and] conveyed away to the Tower of London. Soon after ... he was ... dragged, tied to a horse's tail, through the middle of London to Ulmet [Tyburn] after which he was hung in chains on a gallows... With him were also hanged nine of his neighbours or of his family, who espoused his cause.

According to other contemporary sources, William Longbeard was 'in origin one of the most noble citizens of London', but nonetheless became 'the champion of the poor, it being his wish that every person, both rich and poor, should give according to his property and means, for all the necessities of the state'. In one remarkable and radical speech that provoked outrage and fear throughout the Establishment, he proclaimed: 'I am the saviour of the poor. Oh poor, who have experienced the heaviness of rich men's hands, drink from my wells the waters of the doctrine of salvation, and ... do this joyfully, for the time of your visitation is at hand. For I will divide ... the humble and faithful people from the haughty and treacherous ... as light from darkness.'

John was crowned King in 1199. In 1215, he granted the City of London the right to elect its own Mayor: the 'Mayoral Charter' is now in the Guildhall. The prestige of the position was such that the by-then Mayor, William Hardell, was invited by John to be a witness to the sealing of, and indeed an enforcer or surety of, *Magna Carta*, at Runnymede in Surrey, later in the same year. This was after rebel barons had entered London to force John's hand. Ralph of Coggeshall wrote:

With alliances sworn with the citizens of London via go-betweens ...
the barons came to London and seized it without opposition,

the citizens being busy at Mass. Having entered, the barons captured all of the King's supporters whom they found, depriving them of their goods. They broke into the houses of the Jews, rifling store-houses and strong boxes, and having spent much time in this holy work, abundantly restuffed their own empty purses. Robert FitzWalter, Marshal of the Army of God and Holy Church, and Geoffrey de Mandeville, Earl of Essex and Gloucester, vigilantly and daily reinforced the City walls with stones taken from the houses of the Jews. They could not, however, take the Tower of London, defended against them by a small but brave garrison. As soon as it became known, far and wide, that the barons had seized the royal metropolis, all, save only the earls of Warenne, Arundel, Chester, Pembroke, Ferrers and Salisbury, and amongst the barons only William Brewer ... defected to the baronial party; so that ... the King was seized with such terror that he now dared travel no further than Windsor.

The First Barons' War broke out still later in 1215, when it became clear that John had no intention of abiding by the terms of *Magna Carta*. When John died in 1216, the barons refused to recognise his son Henry III as King, and instead supported the rival claim to the title of the French King Philippe II's son Louis, also known as the Dauphin. The Dauphin and barons suffered a heavy military defeat at the Battle of Lincoln in 1217, after which they were forced to retreat to their power-base in London, there to await reinforcements from France, which in the event never arrived, the transporting fleet being intercepted *en route*. Two prominent Londoners were captured at the battle, the aforementioned Robert FitzWalter, formerly of Baynard's Castle, and Richard de Montfichet, of Montfichet's Tower, both of which had been demolished on John's orders after the baronial conspiracy of 1212, in which FitzWalter had been implicated. The Dauphin then agreed to relinquish his claim to England and end the war, by signing the Treaty of Lambeth, brokered by William Marshall in 1217 (there is a famous alabaster effigy of Marshall in Temple Church). In exchange, the barons and people were given back the liberties that had been taken away under John's unjust rule. The Second Barons' War broke out in 1264. As in the case of the First Baron's War, London remained a barons' stronghold essentially throughout. Following his victory at the Battle of Lewes in 1264, during which the King, Henry III was captured, the barons' leader, Simon de Montfort convened what is widely regarded as England's first representative Parliament in Westminster Hall in 1265 (before this date, Parliament, or its precursor, had met in the Chapter House of Westminster Abbey; and after 1548, it met in the then-secularised Royal Chapel of St Stephen in the Palace of Westminster). De Montfort was killed and Henry freed from captivity at the Battle of Evesham in 1265, which left the royalists holding the upper hand until the eventual cessation of hostilities, according to the terms of the Dictum of Kenilworth, 1267.

The third Horseman of the Apocalypse, Famine, visited during the reign of Henry III in 1257/8, and again during the reign of Edward II in 1314-7. The City of London was subject to a famine of Biblical proportions in 1257/8, as indeed were the entire country and continent. The *Chronicles of the Mayors and Sheriffs* for 1257/8 record: 'In this year, there was a failure of the crops; upon which ... a famine ensued, to such a degree that the people from the villages resorted to the City for food; and there, upon the famine waxing still greater, many thousand people perished.' It is likely that many of the thousands of individuals buried in the crypt-*cum*-charnel house of St Mary Spital, which have recently been shown to date to the middle of the thirteenth century, died during this famine. As to the underlying cause, it has been speculated to have been brought about by a 'volcanic winter' following the explosive eruption of Mount Samalas on the island of Lombok in Indonesia in 1257. Another famine, albeit less well documented in London, affected the country and continent between 1314-7. It, too, appears to have been associated with prolonged bad weather, even in summer months, and associated harvest failure, and to have been compounded by livestock disease and death ('murrain'). Initially, it was the poor who were particularly badly affected, being unable to afford to pay a premium for increasingly scarce foodstuffs, even for the staple, bread, especially after attempts to restrict its price ultimately proved unsuccessful. But, by the summer of 1315, there was essentially nothing for anyone rich or poor to eat anywhere in St Albans, even for King Edward II and his court, who visited the town in August. It has been speculated to have been brought about by either a short-term cooling spike caused by another volcanic eruption, perhaps of Mount Tarawera in New Zealand, or a long-term climatic cooling trend at the transition from the 'Medieval Warm Period' into the 'Little Ice Age', or or a superimposition of the two. The balance between sufficiency and deficiency of food supply was always extremely precarious, and easily tipped. Food shortages would persist well into the post-Medieval period.

The First War of Scottish Independence began with the English conquest of Scotland during the reign of Edward I in 1296, and lasted until the restoration of independence, either *de facto* after the Battle of Bannockburn in 1314, or *de jure* after the Treaty of Edinburgh-Northampton during the reign of Edward II in 1328. One of the principal Scottish leaders, William Wallace ('Braveheart'), was captured by the English at Robroyson near Glasgow in 1305. He was then taken to London, where he was hanged, drawn and quartered for high treason in West Smithfield.

The fourth and final Horseman of the Apocalypse, Plague, visited during the reign of Edward III in 1348-9, and again in 1361 (the so-called *Pestis Secunda*), 1368 (the 'Third Plague'), 1375 (the 'Fourth Plague'), and during the reign of the Lancastrian King Henry VI in 1433-5 (Porter, 2018). It is estimated that around half of the population of the City of London, or 40,000 people, died in the 1348-9 outbreak that came to be known as the Black Death. Twenty-six out of the fifty monks of Westminster Abbey died, and were buried in the cloister (the abbot, Simon Bircheston, also died, and was buried separately, near the Chapter House door, alongside earlier abbots of the late eleventh to twelfth centuries, his epitaph reading in part: 'May this blessed father now flourish with the kind Fathers in the presence of God'). The contemporary chronicler Robert of Avesbury wrote:

The pestilence which had first broken out in the land occupied by the Saracens became so much stronger that, sparing no dominion, it visited with the scourge of sudden death the various parts of all the Kingdoms... [I]t began in England in Dorsetshire ... in the year of the Lord 1348, and immediately advancing from place to place it attacked men without warning... Very many of those who were attacked in the morning it carried out of human affairs before noon. And no one whom it willed to die did it permit to live longer than three or four days... And about the Feast of All Saints [1 November 1348], reaching London, it deprived many of their life daily, and increased to so great an extent that from the feast of the Purification

[2 February 1349] till after Easter [13 April 1349] there were more than two hundred bodies of those who had died buried daily in the cemetery which had been then recently made near Smithfield, besides the bodies which were in other graveyards... The grace of the Holy Spirit finally intervening ... about the feast of Whitsunday [31 May 1349] it ceased at London... In that same year of 1349, about Michaelmas, over six hundred [flagellants] came to London from Flanders ... Sometimes at St Paul's and sometimes at other points in the city they made two daily public appearances... Each had in his right hand a scourge with three tails. Each tail had a knot and through the middle of it there were sometimes sharp nails fixed. They marched naked in a file one behind the other and whipped themselves with these scourges on their naked and bleeding bodies. Four of them would chant in their native tongue and, another four would chant in response like a litany. Thrice they would all cast themselves on the ground in this sort of procession, stretching out their hands like the arms of a cross.

The horror of the Black Death can hardly be imagined. The many thousands of dead were buried, with little ceremony or none, in plague pits in East Smithfield, in what were to become the grounds of the Cistercian abbey of St Mary Graces, founded in 1350; and at West Smithfield, in what were to become the grounds of the Carthusian monastery of Charterhouse, founded in 1371. As Stow put it, 'A great pestilence ... overspread all England, so wasting the people that scarce the tenth person of all sorts was left alive, and churchyards were not sufficient to receive the dead, but men were forced to choose out certain fields for burial.' Some have recently been unearthed in archaeological excavations, and on analysis have been found to contain traces of the plague bacillus *Yersinia pestis* (Callaway, 2011).

In the immediate aftermath of the Black Death of 1348-9, the demand for labour came to exceed by far the supply, in both city and countryside. At the same time, the workforce had its wages frozen, under the 'Ordinance of Labourers' of 1349 and then became subject to understandably even more unpopular, and extremely unjustly enforced, poll taxes, in 1377, 1379 and 1381. Civil unrest followed in the Peasants' Revolt of 1381. This came to a head in a confrontation, at West Smithfield (*Figure 9c*), between on the one side a thousands-strong peasant mob and on the other heavily armed knights and henchmen, officers of the City, and the then boy-king Richard II. By this time, the mob had already slaked its blood-thirst by sacking some official buildings in the City, including the Tower of London and John of Gaunt's Savoy Palace, and killing many of their occupants, together with many other innocent bystanders – especially foreigners. Among the dead were Robert Hales, the Lord High Treasurer, who had introduced the Poll Tax, and Simon Sudbury, the Archbishop of Canterbury; both unceremoniously beheaded on Tower Hill. As well as being the Treasurer, Hales was the Prior of the Priory of St John in Clerkenwell. Its buildings, too, were deliberately targeted during the revolt. It is significant that no attempt was made to harm the King, whose perceived status from birth was not only royal but also essentially divine and sacrosanct, as indicated by the symbology of the Wilton Diptych (in the National Gallery). The French chronicler Jean Froissart (*c.* 1337-*c.* 1405) wrote, in the second of his *Chroniques*, completed in 1388:

This day all the rabble ... assembled under Wat Tyler, John Straw and John Ball, at a place called Smithfield... There were present about 20,000 ... breakfasting, and drinking Rhenish wine and Malmsey Madeira ... without paying for anything... [W]hen the King, attended by sixty horses ... arrived before the Abbey of St Bartholomew ... and saw the crowd of people, he stopped, saying that he would ... endeavour to appease them. Wat Tyler ... was only desirous of a riot... The Mayor of London [the fishmonger William Walworth], with about twelve men, rode forward, armed under their robes ... seeing Tyler's manner of behaving... [T]he Mayor ... supported by the King ... then drew a kind of scimitar [now in the Fishmongers' Hall], and struck Tyler such a blow on the head as felled him to his horse's feet. As soon as the rebel was down, he was surrounded on all sides, in order that his own men might not see him; and one of the King's squires, by name John Standwich, immediately leaped from his horse, and drawing his sword, thrust it into his belly, so that he died. When the rebels found that their leader was dead, they drew up in a sort of battle array, each man having his bow bent before him. The King at this time ... hazarded much, though it turned out most fortunately for him; for ... he left his attendants, giving orders that no one should follow him, and riding up to the rebels, ... said 'Gentlemen, ... I am your King, remain peaceable.' The greater part, on hearing these words, were quite ashamed, and those among them who were inclined for peace began to slip away.

Two further crises followed the Peasants' Revolt during the course of Richard II's reign, as chronicled by Froissart. The first was a series of power struggles with Parliament, and with his uncle, Thomas of Woodstock, the Duke of Gloucester, and the other Lords Appellant, in 1386-8. At this time, the King, and his Chancellor, Michael de la Pole, sought an unprecedentedly high rise in taxes to continue to fund the war against France that had begun in 1337 (and that would only end in 1453, which is why it is now known as the Hundred Years' War). Parliament – the 'Wonderful Parliament' – refused to give its consent unless the unpopular Chancellor was removed from power, whereupon the King famously responded that he would not dismiss as much as a scullion from his kitchen at the request of Parliament, and only eventually acceded to the request when threatened with deposition. Richard was so incensed by this curbing of his prerogative powers that he sought, and secured, a legal ruling from Chief Justice Robert Tresilian to the effect that Parliament's conduct in the matter had been unlawful and treasonable. He also went on a 'gyration' of the country to garner support for his cause, and began to establish a military power-base in the north, at Chester. On his return to London, he found himself confronted by the Dukes of Gloucester, Arundel and Warwick, who had in turn brought an appeal of treason against de la Pole, Tresilian and two other loyalists, Nicholas Brembre, the Mayor of London, and Alexander Neville, the Archbishop of York. According to Froissart, the King had earlier been advised by Brembre that 'many Londoners' supported him, encouraging him to march on the capital, 'to test the temper of the citizens [with] fifteen thousand men'. In the event, Londoners resisted his advance, and Brembre fled to Wales, but was captured and subsequently beheaded in the capital on 20 February 1388. The King attempted to delay the trial proceedings in anticipation of the arrival of supporting troops from Chester, whereupon Gloucester, Arundel and Warwick joined forces with the Earl of Derby (Henry Bolingbroke), and the Earl of Nottingham, to form the Lords Appellant, and intercepted, and routed, the King's troops at Radcot Bridge. At this, Richard no longer had any choice but to comply with the appellants' demands. Tresilian and Brembre were executed, and de la Pole, who had fled the country, was sentenced to death *in absentia*, by the 'Merciless Parliament' of 1388. The King's circle of favourites was broken.

The second crisis of the latter part of Richard's reign witnessed the King's eventual decline and deposition, between 1397-9. It began with his attempt to re-assert his authority after the first crisis, in the so-called 'Tyranny'. In 1397, he had Gloucester, Arundel and Warwick arrested on charges of treason: Gloucester either died or was killed on the King's instructions, while awaiting trial; Arundel was tried, convicted and executed; and Warwick tried, convicted and sentenced to death, although his sentence was later commuted to life imprisonment. The King then set about the systematic persecution of the appellants' supporters, fining them, and at the same time distributing largesse to his own followers. In 1398, he convened a packed 'Parliament of Shrewsbury', which overturned all the earlier rulings of the 'Merciless Parliament' and essentially made the King once more an absolute monarch. However, the House of Lancaster, personified by John of Gaunt and his son Henry Bolingbroke, now Earl of Hereford, remained a formidable opponent. Richard attempted to resolve this by ordering Bolingbroke into exile in France, initially for ten years, and eventually for life. But in 1399, Bolingbroke returned from exile to mount a challenge to the King, landing in the north of England and there forging an important strategic alliance with Henry Percy, Earl of Northumberland. He, Bolingbroke, then marched south with a strong and ever-growing force, encountering little Royalist resistance along the way, the King and much of the nobility being in Ireland. When the King eventually returned to England, he found himself facing overwhelming odds and was forced to surrender himself to Bolingbroke, who had him imprisoned in the Tower of London, and eventually deposed, after hearings before an assembly of Lords and Commons at Westminster Hall, on 1 October 1399. Richard, is thought to have been allowed to starve to death in captivity in Pontefract Castle on or around 14 February 1400.

Lancastrian and Yorkist History, and the Wars of the Roses
The Lancastrian Henry of Bolingbroke was formally crowned King Henry IV on the feast day of St Edward the Confessor, 13 October, although the heir-presumptive had been Edmund Mortimer, Earl of March, who was descended from Edward III. The Welsh Revolt against English rule broke out in 1400, and ended in defeat for the

rebels during the reign of Henry's son Henry V in 1415. Its principal leader, Owain Glyndwr, the anglicised version of whose name is Owen Glendower, went into hiding in 1415, never to be seen or heard of again. Owain's lieutenant Rhys Ddu was captured on a raid into Shropshire in 1410, brought to London, 'laid on a hurdle and so drawn forth to Tyburn through the City' and there 'hanged and let down again ... his head ... smitten off and his body quartered and sent to four towns and his head set on London Bridge'. Owain's daughter Catrin and her children had previously been captured by the English at the Siege of Harlech in 1409. They had then been taken to London, where they were imprisoned in the Tower, and most if not all of them died there in 1413, under circumstances best described as mysterious (the children had a claim to the English throne through their late father, the aforementioned Edmund Mortimer, and some suspect that they were done to death so as to prevent them from making any such claim). Surviving records indicate that Catrin and two of her daughters were buried not in the Tower but in the churchyard of St Swithin London Stone on the other side of the city (there are no records of what became of her other daughter, or of her son Lionel). A modern Gelligaer bluestone sculpture by Nic Stradlyn-John and Richard Renshaw, inscribed with a Welsh *englyn* by Menna Elfyn, marks the spot. Freely (by me) rendered into English, the *englyn* reads: 'In the Tower, now her home,/Her heart-song turns to longing:/The exile's silent lament.'

The attempt of the Lollard Revolt of 1413/4 to overthrow the established church came to nothing when the supporters of the movement, gathered at St Giles-in-the-Fields on the western outskirts of the City of London, were betrayed and dispersed. Its local leader, Sir John Oldcastle, was later put to death at St Giles – by hanging in chains over a low fire – in 1417. Another Lollard Priest, William Taylor, was burnt at the stake for heresy in West Smithfield in 1423.

Henry V was crowned King in 1413. A month after his famous victory over the French at the Battle of Agincourt in 1415, he made a triumphal return to London. An anonymous author wrote the following eye-witness account:

[T]he citizens went out to meet the King at the brow of Blackheath, ... the mayor and ... aldermen in scarlet, and the ... lesser citizens in red cloaks with red-and-white party-coloured hoods, to the number of about 20,000... And when the King came through the midst of them ... and the citizens had given glory and honour to God, and congratulations to the King ... the citizens rode before him towards the city, and the King followed... When they arrived at the ... bridge ... there placed on the top of the tower was an enormous figure, with ... the keys of the city hanging from a staff... And when they reached the ... aqueduct in Cornhill they found the tower hidden under a scarlet cloth stretched in the form of a tent, on spears hidden under the cloth. Surrounding [it] were the arms of St George, St Edward, St Edmund and of England ... inset with this pious legend: 'Since the King hopes in the Lord and in the mercy of the highest, he shall not be moved'. Under a covering was a band of venerable white-haired prophets ... who released, when the King came by, sparrows and other small birds in great cloud as a ... thanksgiving to God for the victory He had given... Then they went on to the tower of the conduit at the entrance to Cheapside which was decked with an awning of green ... and erected to resemble a building... And when they came to the [Eleanor] cross in Cheapside ... it was hidden by a beautiful castle of wood... And when they came to the tower the conduit at the exit to Cheapside towards St Paul's ... above the tower was stretched a canopy sky-blue in colour ... adorned by an archangel in shining gold [and below] was a figure of majesty represented by a sun darting out flashing rays... Such was the dense throng of people in Cheapside ... that a bigger or more impressive crowd had never gathered before in London. But the King himself went along, amidst ... the citizens, dressed in a purple robe, not with a haughty look and a pompous train ... but with a serious countenance and a reverend pace accompanied by only a few of his most faithful servants; following him, guarded by knights, were the captured dukes, counts and the marshal. From his silent face and ... sober pace it could be inferred that the King ... was giving thanks and glory to God alone and not to man. And when he had visited the sanctuary of SS Peter and Paul [Westminster Abbey], he rode away to his palace of Westminster, escorted by his citizens.

Henry VI was crowned King in 1422. During the course of his reign, in 1450 Jack Cade, alias Mortimer, and thousands of armed supporters entered London 'to punish evil ministers and procure a redress of grievances'. Cade went on to strike the 'London Stone' on Cannon

Street with his sword, and declare himself 'Lord of this City' (an act immortalised by Shakespeare in *Henry VI, Part II*); and in this capacity to oversee the show-trial at the Guildhall and subsequent execution on Cheapside of the corrupt Lord High Treasurer, James Fiennes, Baron of Saye and Sele, and his son-in-law William Crowmer. Unfortunately for Cade, in succeeding days he lost what support he had for his cause among the citizens of London, as his followers descended into drunken rioting and looting in the City. Eventually, the citizens drove him and his followers from the City after a pitched battle on London Bridge, during which scores of combatants were killed. Cade was later captured and executed in Sussex, whereupon his body was brought to London and beheaded and quartered in the King's Bench Prison in Southwark, and his head was put upon a pike on London Bridge. Thus ended the 'Harvest of the Heads'.

The Yorkist Edward IV was crowned King in 1461, after the overthrow of the Lancastrian Henry VI during the Wars of the Roses. For a brief period in 1470-1, Edward IV was forced into exile, following a falling-out with two of his principal supporters, his brother George, Duke of Clarence, and Richard Neville, the Earl of Warwick, known as Warwick the Kingmaker, and during this period Henry VI was readepted to the throne.

During the Wars of the Roses between the Lancastrians and Yorkists 1455-85, London was an important centre of political machinations; and the Tower, at least according to some accounts, the scene of a series of chilling politically motivated murders, in forgotten dreadful cubicles behind massive locked doors. It appears that Henry VI was done to death here, possibly on the orders of Edward IV, in 1471; and that George, Duke of Clarence was killed here, possibly on the orders either of his elder brother, Edward IV, or his younger brother Richard, Duke of Gloucester, in 1478 (by drowning in a butt of Malmsey wine). It also appears that the recently deceased Edward IV's sons, Edward V and Richard, Duke of York, the 'Princes in the Tower', were murdered here, possibly on the orders of their uncle, Richard, Duke of Gloucester – the future Richard III – in 1483. This accusation is viewed as a calumny by many today, but it appears that the deaths of his nephews removed any obstacles standing between Richard and the crown, which he was duly eventually offered in Baynard's Castle in 1483.

There was some military action on the outskirts of London, in the Battles of St Albans in 1455 and 1461, and of Barnet in 1471.

The Battle of Barnet was fought on 14 April 1471 between a Yorkist army under Edward IV and a Lancastrian army under the Earl of Warwick. Earlier, Edward had sallied forth from Bishopsgate in the City of London and marched ten miles or so up the Great North Road to meet Warwick's advance from the north, battle lines being drawn a little to the north of Barnet, at that time a small market town in Hertfordshire: the Yorkists to the south, the Lancastrians to the north. The night before the battle, the two sides bombarded each other with artillery, such that on the morning of the day of the battle, the air was thick with smoke as well as fog, and visibility was poor. Historical accounts of the battle are correspondingly unclear, and no systematic archaeological survey of the battle site has yet been undertaken that might clarify the course of events (as in the cases of Towton and Bosworth Field). The consensus among historians is that the Lancastrian army got the better of the early exchanges, its right, under the Earl of Oxford, turning the Yorkist left, forcing it to flee to the south and then pursuing it into Barnet and ransacking the town. Oxford's men later returned to the field of battle from the south, only to be fired on by their fellow Lancastrians under Montague, who, in the smoke, fog and general confusion had mistaken them for Yorkists (their banners also evidently resembled those of the Yorkists). The Lancastrians were then themselves turned by the Yorkists, and pursued and routed; Warwick was killed in the ensuing melee, as depicted in the *Ghent Manuscript*; and the Yorkists won a decisive victory. John Paston, a Lancastrian, wrote in a letter to his mother: [M]y brother ... is alive and fareth well, and in no peril of death: nevertheless he is hurt with an Arrow on his right arm, beneath the elbow; and I have sent him to a Surgeon, which hath dressed him, and he telleth me that he trusteth that he shall be whole within right short time... [A]s for me, I am in good case blessed be God; and in no jeopardy of my life... [T]he world, I assure you, is right queasy [unsettled].'

Most of the dead, from both sides, numbering somewhere between 1,500 and 4,000, were buried on the battlefield, possibly where the essentially late fifteenth-century Monken Hadley Church now stands (Fabian's *Great Chronicle of London* refers to the construction of a 'lytyll Chappell' at the burial site). Some noblemen were taken back to London to be buried in Austin Friars Priory; and Warwick's body was for a while put on display in St Paul's, where, according to von Wesel, it was seen by 'many thousands'. The battlefield site is marked by an eighteenth-century obelisk bearing the inscription 'Here was fought the Famous Battle Between Edward the 4th and the Earl of Warwick on April 14th, 1471, in which the Earl was Defeated and Slain.' Many of the artefacts recovered from the site over the centuries may be seen in the Barnet Museum, including cannonballs, various types of arrowhead, and spurs. The Battle of Barnet was reportedly one of the earliest engagements to have involved the use of handguns, although as yet no physical evidence has been recovered to substantiate this. *Warkworth's Chronicle* recounts that Edward had '300 Flemings handgunners', armed with arquebuses, in his army.

There was also some action in the City. On 2 July 1460, a Yorkist army arrived at the gates of London and was admitted by Aldermen sympathetic to their cause. At this, the Lancastrian garrison in the Tower, under Thomas, the Seventh Baron Scales, indiscriminately opened fire on the City in an ultimately unsuccessful attempt to prevent its occupation, using both conventional and chemical weapons from the Royal Armoury, causing both combatant and civilian casualties, and occasioning extreme public outrage, ultimately resulting in Scales's summary execution (as a contemporary chronicler put it: 'They that were within the Tower cast wildfire into the City, and shot in small guns, and burned and hurt men and women and children in the streets'). The chemical weapon, let loose from a primitive and unreliable flame-thrower, was 'Greek fire' or 'wildfire', which may be thought of as a form of napalm, that stuck and set fire to everything – and everyone – it came into contact with, and flared up even more fiercely if water was cast onto it, the base ingredient almost certainly being naphtha.

On 14 May 1471, shortly after the Battle of Barnet, London's by then Yorkist garrison was bombarded and then assaulted, as the contemporary *Chronicle of London* put it, 'on alle sydys', by Lancastrian forces under the privateer Thomas Nevill, illegitimate son of William Nevill, Lord Fauconberg, and otherwise known as the Bastard Fauconberg. In response, the Mayor, John Stockton, and his Sheriffs, John Crosby and John Ward, rode from gate to gate to rally the City's defences, 'in alle haast with a Trumpett' (Crosby was later knighted for his role in the City's defence: his memorial in the church of St Helen Bishopsgate shows him in armour). And for the most part the defences held firm. Aldgate came under the most sustained attack, 'with mighty shott of hand Gunnys & sharp shott of arrowis'. Indeed, some attackers even managed to enter the City there, only to be held up by defenders under the Recorder of the City, Thomas Ursewyk, and an Alderman named John Basset, and then to be forced to retreat by the arrival of defensive reinforcements from the Tower of London, 'which dyscomffortid the Rebellys'. The attack had failed, and the attackers who had evaded capture took to their ships and sailed out to the safety of the Thames estuary. Many of those who had been captured were summarily executed, including Spysyng and Quyntyn.

Social History

The social history of Medieval London is discussed by, among others, Porter (2000) and Mount (2014) (see also 'Further Reading'). The role of women in Medieval society – in London and elsewhere – is discussed by Power (1975), Leyser (1995) and Telford (2018). The lives of almost all women in the Medieval period – other than those from the higher strata of society, that is, of the aristocracy and higher positions of the church – would have revolved around the daily grind of managing their households, and providing food and care for their families, and they would have had little time for extraneous activities or interests. Moreover, they would have enjoyed less freedom under the law than in Saxon times. Indeed, under the Medieval Law of Coverture, a married woman, or *femme covert*, had no legal rights whatsoever independent of her husband, and was essentially his chattel. An unmarried woman or widow, or *femme sole*, though, was at least legally allowed to manage her own business. And there is evidence that, in London and some other towns, a *femme covert* might be permitted to adopt the more privileged status of a *femme sole* to enable her to do so.

Religion

Medieval Londoners were God-fearing folk, and one could argue that they had cause to be. The sporadic and apocalyptic outbreaks of famine and plague must have seemed to have been visited upon them by a vengeful God. Life could also be cut painfully short by other diseases, accidents, and acts of violence; and the deaths of mother and/or baby in the act of childbirth would have been distressingly common. Infant mortality was shockingly high. Faith at least offered hope of life eternal.

The predominant religion was of course Catholicism, which pervaded all areas of life, even the very air, with its incense and incantations. Note, though, that the seeds of the post-Medieval Protestant Reformation may be said to have been sown with the so-called Lollardy of the late fourteenth to fifteenth centuries, which has been referred to as the 'Morning Star of the Reformation', and which similarly sought to restrict the secular wealth and power of the established church, and to return to apostolic poverty and mission. There was a major phase of church building and rebuilding, perhaps as an act of penance, to assuage the guilt of the conqueror and oppressor, beginning in the late eleventh and twelfth centuries (see also 'Building Works' below). By the end of the thirteenth century there were around 100 churches in the City, as recorded in the *Taxatio Ecclesiastica* of Pope Nicholas IV of 1291 – some of the associated parishes constituted only a few streets. Late parishioners' bequests for 'Chantries', or prayers to be chanted for those in Purgatory, were often spent on extravagant embellishments.

Further religious or monastic houses began to be established in and around the City in the twelfth to thirteenth centuries, among them those of the hermit monks and nuns of the Benedictine, Cluniac and Carthusian orders; the mendicant friars of the Carmelite, Dominican and Franciscan orders (the White, Black and Grey Friars, respectively); the monk- and nun-like regular and friar-like secular canons and canonesses of the Augustinan or Austin orders; and the Knights Templar and Hospitallers. The monks and nuns following Benedictine rule foreswore earthly delights, and instead dedicated their lives to divine service, and the rhythms of their days were tuned to the Liturgy of the Hours: matins in the middle of the night; lauds at dawn; prime in the first hour; terce in the third; sext in the sixth; none in the ninth; vespers 'at the lighting of the lamps', at dusk; and compline before retiring at night. The monastic houses came to dominate not only the religious life but also the philosophical and indeed even the physical life of the City, becoming wealthy and powerful in the process, and making many enemies as well as friends. The Knights Templar and Hospitaller came into being in the twelfth century, as Orders of 'fighting monks' tasked principally with the protection of Christians on pilgrimage to the Holy Land, and with participation in Crusades, and incidentally with infrastructure and finance. The Knights Templar in particular became immensely wealthy and powerful, and at the same time the subject of much mistrust, on account of the secrecy surrounding their activity. Indeed, eventually, on 13 October 1307 – the original unlucky

Friday the thirteenth – the leaders of the Order were arrested on a variety of charges, at least some no doubt trumped up by debtors and other vested interests, under a warrant reading 'God is not pleased. We have enemies of the faith in the Kingdom' ('Dieu n'est pas content, nous avons des ennemis de la foi dans le Royaume'). They were later tortured into confessing to having 'spat three times on the Cross' ('craché trois fois sur la Croix'), and burned at the stake, and the entire Order was eventually disbanded, essentially to be subsumed into that of the Knights Hospitaller. In 1237, Matthew Paris chronicled the departure of a party of Knights Hospitaller from the Priory of St John in Clerkenwell to the Holy Land: 'They ... set out from their house [and] proceeded in good order, with about thirty shields uncovered, with spears raised, and preceded by their banner, through the midst of the City, towards the bridge, that they might obtain the blessings of the spectators, and, bowing their heads with their cowls lowered, commended themselves to the prayers of all.' The Priory had been founded by Jordan de Briset almost a century earlier, in 1140.

Medieval London would have been full of pilgrims. London was a site of pilgrimage in its own right, with large numbers flocking each year to the shrine of Edward the Confessor in Westminster Abbey, or to lesser shrines in Bermondsey Abbey, Syon Abbey, Our Lady of Willesden or St Anthony's Hospital. It would also have been the point of departure for local pilgrims on their way to other sites; for example, the shrines of Henry VI in Windsor Castle, St Alban in St Albans Abbey, St Swithun in Winchester Cathedral, St John in Beverley Minster, or that of Our Lady of Walsingham in Walsingham Priory (not to mention Santiago de Compostela, Rome or the Holy Land). Perhaps most importantly, though, London would have been a gathering-point on the pilgrimage route from the north to the shrine of St Thomas Becket in Canterbury Cathedral ('The Pilgrim's Way'). The 'turbulent priest' Thomas Becket, the Archbishop of Canterbury, was murdered in Canterbury Cathedral on Tuesday 29 December, 1170 by knights acting on what they had interpreted as an instruction from the King, Henry II. The site became an important one of pilgrimage throughout the later Middle Ages (the penitent Henry making the journey barefoot – at least from the hospital of St Nicholas in Harbledown – in 1174, the year after Thomas was made a saint). The practice ceased after the Reformation under Henry VIII in the sixteenth century, when images of Becket were ordered to be 'putte downe and auoyded out of all churches, chapelles and other places', and a painter from Southwark was paid for 'defasynge' diverse examples in the chapel on London Bridge by then rededicated to St Thomas the Apostle rather than the Martyr. However, it may be said to have resumed in later centuries. Research published by the Chaucer Society in the nineteenth century suggests that the route taken by pilgrims from London to Canterbury ran more or less along the line of the old Roman road of Watling Street – or its modern equivalent, the A2 – through Dartford, Rochester and Faversham (Rochester is mentioned in the Monk's prologue, Sittingbourne in the Wife of Bath's prologue, and Boughton-under-Blean, which is near Faversham, in the Canon Yeoman's prologue, in *The Canterbury Tales*). The journey along this 58-mile route would have taken about four days, with overnight stops at each of the three aforementioned towns. It would have involved travelling 16 miles on the first day (London to Dartford); 14 on the second (Dartford to Rochester), 18 on the third (Rochester to Faversham) and 10 on the fourth (Faversham to Canterbury). The first day's journey, from the City of London to Dartford, would have been by way of London Bridge, Borough High Street, Tabard Street, the Old Kent Road, Deptford, Blackheath, Shooters Hill, Welling, East Wickham, Bexley and Crayford. Sufficient numbers of pilgrim souvenirs, in the form of badges, free-standing figures, *ampullae* and reliquary *chasses*, have been found in Thames-side locations in London to suggest that they were deliberately deposited there in accordance with some forgotten rite (*Figure 10c*).

A minority community of Jews became established in England in the late eleventh century, during the reign of the Norman King William I, many of its members originating from Rouen in Normandy, and practising usury, which Canon Law forbade for Christians. At this time, a number of synagogues were built in and around Old Jewry in the heart of the City of London, and the remains of Jewish ritual baths or *mikvaot* (sing. *mikvah* or *mikveh*) have been found here. Tragically, the Jews of England became subject in the late twelfth and thirteenth centuries to a series of what in later times would be referred to as pogroms or purges. To cite a single example, in 1278, around 680 Jews were arrested in London and detained in the Tower, on suspicion of the capital offence of coin clipping and counterfeiting, of whom 300 were subsequently hanged. Eventually, all the Jews of England were ordered, under the Edict of Expulsion issued by

Edward I on the day of the Fast of Tisha B'Av, 18 July 1290, to be expelled by 1 November of that year. On the actual day of the expulsion, one ship's captain had his Jewish passengers from London disembark on a sandbank at Queenborough in the Thames estuary, and then left them there to drown on the rising tide – for which terrible crime he was later hanged.

Food and Drink

The staple foods of the day were those of the butcher – or on holy days the fishmonger – and baker. The rich gorged themselves on meat, and as FitzStephen put it: 'Those with a fancy for delicacies can obtain for themselves the meat of goose, guinea-hen or woodcock … all set out in front of them.' The poor, whose wages were as little as 1s or 12d/week or less in 1300, subsisted on 'potage', a sort of cereal and vegetable stew that enabled them to eke out their meagre supplies of meat: for them, the only affordable meats would have been suet or marrowbone, typically at 1d per lb., chicken at 1½d each, and rabbit, at 2d each (Rappaport, 1989). Cooked meat and other ready-to-eat foods were sold on the street by hawkers ('One cryd hot shepes feete./One cryd mackerel./One rybbs of befe, and many a pye'). The relationship with meat animals was intimate: people lived with their livestock and pigs ran wild in the streets, creating a considerable public nuisance. Little of the animal was wasted, everything edible being eaten, the fat rendered to make tallow and the hide tanned to make leather. Herbs and and a limited range of spices were widely used in cooking to mask the 'corrupt savours' of foods that had started to spoil – at a time when the only means of preserving were pickling and salting. Dishes could be sweetened either with honey, perhaps purchased on Honey Lane, off Cheapside, in London, or with sugar, although obviously only after it was introduced from the Moorish World in the fourteenth century. (Potatoes were only introduced, from the New World, in the post-Medieval period, in the late sixteenth century.)

Water was drawn from the City's rivers, or from springs or wells. In FitzStephen's time, it was pure and clean. Later, though, 'the tide from the sea prevailed to such a degree that the water of the Thames was salt; so much so that many folks complained of the ale tasting like salt' – and obviously they couldn't have that! By the beginning of the thirteenth century, the water from the Thames had become so contaminated by waste from ships and from shore as to be not only unpalatable but unsafe to drink, for fear of contracting a water-borne disease such as Bloody Flux (dysentery). A supply had to be brought in from outside. A (lead!) pipeline was built, by public subscription, in 1236, to bring water from a spring at Tyburn, roughly opposite where Bond Street tube station now stands, to the so-called Little Conduit, Standard and Great Conduit on Cheapside, about three miles away (sections have recently been discovered 2 metres below Medieval street level in Paternoster Row and in Poultry). Most people collected water from the conduits themselves, although some had it delivered to them – in buckets suspended from shoulder-yokes – by water-carriers or 'cobs' (of whom there were 4,000 by 1600), and the few that could afford it had a private supply piped directly to their homes or businesses in specially installed 'quills'. The pipeline was extended at either end in the fifteenth century so as to run from Oxlese, near where Paddington station now stands, to Cornhill, about six miles away. The so-called Devil's Conduit under Queen's Square probably dates to around the same time; a photograph taken in 1910, shortly before its demolition in 1911-3, shows it to contain graffiti from 1411. The Aldermanbury Conduit under Aldermanbury Square dates to 1471.

Ale and beer, or 'liquid bread', became a staple in the City, as soon as it was unsafe to drink the water – 'small beer' even for breakfast (beer was brewed with hops, which first begun to be imported from the Low Countries in the late Medieval period). Wine was also imbibed in quantity. When King Edward I and his wife Eleanor of Castile were crowned at Westminster on the Sunday after the feast of the Assumption in 1274, 'the Conduit in Chepe ran all the day with red and white wine to drink, for all such who wished.' Purpose-built drinking establishments began to spring up in and around the City in the Medieval period. Among them were the Tabard of 1304, on Borough High Street in Southwark; the Bull Head of 1307, the Nag's Head of 1356, the Star of 1405, and the Mitre of 1461, all on Cheapside; the Pope's Head of 1318, and the Cardinal's Cap of 1369, on Lombard Street; the Bear of 1319 at Bridge Foot; the Swan of 1413, on Old Fish Street; the King's Head of 1417, and the Sun of 1429, on New Fish Street; the Bell of 1464, on King Street [Whitehall] in Westminster; and the King's Head of 1472, on Chancery Lane. The Tabard was written about by Chaucer. It was burned down in the Great Fire of Southwark in 1676, and rebuilt as a coaching-inn in 1677, only to be demolished in 1873, after the arrival of the railway at nearby London Bridge rendered most such establishments surplus to requirements (only the George of 1677 is still standing). Its former site is marked by a Blue Plaque in Talbot Yard.

Sanitation

Which brings us to the indelicate matter of waste, and the disposal thereof. That is to say, human and animal waste, food waste, and the equally if not even more noxious by-products of the City's cottage industries (butchery, tallow chandlery, tannery, soap manufacture, glass manufacture, and so on). Originally, essentially all of the above was simply dumped in the streets, to be washed downhill in gutters and into the Thames or one of its tributaries – one of the streets thus coming to be known as Shiteburn Lane (and later, so as to shield the delicate from shock or at least appease its inhabitants, Sherborne Lane). To be fair, some public latrines were built directly over the Thames or its tributaries, thereby at least cutting out the middle man, so to speak. Eventually, though, this practice was outlawed as the streets became breeding grounds for vermin and disease, not to mention evil-smelling, and exceedingly unpleasant underfoot – whence the invention of the 'patten', the platform sole of the day. After the mid-fourteenth century, waste was compelled to be collected by rakers and carters, and disposed of further afield 'without throwing anything into the Thames for the saving of the body of the river ... and also for avoiding the filthiness that is increasing in the water and upon the Banks of the Thames, to the great abomination and damage of the people', and anyone guilty of any violation was punished by 'prison for his body, and other heavy punishment as well, at the discretion of the Mayor and the Aldermen'. Some was carried down the Thames, in 'dung-boats' to be dumped, some deposited in land-fill sites outside the City, and some spread as fertiliser on surrounding fields. Nonetheless, a considerable amount of damage had already been done to the environment and to public health, and the Fleet and Walbrook had effectively become dead rivers, the post-Saxon history of the former being described as 'a decline from a river to a brook, from a brook to a ditch, and from a ditch to a drain'.

Environmental archaeological examination of Medieval Fleet deposits from a site in Tudor Street revealed the existence of 140 species of mainly micro-organisms in one early layer, indicating – apart from nematode worms from human faeces – a generally healthy condition;

but only two stress-tolerant and opportunistic species in a second, later layer, indicating increasing toxicity; and none at all in a third, latest layer, indicating the total eradication of all life, as described in the archive records for 1343 (Boyd, 1981).

All in all, Medieval London was a City of crowding and clamour and squalor and stench. Nosegays and pomanders notwithstanding.

Medical Matters

The diagnosis and treatment of disease in Medieval England would have been based essentially on Galenic principles – as in Roman times. Diseases would have been diagnosed on the basis of perceived imbalances in the four humours, namely choleric (yellow bile), melancholic (black bile), phlegmatic (phlegm) and sanguine (blood) and treated according to the 'theory of opposites', for example, in the case of excesses, by blood-letting or purging, through the use of herbal concoctions. Sadly, the mainly herbal treatments administered by monks, apothecaries and physicians, were of limited efficacy against the diseases of the day, including ague, plague, leprosy, and consumption.

Quartan Ague, the commonest strain, was diagnosed by a high fever recurring every fourth day. It is now known to be caused by the parasitic protozoan *Plasmodium malariae*, in turn transmitted by the bite of an infected mosquito of the genus *Anopheles*. In the Medieval period, it was thought to be associated with harmful airs associated with stagnant water (whence 'Mal-aria'). There is actually something in this, as stagnant water provides the perfect habitat for the vector mosquito. There was a major epidemic in 1241 after the great floods of that year, as chronicled by Matthew Paris: 'Thus the year passed away, generating epidemics and quartan agues.'

Bubonic Plague (see also above) was diagnosed by painful swellings or buboes in the groin or armpit. It is now known to be caused by the bacterium *Yersinia pestis*, in turn generally transmitted by the bite of an infected rat-flea of the species *Xenopsylla cheopis*, such as was common in the conditions in which people, livestock, pets and vermin lived, cheek-by-jowl, in London in the Medieval to post-Medieval period. In that period, it was thought to be spread by cats and dogs, which were therefore rounded up and killed in large numbers (the resulting reduction in predation ironically allowing the real culrits, rats to proliferate). The 1348-9 outbreak, now referred to as the Black Death, caused so many deaths in such a short time that epidemiologists suspect that it was a particularly deadly and infectious – possibly pneumonic – strain of the disease, capable of being passed directly from one infected person to another without the involvement of the vector flea (Sloane, 2011). Significantly in this context, the Black Death was able to continue to spread and even to spike over the winter of 1348-9, when the vector flea would have been inactive, as it is everywhere today at temperatures of less than 10°C.

Leprosy was diagnosed by the loss of sensitivity to pain and by the consequent loss of parts of extremities due to repeated injuries or infections. It is now known to be an infection caused by the bacterium *Mycobacterium leprae* or *M. lepromatosis*, and to be spread from person to person. In the Middle Ages, sufferers were regarded as unclean, and stigmatised by being made to carry a bell with which to announce their presence. Indeed, all lepers were banished and banned from the City of London under a Royal Edict issued by Edward III in 1346, which read, in part: 'all leprose persons inhabiting ... should auoid within fifteen dayes [and] no man suffer any such leprose person to abide within his house, vpon paine to forfeite his said house, and to incurre the Kinges further displeasure.' An entry in the *Letter-Book* of 1372 read:

John Mayn, who had oftentimes been commanded to depart from the City ... and avoid the common conversation of mankind – seeing that he ... was smitten with the blemish of leprosy ... was [ordered] before the mayor and aldermen [to] depart forthwith [and] not return ... on pain of undergoing the punishment of the pillory.

Even quite intricate surgical operations were evidently skilfully performed, and most patients survived the actual surgery, although sadly many succumbed to uncontrollable infection afterwards. Operations performed by monks were proscribed by a Papal Decree issued by Boniface VIII after the Council of Tours in 1163 (*Ecclesia abhorret a sanguine*). After this date, they came to be undertaken by Barber-Surgeons.

Some twenty-five hospitals, mainly attached to monastic houses, sprang up around the City in the Medieval period (Barnett & Jay, 2008), a few of which survived the Dissolution and into the post-Medieval, including St Mary of Bethlehem, St Bartholomew's and St Thomas's. They are perhaps best thought of as places to which patients would go to in anticipation of compassionate care ('hospitality'), if not necessarily effective treatment. Some of the hospitals specialised in the treatment of particular types of patient, for example, St Mary of Bethlehem, or 'Bedlam', in the treatment of mentally ill persons; Elsing Spital, in the treatment of blind persons; St Anthony's Hospital, in the treatment of those suffering from 'St Anthony's Fire', or ergotism, a disease caused by eating cereals contaminated by an alkaloid-secreting fungus; and the 'Lazar(us) Houses' of St Giles-in-the-Fields, Westminster, Knightbridge to the west of the City of London, Kingsland to the north, Mile End to the east, and Southwark to the south, in the treatment of lepers. The sites of the leper hospitals were deliberately chosen so as to allow a degree of social isolation, and yet at the same time to provide the opportunity for the inmates to beg for alms from the occasional passers-by. St Giles-in-the-Fields was quite literally in the fields between the Cities of London and Westminster.

The Priory of St Mary of Bethlehem was originally built just outside Bishopsgate in 1247, part of it becoming a hospital in 1329/30, a hospital for the mentally ill, of a sort, purportedly as long ago as 1377, and demonstrably as long ago as 1403, and infamous for the shameful ill-treatment of its inmates by all and sundry in the unenlightened times that followed.

Population
From various accounts, it appears that the population of London was of the order of 10-15,000 at the time of the *Domesday* survey in 1086, 40,000 a century later in 1180, 80,000 in 1300, and 40,000 in 1377, after the Black Death (the *Domesday* survey was undertaken by the Normans principally to determine who owned what, and what taxes they were liable for). The death rate among native Londoners tended to exceed the birth rate, significantly so during outbreaks of plague, such that the city's population could only be maintained and grown by immigration, either from elsewhere in England and Scotland, from Europe, for example from Normandy, Gascony, Flanders and Lombardy, or indeed from even further afield (Bolton, 1998). The subsidy rolls of 1292 and 1319 record primarily French, Flemish/Dutch, Italian and German 'aliens' or 'strangers'. Those of 1440 and 1483 record primarily German aliens, numbering 1,307 out of a total

of 2,540, but also French, Flemish/Dutch, Italian (Genoese, Venetian and Lucchian), Spanish and other, including Indian. By this time, there were already over 100 'aliens' in each of the wards of Bishopsgate, Broad Street, Cripplegate, Dowgate (where the 'Steelyard' was), Farringdon, Langbourn, Portsoken and Tower (Ross & Clark, 2008).

Administration and Governance

Under the Normans, and indeed the Plantagenets, the City of London remained outwardly little changed, at least initially, still largely confined within the Roman walls and laid out according to the Saxon street plan. There were, though, sweeping changes to the way the City, and indeed the country, was run, at least initially, under the autocratic Feudal System. Under the system, the King and his place-men, the barons and knights, essentially owned all the land; and granted the peasantry, that is to say, in descending order of status, the manorial serfs, villeins, and bordars, access to it only in exchange for rent, labour, produce or services, or for some combination thereof. At the time of the *Domesday* in 1086, the population of England was 2,000,000, of which, considerably less than 1% belonged to the royal, noble and ecclesiastical elite, and 20% were classified as semi-free serfs, 40% as villeins, and 30% as bordars, also known as cottars (all numbers are approximate). Also at this time, 10% of the population were slaves, owned and sold like chattels. However, shortly afterwards, in 1102, the Church Council of London issued a decree ordering 'Let no man dare hereafter to engage in the infamous business, prevalent in England, of selling men like animals.' And by the turn of the twelfth and thirteenth centuries, slavery appears to have been effectively eliminated (most former slaves by this time having been granted small-holdings, and become bordars). Under the Normans and Plantagenets, the ruling elite, though powerful, was small, and more than a little wary of the large and potentially rebellious population now nominally under its control. In consequence, successive kings made a series of placatory political moves to maintain and even extend the rights and privileges that the City had enjoyed under the Saxon King Edward the Confessor. But lest the City get ideas above its station, there were everywhere within it and without reminders of the Royal presence, and of where the real power lay: the Tower of London and the gallows and scaffold on Tower Hill, in the east; and Baynard's Castle, Montfichet's Tower and the Royal Wardrobe, in the west.

As noted above, the City of London became at least in part self-governing in Medieval times, under the Corporation and its officials, namely the Mayor, Sheriffs (Shire-Reeves), Aldermen and Common Councilmen, who were initially appointed and subsequently elected, albeit elected by, and from within, a wealthy and influential elite, including representatives of the trades guilds or Livery Companies. Perhaps the most famous of London's Mayors was Richard or Dick Whittington (c. 1354-1423). Whittington, a Mercer, was appointed Mayor in 1397, on the death of the incumbent, and elected to the post on a further three occasions, in 1397, 1406 and 1419. Among the many public works undertaken by Whittington, in or out of public office, were the reconstruction of the Guildhall; the conversion into a Market and Garner of the Leaden Hall; the establishment of the College of St Spirit and St Mary, on what is now College Hill, where he lived; the reconstruction of the church of St Michael Paternoster Royal, also on College Hill; the reconstruction of Newgate Prison, which had been damaged during the Peasants' Revolt; and the bequest of a library valued at £400 to Christ Church Newgate Street. Not to mention the construction of a 128-seater public lavatory, popularly known as 'Whittington's Longhouse', in the parish of St Martin Vintry! *Magna Carta* of 1215 had granted the City 'all its ancient liberties and free customs, both by land and by water'. In exchange, the Crown required that, each year, the newly elected Mayor present himself at court to ceremonially demonstrate his allegiance. This event eventually became the Lord Mayor's Show we know today. The associated parade of the mayor and his entourage from the City to Westminster used to take place on the Feast of St Simon and St Jude at the end of October, whereas now it takes place on the second Saturday in November. The parade also used to take place on the water, whereas now it takes place on land – although the mobile stages are referred to as 'floats'. It travels, accompanied by much pomp, from the Lord Mayor's official residence, Mansion House, past St Paul's Cathedral to the Royal Courts of Justice, where the Cities of London and Westminster meet.

The Corporation became responsible for the infrastructure of the City and the health and welfare of its citizens, including the maintainence of the City walls, communal buildings and gardens; the oversight of industrial activity within the walls; street-cleaning; the provision of water-supply and sewage systems; and the implementation of measures to prevent or control disease – at least insofar as this was possible. It also became at least partially responsible for the more general prosperity and orderliness of the City, including the education of the populace, and the maintenance, if not the establishment, of the law.

The Corporation and its benefactors, many of them associated with burgeoning trades guilds or Livery Companies, with vested interests in vocational training, were responsible for founding a number of educational establishments from the twelfth century onwards, some of which are still running (although none on their original sites) (FitzStephen, 1183). The City of London School was founded through the benefaction of the Town Clerk, John Carpenter, in 1442, on a site adjacent to the Guildhall; and the school attached to St Paul's Cathedral was re-founded by Dean John Colet in 1511. St Peter's College, or Westminster School, attached to Westminster Abbey, was founded in the twelfth century. Literacy rates have been estimated to have been of the order of 50% by the end of the Medieval period or beginning of the post-Medieval. Functional literacy rates would have been even higher.

The law of the land was established centrally, by Parliament. It was essentially maintained locally, through the fore-runners of the police, namely the sergeants and constables or night-watchmen, and through the courts. As the then Mayor, Henry Galeys, put it, in his *Provision for the Safe-Keeping of the City*, in 1282:

> As to the safe-keeping of the City: All the gates of the City are to be open by day; and at each gate there are to be two serjeants to open the same, skilful men, and fluent of speech, who are to keep a good watch upon persons coming in and going out that so no evil may befall the City. At every parish church, curfew is to be rung at the same hour as at St Martin's le Grand; so that they begin together, and end together; and then all the gates are to be shut, as well as taverns for wine or for ale; and no one is then to go about by the alleys or ways. Six persons are to watch in each ward by night, of the most competent men of the ward thereto; and the two serjeants who guard the gates by day, are to lie at night either within the gates, on near thereto.

There were only a few dozen sergeants (including one for each of the twenty-five wards, and a comparable total based at the Guildhall), and a few score constables or night-watchmen, to police a population of a few tens of thousands. They had to deal with every type of crime, from petty theft, through adulteration or false weighing of foodstuffs (or other breaches of manufacturing and retail regulations), to counterfeiting currency, assault and murder.

The right of every Englishman accused of a crime to a trial by jury in a court of law was first codified in *Magna Carta* of 1215, the great charter that ultimately gave rise to our modern legal and – democratic – parliamentary systems: two of the four surviving copies of which are now in the British Library in London. This and some of the other provisions of *Magna Carta* that have resonated down the centuries read – rather wonderfully – as follows:

> 39 – No man shall be taken or imprisoned ... or outlawed or exiled or in any way ruined, nor will we go or send against him, except by the lawful judgement of his peers... 40 – To no one will we sell, to no one will we deny right or justice... 52 – If anyone has been ... deprived by us without lawful judgement of his peers of lands, castles, liberties or ... rights, we will restore them to him at once... 61 ['The Security Clause'] We give and grant ... the following security: namely, that the barons shall choose any twenty-five barons of the realm that they wich, who with all their might are to observe ... and cause to be observed the peace and liberties which we have granted and confirmed to them by this our present charter... 62 – Wherefore we wish and firmly command that the English church shall be free, and the men in our realm shall have and hold all the aforesaid liberties, rights and concessions well and peacefully, freely and quietly, fully and completely ... in all things and places for ever, as is aforesaid... Given under our hand in the meadow which is called Runnymede on the fifteenth day of June in the seventeenth year of our reign.

The right to legal counsel and representation, by attorneys (solicitors) and pleaders-before-court (barristers), became established in the later thirteenth century; formal training of pleaders-before-court, in the Inns of Court, strategically situated between the Cities of London to the east and Westminster to the west, at Temple in the early fourteenth, at Gray's Inn in the late fourteenth, and at Lincoln's Inn, in its present location, in the fifteenth. John Fortescue, a sometime Governor of Lincoln's Inn, wrote of the Inns of Court in 1470:

In England, laws are learned in three languages, namely English [which was in fact the everyday language of the court from the late fourteenth century onwards], French and Latin [and] not in universities, but in a certain public academy situated near the King's courts [in Westminster]. That academy is not situated in the city, where the tumult could disturb the student's quiet, but in a suburb. There are in this academy ten lesser Inns of Chancery to each of [which] at least a hundred belong. These students are for the most part young men learning the elements of the law, who, becoming proficient as they mature, are absorbed into the greater Inns of Court, of which there are four in number, and to the least of which belong 200 students or more. ... [I]n these greater inns there can no student be maintained for less expenses by the year than 20 marks. And if he have a servant to wait upon him, as most of them have, then so much the greater will his charges be. Now by reason of these charges the children only of noble men do study the laws... For the poor and common sort of the people are not able to bear so great charges ... and merchant men can seldom find in their hearts to hinder their merchandise with so great yearly expenses. And thus it falleth out that there is scant any man found within the ... laws, except he be a gentleman born... Wherefore they more than any other kind of men have a special regard to their nobility and to the preservation of their honour and fame. And to speak uprightly there is in these greater inns, yea and in the lesser too, beside the study of the laws, as it were an university or school of all commendable qualities requisite for noble men. There they learn to sing, and to exercise themselves in all kinds of harmony. There also they practise dancing, and other noble men's pastimes, as they do which are brought up in the King's house.

The law was upheld through a judicial system that placed particular emphasis on punishment as a deterrent to crime, although in its defence it also at least attempted to make the punishment fit the crime, with the least serious or petty crimes punishable by fines or corporal punishment, and only the perceived most serious – of which it has to be admitted there were scores – by capital punishment (Wright, 2017).

Corporal punishment included the use of the pillories and stocks, which restrained convicted criminals and allowed them to be harangued or to have missiles thrown at them by the general public. In 1327: 'John Brid, baker, was ... put upon the pillory, with ... dough hung from [his neck]; ... until vespers at St Paul's ... be ended,' for 'falsehood, malice and deceit, by him committed, to the nuisance of the common people', for stealing dough from persons using his premises to bake their bread. Capital punishment took one of a number of forms, for example, hanging, for murderers, and also for common thieves – of any article valued at over 1s – and other felons; boiling, for poisoners; burning, for religious dissenters; *peine forte e dure* (pressing, under increasingly heavy weights), for those accused who refused to confess; beheading, for those of noble birth; and, most gruesomely, hanging, drawing (disembowelling) and quartering, with or without the refinement of castrating, for traitors, that is, those found guilty of high treason. Executions were carried out not only in prison but also in public, in various parts of the city, most famously on Tower Hill and in West Smithfield, or at Tyburn, at the western end of Oxford Street, near the modern Marble Arch. Among those executed at West Smithfield were William Wallace, the Scottish freedom fighter, who was hanged, drawn and quartered here in 1305, for high treason; and one Margery Jordemaine, the 'Witch of Eye', who was burned at the stake here in 1441 for allegedly plotting to kill the then King, Henry VI, by means of witchcraft. Contrary to popular belief, comparatively few women were burned for witchcraft in Medieval England (although many more were hanged).

Interestingly, imprisonment was originally only for those awaiting trial, sentencing, or sentence of execution, and not intended as a punishment in its own right, although in actual practice it was such, on account partly of the inhumane conditions under which prisoners were kept, and partly of the brutal treatment meted out to them. Most of London's many prisons were deliberately located outside the walls – and jurisdiction – of the City, so as not to sully its gilded streets (the same also being true, incidentally, of other undesirable buildings, industries and activities, not to mention persons). Some of the more famous – or infamous – ones were on the south side of the river in Southwark, including at one time or another the Borough Compter, Clink, King's Bench, Horsemonger Lane, first and second Marshalsea, and White Lion. The surviving part of the wall of the second, nineteenth-century Marshalsea Prison, where Dickens's father was incarcerated for debt, may still be seen, adjacent to the church of St George the Martyr. There were also the Bridewell and Fleet to the west, and the Tothill Bridewell in Westminster (one of the surviving gates of the Tothill Bridewell may still be seen, in Little Sanctuary, a short distance from its original location). Perhaps the most infamous prison of all, Newgate, on the western edge of the City, was originally built in 1188 and rebuilt in 1236, and again, at the behest of Dick Whittington, in 1422, after having been destroyed during the Peasants' Revolt of 1381. Newgate became a byword for everything bad about the prison system, with Dick Whittington writing in 1419 'by reason of the foetid ... atmosphere ... in the heinous gaol ... many persons are now dead who would be alive' (many more would die here yet, of 'Gaol Fever', or typhus). Throughout the Medieval period, condemned prisoners were dragged on a pallet all the way from Newgate, past baying crowds, to Tyburn to be executed, some of them being allowed to stop at a tavern on the way to drink themselves into a merciful early oblivion.

Trade and Commerce

Trade prospered alongside religiosity in the Medieval City of London, as it always had, always would and no doubt always will – although the relationship between the two was at times strained, like that between an errant child and its parents. Throughout the Medieval and post-Medieval periods, only Freemen of the City were entitled to trade here (from the early fourteenth century onwards, Freemen had to be members of one or other of the Livery Companies). Freedom of the City was acquired by one of three means: servitude (apprenticeship), patrimony (inheritance), or redemption (purchase).

The City had become an important port and trading centre, through which a significant proportion of the entire country's imports and exports were channelled. The waterfront, the Port of London, much of it then recently reclaimed, bristled with bustling wharves, some trade flowing to the downstream side of London Bridge after the drawbridge that allowed large vessels to pass upstream became unusable in the fifteenth or sixteenth century.

A prodigious range of comestible and manufactured goods was imported from all over the known Old World, from the the lands bordering the English Channel, North Sea and Baltic; and further afield, from those bordering the Mediterranean, or linked to the latter by the Silk or Spice Routes. These included fresh fish from the

Thames, imported to Queenhithe and Billingsgate, and shellfish to Oystergate (oysters were an important source of protein, especially for the poor, and discarded oyster shells are still common finds on the foreshore of the Thames); wine from Gascony, to Vintry; and 'Baltic goods', including timber, amber, 'Stockholm Tar' and what FitzStephen described as 'sable, vair and miniver from the far lands where Russ and Norseman dwell', to Dowgate. FitzStephen also listed 'Gold from Arabia; from Sabaea spice and incense; from the Scythians arms of steel well-tempered; oil from the rich groves of palm that spring from the fat lands of Babylon; fine gems from Nile; [and] from China crimson silks'. Significant numbers of fritware (stone-paste) containers for exotic goods, known as *albarelli* (sing. *albarello*), likely to have been imported from the Islamic World, have been found in archaeological excavations at Plantation Place, off Fenchurch Street (Pitt *et al.*, 2013). 'Stockfish' (dried) were sold at the Stocks Market; meat at the 'shambles' on Newgate Street; poultry on Poultry; grain at Cornhill; bread, milk and honey and a range of general and exotic goods in the shops and selds on Cheapside and Eastcheap; and general and exotic goods at the covered market on Leadenhall Street, and at open-air fairs. Wool and, later, finished woollen cloth were the most important exports, chiefly to the Low Countries, and the trade was enormously lucrative. Sheepskins and other animal hides, food-stuffs, and Cornish tin were also exported.

The trade with the ports on the coasts of the North Sea and Baltic came to be controlled by an alliance called the Hanseatic League, which was formally founded in 1241, and which had its London headquarters at the Steelyard, which was essentially a semi-autonomous enclave of Germany. The relationship between the Hanse and local merchants was sometimes strained. In 1388, the following writ was issued in Westminster, when the London merchants complained that their servants and goods had been 'arrested in Stralsund ... the King commands the mayor and sheriffs of London to arrest all the men ... of ... Germany ... in ... London ... and to detain them until they ... answer to such charges as may be made against them on behalf of the King.'

The Custom House was originally built at least as long ago as 1377, in Billingsgate, close to the centre of activity on the waterfront, its purpose being to collect the duties payable on exports of wool, and subsequently rebuilt, following a fire, in 1559. It was burned down in the Great Fire in 1666, and rebuilt yet again, by Christopher Wren, in 1668-71. Wren's building was destroyed in an explosion in 1714, and rebuilt by Thomas Ripley; Ripley's building in turn burned down in 1814. The present Custom House was built by David Laing in 1814-7 and rebuilt following a partial collapse caused by the rotting of the beech-wood foundation piles by Robert Smirke in 1825. Perhaps surprisingly, given its previous history, it survived the Blitz unscathed. It is designed to be, and is, best viewed from the river rather than from the road.

Trades guilds, or Livery Companies, began to be founded from the turn of the thirteenth and fourteenth centuries onwards, in part an attempt to control the freedom to trade at a time of comparative over-population and shortage of work. The Livery Companies established working practices and standards. In 1671, the Mayor's Court in the Guildhall ordered that defective spectacles discovered in the possession of one Elizabeth Bagnall be 'with a hammber broken all in pieces' by the Master of the Company of Spectacle-Makers 'on the remaining parte of London Stone' (damaged during the Great Fire five years earlier). The Livery Companies also provided apprenticeships for members at the beginning of their working lives and alms for those at the end of theirs. The twelve 'Great' Livery Companies, whose coats-of-arms adorn the walls of the Great Hall of the Guildhall, are, in order of precedence, the Mercers', Grocers', Drapers', Fishmongers', Goldsmiths', Skinners', Merchant Taylors', Haberdashers', Salters', Ironmongers', Vintners' and Clothworkers'. The Skinners' and Merchant Taylors' each alternate between sixth and seventh in the order of precedence, in accordance with the 'Billesdon Award', a ruling made by the then-mayor Robert Billesdon in 1484 to end their long-running dispute (Lang, 1984). To this day, any such state of confusion is referred to as 'at sixes and sevens'.

Wealth and Poverty
As time went by, City traders grew rich, in some cases fabulously so. In contrast, although some unskilled 'working-class' people made money by supplying the demands of the burgeoning bourgeoisie for fancy goods and services, most remained grindingly poor, and deprived of any real opportunity of social mobility. There was never an equitable distribution or redistribution of wealth, although there was at least

an informal system of charitable patronage and donation from the churches, from other rich institutions such as the Livery Companies, and from rich individuals. The rich burned wax candles, the poor, tallow (rendered animal fat). All would appear to have lived rather uneasily cheek by jowl. Though there is a certain amount of evidence from tax records of concentrations of wealth in the wards in the centre of the City, and of poverty in those around its margins and without the walls, in both the Medieval and post-Medieval periods. For ward maps, see Hyde (1999).

Entertainment and Culture

For the entertainment of the many and the edification of the few, there was at West Smithfield archery, wrestling and cock-fighting, a weekly horse fair, and an annual Bartholomew Fair every August from the twelfth century, and there were also regular jousting tournaments from the fourteenth. At East Smithfield, there was another fair, on Undershaft an annual May Fair; and on Cheapside further tournaments. In the Tower of London from the thirteenth century there was, bizarrely, a menagerie of elephants, lions, bears and other exotic beasts. Louis IX of France presented Henry III with an African elephant in 1255, which became one of the prize exhibits in the menagerie before it died in 1257, likely of a surfeit of the red wine fed to it by its keeper, one Henri(cus) de Flor. Surviving records indicate that the cost of transporting the elephant to the Tower, building a special house for it and feeding it was well over £50, at a time when a knight could live comfortably for a year on £15. Visitors to the menagerie were allowed 'free' entry if they presented the warders with a cat or dog to feed to the lions. The polar bear was able to feed itself by fishing in the Thames (at the end of a long tether). On Bankside in Southwark, from the mid-fifteenth century, there was animal-baiting. The oldest record of the royal office of 'Master of the Bears' is from 1484, which was during the reign of the last Plantagenet King, Richard III, who appointed a 'Master, Guyder and Ruler of all our Bears', which rather begs the question, how many were there?

On Moorfields in the winter, when the Walbrook froze over, which it did repeatedly in the Medieval period, there was improvised ice-skating as described by Fitzstephen: '[T]he younger crowd ... equip each of their feet with an animal's shin-bone, attaching it to the underside of their footwear; using hand-held poles reinforced with metal tips, which they periodically thrust against the ice, they propel themselves along as swiftly as a bird in flight or a bolt shot from a crossbow.' On the Thames, when it repeatedly froze over between the twelfth and nineteenth centuries, there were impromptu 'frost fairs'. Records indicate that in all the river froze over nearly forty times between 1142 and 1895, becoming the site of the fairs for certain in 1564-65, 1683-84, 1715-16, 1739-40, 1788-89 and 1813-14, and possibly in other years. Everywhere, all the time, there was drinking, gambling, and rough sport. Repeated attempts were made over the years to ban football. In 1314, the Mayor of London, Nicholas de Farndone, issued the following order: 'And whereas there is great uproar in the City, through certain tumults arising from the striking of great footballs in the fields of the public, from which many evils perchance may arise, which may God forbid, we do command and do forbid, on the King's behalf, on pain of imprisonment, that such game be practices from henceforth within the city.' Wrestling within the bounds of St Paul's was also proscribed in the fifteenth century! 'That no manne ne childe, of what estate or condicion that he be, be so hardy as to wrestell, or make any wrestlyng, within the seintury ne the boundes of Poules, ne in non other open place within the Citee of London, up peyne of emprisonement of fourty days, & making fyn un-to the chaumbre after the discrecioun of the Mair & Aldermen.'

There were of course 'stew-houses', or brothels. A set of 'Ordinances for the Governance of the Stews' was issued as long ago as 1161, and a 'Proclamation as to Street Walkers by Night, and Women of Bad Repute' in 1393. The latter read in part as follows:

> Whereas many and divers affrays, broils and dissensions have arisen in times past, and many men have been slain and murdered by reason of the frequent resort of, and consorting with, common harlots ... we do by our command forbid ... that any such women shall go about ... the ... city ... but they are to keep themselves to the places thereunto assigned, that is to say, the Stews on the other side of the Thames [on Bankside in Southwark], and Cokkeslane [Cock Lane].

There were also occasional royal spectacles and civic ceremonials such as the Lord Mayor's Show, and miracle, mystery or morality plays, 'holy plays, representations of miracles, which holy confessors have wrought, or representations of torments wherein the constancy of martyrs appeared', from at least as long ago as the twelfth century (FitzStephen, 1183); and Creation and Passion performances staged by the City clerks and apprentices at the Clerks' Well in Clerkenwell in the fourteenth and fifteenth.

London was the home of the courtier, diplomat, bureaucrat, poet and author Geoffrey Chaucer (1342?-1400), and figured prominently in his famously bawdy works, which were originally written in Middle English, and of his fellow Ricardian poet and friend John Gower (1330-1408), the inventor of the iambic tetrameter. (Chaucer is buried in Westminster Abbey; Gower in Southwark Cathedral.) Chaucer was variously employed as a *Varlet de Chambre* by Edward III, between 1367-74; as the 'Comptroller of the Customs and Subside of Wools, Skins and Tanned Hides' by Edward III and Richard II, between 1374-86; and as Clerk of the King's Works by Richard II, between 1389-91 (he is also thought to have studied Law at the Inner Temple, around 1366).

In the course of his employment, in 1373, he is thought to have come into contact with Petrarch and Bocaccio, and to have been introduced to Italian poetry in Italy. Between 1374 and 1386, he would undoubtedly have met travellers from all over the country and continent at his then place of work at the Custom House on the river-front in Billingsgate, including those making the pilgrimage to the shrine of St Thomas Becket in Canterbury Cathedral, some of them perhaps providing inspiration for the colourful characters he wrote about in the *Canterbury Tales*.

He would appear to have written *The House of Fame, The Legend of Good Women, Parlement of Foules*, and *Troilus and Criseyde*, and also at least to have begun to write *The Canterbury Tales* at this time, at his lodgings in Aldgate. Earlier, in 1369, he had written *The Book of the Duchess* in honour of his mentor John of Gaunt's wife Blanche of Lancaster (who died of the plague that year).

Dress
Contemporary representations – most of them, it has to be acknowledged, of the rich – indicate that the everyday dress of both men and women essentially throughout the Middle Ages consisted of various types of gown. The materials from which the gowns were

5. Memorial to John and Mary Oteswich, church of St Helen (*c.* 1400).

made varied across society, with the wearing of expensive fabrics and furs restricted to the ruling classes, and that of cloth-of-gold to royalty, as stipulated by the Sumptuary Laws (and the later 'Acts of Apparel').

Materials that have been found during the course of archaeological excavations in London include variously woven sheeps' wool, goats' hair, linen, silk and velvet; variously dyed with madder and kermes (shades of red), weld (yellow), woad (light blue), indigo (dark blue) and indigo purple.

The cuts as a general rule tended to become shorter and closer through time. In the church of St Helen, there is a memorial to the gentleman John (de) Oteswich and his wife Mary that is thought to date to the end of the fourteenth century (*Figure 5*). It depicts John wearing a long, loose gown with flared sleeves of a type known as a 'houppelande', carrying on his belt a short sword on his left hip and a sort of man-bag known as a 'scrip' on his right. Mary wears a similar gown, covered by a 'coat-hardie' and a veiled head-dress or wimple.

The Medieval men and women of London were clearly concerned not only about their clothes, but also their hair, eyebrows, ears and nails, as evidenced by the discoveries in archaeological excavations of diverse accessories including girdles, buckles, strap-ends, mounts, brooches, buttons, lace chapes, pins, beads, chains, pendants, rings, bells, purses, cased mirrors, combs, cosmetic implements and sets, and needle-cases (Egan & Pritchard, 2002). The physical evidence is supported by literary sources – the Carpenter's wife in Chaucer's *Canterbury Tales* plucked and darkened her eyebrows!

Throughout Europe, men's shoes became increasingly elongated and pointed at the toe from the twelfth century to the fifteenth, to such an extreme extent in the late fourteenth to fifteenth that the points had to be tied to the wearers' legs to prevent tripping! Such shoes, known as 'crakows' or 'poulaines', after Krakow in Poland, became particularly popular in England after the marriage of Richard II to Anne of Bohemia in 1382, though their wearing was subsequently restricted to Lords, Esquires and Gentlemen by a Sumptuary Law in 1463, and eventually banned altogether in 1465. An anonymous monk of Evesham wrote in 1394: 'With this Queen there came from Bohemia into England those accursed vices ... half a yard in length, thus it was necessary for them to be tied to the shin with chains of silver before they could walk with them.' Fine fourteenth-century examples have been found on the foreshore of the Thames near the second Baynard's Castle, built in 1338, and the Royal Wardrobe, built in around 1361, that would have been worn by high-status individuals associated with these buildings (their impracticality would have ruled out their use by working men).

Building Works

The Normans built the first stone buildings within and without the walls of the City for hundreds of years. These included a number intended to symbolise their sovereign authority over the Saxons: the White Tower in the Tower of London, built of Caen Stone from 1076-1101 onwards; the first Baynard's Castle and Montfichet's Tower, also built in the late eleventh century; and, further afield, Windsor Castle, built between 1070-86. The first Baynard's Castle and Montfichet's Tower were both built, a little to the south-west of St Paul's, in the late eleventh century (Baynard's Castle by Ralph Baynard, and Montfichet's Tower by Richard de Montfichet, both of them Norman noblemen). Both buildings were demolished in the early thirteenth (Blackfriars Priory was built on the site of the first Baynard's Castle in in 1276).

The Normans also initiated a major phase of building churches and other religious houses in the late eleventh to early twelfth centuries, in the Norman or Romanesque style. The collegiate church and monastery of St Martin-le-Grand was originally founded by two brothers, Ingelric and Girard, in around 1056; the parish church of St Mary-le-Bow, or Bow Church, by the Norman King William I's Archbishop of Canterbury, Lanfranc, around 1077-87; the Cluniac Priory and Abbey of St Saviour, or Bermondsey Abbey, in 1082; the parish church of St Mary-at-Lambeth sometime before 1086; what is now known as Old St Paul's, by Bishop Maurice and his successors sometime after 1087; the parish church of St Giles Cripplegate in around 1100; Holy Trinity Priory, by the Canons of Augustine, in 1108; the Augustinian Priory of St Bartholomew in 1123; the Priory of the Order of the Hospital of St John of Jerusalem, in Clerkenwell, the English home of the Knights Hospitaller, in 1144; the Augustinian Priory of St Mary, also in Clerkenwell, in 1145; the Royal Hospital of St Katharine by the Tower, in 1148; and the round nave of Temple Church, the English home of the Knights Templar, modelled on the Church of the Holy Sepulchre in Jerusalem, in 1160-85. The nunnery of St Mary Overie (Southwark Cathedral) was refounded as a priory in 1106. Important new secular public buildings of the Norman period included Westminster Hall, built 1097-99; and the Guildhall, built sometime before 1128

Later, the Plantagenets added inner and outer curtain walls to the Tower of London in the thirteenth to early fourteenth centuries; built Savoy Palace in the early fourteenth, in 1324; the second Baynard's Castle also in the early fourteenth, in around 1338; and the Royal Wardrobe in the late fourteenth, in 1361; in Westminster, the Jewel Tower (part of the Palace of Westminster), in 1365-6; and further afield, a manor-house on the then-waterfront in Rotherhithe in 1349-53. Also further afield, a succession of Plantagenet Kings extended Windsor Castle. The second Baynard's Castle was built in a river-front location around 1338, and rebuilt around 1428, and possibly again in the late fifteenth. It was used by a succession of Kings and Queens in the late fifteenth to sixteenth centuries, before being destroyed in the Great Fire in the seventeenth. It was the London headquarters of the House of York during the Wars of the Roses. According to the chronicler

Fabian, The Earl of March was hailed King Edward IV here, before he was formally crowned in Westminster Abbey, in 1461:

> [T]he Earls of March and Warwick with a great power of men, ... entered into the City of London, the which was of the citizens joyously received, and ... the said earl caused to be mustered his people ... whereupon it was demanded of the said people whether ... Henry [VI] were worthy to reign as king any longer or no. Whereunto the people cried hugely and said Nay, Nay. And after it was asked of them whether they would have the Earl of March as their king and they cried with one voice, Yea, Yea. After the which admission thus by the commons assented, certain captains were assigned to bear report unto the said Earl of March then being lodged in his place called Baynard's Castle.

In 1483, Richard III is believed to have asserted his claim to the throne here. The Plantagenets also continued the church and religious house building or rebuilding programme in the later Medieval, in the Gothic style. All Hallows Staining, Austin Friars Priory, Blackfriars Priory, the Charterhouse, Greyfriars Priory, Holywell Priory, St Andrew Undershaft, St Clare without Aldgate (also known as Holy Trinity Minories), St Ethelburga, St Etheldreda, St Helen, St Katharine Cree, St Leonard Shoreditch, St Mary Aldermary, St Mary-at-Hill, St Mary Graces, St Mary-le-Strand, St Mary of Bethlehem ('Bedlam'), St Mary Rotherhithe, St Mary Spital, St Mary within Cripplegate (also known as Elsing Spital), St Mary Magdalene Bermondsey, St Olave Hart Street, St Sepulchre, the rectangular chancel of Temple Church, possibly modelled on the Second Temple of Solomon, or on the Temple of the Lord (otherwise known as the Dome of the Rock) in Jerusalem, Whitefriars Priory and Winchester Palace, among others, were all built at this time; and St Giles Cripplegate, St Mary-at-Lambeth, St Mary Overie (Southwark Cathedral), Old St Paul's, and Westminster Abbey, among others, rebuilt or extended. Old St Paul's was evidently an impressive building by the end of the Medieval period, measuring some 600 ft in length, and, according to some estimates, over 500 ft in height, inclusive of the spire, which was destroyed by lightning in 1444 and rebuilt in 1462 (only to be destroyed by lightning again in 1561). The old Chapter House, built in 1332 by the Master Mason

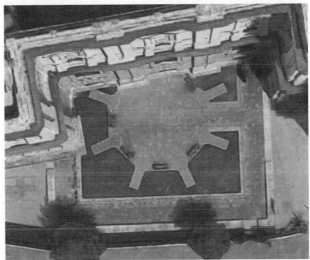

Above: 6. Chapter House, Old St Paul's (1332) by Hollar.

Right: 7. Aerial view of the footings of Chapter House, Old St Paul's.

William Ramsay, who would die of the Black Death in 1349, was the earliest example in London of the Perpendicular Gothic style that was to remain the fashion for the next two hundred years (*Figure 6*). Sadly, only the octagonal outline of the foundations survives, in the churchyard on the south side of the cathedral (*Figure 7*). Perhaps even more sadly, the celebrated wall-painting of the Dance of Death in the Pardon Cloister of the north side of the cathedral, commissioned by John Carpenter during his tenure as Town Clerk

1417-38, was destroyed in 1549 on the orders of Protector Somerset. The painting is said to have been based on the *Danse Macabre* in the *Cimetière des Innocents* in Paris. According to Stow, 'the metres, or posey of this dance, were translated out of French into English by John Lidgate, monk of Bury.' The Master Mason Henry (de) Reyns, generally known simply as Master Henry (fl. 1243-53), is known to have worked extensively on the reconstruction of Westminster Abbey under Henry III in the thirteenth century and also, incidentally, on the Tower of London. The Master Mason Henry Yevele (*c.* 1320-1400) worked at Westminster Abbey in the fourteenth century on, among other things, the tombs of Edward III and Richard II, as well as on the tomb of John of Gaunt in Old St Paul's, on the Charterhouse and also the Tower of London, the Savoy Palace, and the Palace of Westminster, including the Jewel Tower and Westminster Hall.

Important new secular public building works of the Plantagenet period included London Bridge, rebuilt 1176-1209; Westminster Hall, rebuilt in 1394-1401, in part by Hugh Herland (c. 1330-c. 1411), who was responsible for the spectacular hammerbeam roof; its City rival, the Guildhall, rebuilt in 1411-30, by John Croxton(e) (fl. 1411-47). Incidentally, Herland also worked on the Tower of London and Westminster Abbey, Croxton(e), on Leadenhall Market and Garner (granary).

New private buildings of the period included a number of Inns of Court and Livery Company Halls. Some of the latter, such as the Merchant Taylors', were particularly grand, including gardens, grounds and alms-houses – for 'decayed' members of the company – as well as Great Halls (and kitchens), offices and private chapels. New private residences included that of the wealthy grocer and twice Mayor Stephen Browne, in Billingsgate, which was evidently sufficiently grand as to have included its own quay; and that of the wealthy grocer John Crosby, immediately south of the church of St Helen on Bishopsgate, later owned by Richard, Duke of Gloucester (the future Richard III), Thomas More, and Walter Ralegh, which Stow described as 'very large and beautiful'. The cheaper ones of the common man, such as those recently excavated on Poultry, were evidently built out of timber and thatch in the eleventh and twelfth centuries, and of stone (or brick) and tile from the thirteenth onwards, after the use of combustible materials in construction was banned by the Mayor – Henry FitzAilwyn de

Londonestone – following the terrible fire of 1212, in which thousands of people died.

The Medieval street layout, so organically developed or evolved and so modified after the Roman and Saxon ones as to be unrecognisable, was less in the form of a grid than of an intricate, almost beguiling, maze or web, although there were streets parallel and perpendicular to the river, some of the latter on reclaimed land. The intricately intermingled alleyways and courtyards were the capillaries and alveoli of the City, where persons might pause albeit fleetingly among the seething mass to rest and refresh body and soul, the lanes and thoroughfares its veins and arteries, moving people and trade far and wide. Horse-drawn carts and wagons were widely used to transport goods.

Surviving Structures

Essentially nothing now remains of the the majority of the Medieval seats of power, religious houses and secular buildings that stood within and without the walls of the City of London before the Great Fire. However, the Tower of London, which survived the fire, is substantially intact within the walls of the City, the Chapel of St John in the White Tower representing a fine example of the Norman or Romanesque architectural style (*Figures 11c, 12c, 13c*). And on nearby Tower Hill are the remaining ruins of the Medieval Postern Gate. The Jewel Tower, part of the Palace of Westminster, also stands, in the City of Westminster (*Figure 8*) and the footings and some of the standing structure of Edward III's manor-house, in Rotherhithe (*Figure 9*).

Moreover, of the ninety-seven parish churches within the walls of the City, eight, – All Hallows Barking, All Hallows Staining, St Alphage, St Andrew Undershaft, St Ethelburga, St Helen (*Figure 10*), St Katharine Cree and St Olave Hart Street – survived the fire and survive still, with at least some pre-fire structures standing above ground (St Alban Wood Street, St Mary Aldermary, St Dunstan-in-the-East, St Mary-at-Hill and St Michael Cornhill were rebuilt after the fire incorporating into their designs significant portions of the pre-fire structures). St Helen, re-built in 1210, stands as an exemplar of the Early English Gothic architectural style of the early thirteenth century. A further five churches – All Hallows on the Wall, St James Duke's Place, St Katherine Coleman, St Martin Outwich and St Peter-le-Poer – were also undamaged in the fire but either demolished or rebuilt afterwards. Forty-nine were burned down in the fire and rebuilt afterwards and thirty-five were burned down and not rebuilt. Without the walls, St Bartholomew the Great, St Bartholomew the Less, St Etheldreda (*Figure 11*), St Giles Cripplegate, St Margaret Westminster, St Mary Overie (Southwark Cathedral) (*Figure 12*), Temple Church and Westminster Abbey also still stand. St Etheldreda, built in 1294, is an exemplar of the Decorated Gothic style of the late thirteenth century, which was never as flamboyant as on the continent. Rather further afield, ten miles or so to the north-west, stands St Martin Ruislip, with its late Medieval wall-painting depicting the Seven Deadly Sins that miraculously survived the Reformation (*Figure 13*). Precious fragments remain of Bermondsey Abbey, Blackfriars Priory (*Figure 14*), the Charterhouse (*Figure 15*), Holy Trinity Priory (*Figure 16*), the Priory of St John (*Figures 17, 18*), the Priory of St Mary Spital (*Figure 19*), Whitefriars Priory (*Figure 20*) and Winchester Palace (*Figure 21*) that survived the Reformation and Dissolution. The surviving parts of the 'rambling nest' of Medieval and Renaissance buildings in the Charterhouse that date back to the monastic period include not only the doorway to Cell B in the Norfolk Cloister, with its *guichet* or serving hatch, but also some stone buildings in Wash-House Court. Many of the buildings, fragments of buildings, and fitments on the site sustained damage during the Blitz and had to be restored in the post-war period (by Seely and Paget).

Furthermore, Westminster Hall still stands (*Figure 22*); as do the Guildhall, in the City of London (*Figure 23*); the Hall of Barnard's Inn, one of the Inns of Court, without the City walls (*Figure 24*); and parts of the Merchant Taylors' Hall, one of the Livery Companies' Halls, within. Westminster Hall is fortunate to still exist as it must have come close to being washed away by the great flood of 1241 chronicled by Matthew Paris, during which 'such deluges of rain fell, that the river Thames, overflowing its usual bounds and its ancient banks, spread itself over the country towards Lambeth ... and took possession, far and wide, of the houses and fields in that part ... people rode into the great hall at Westminster on horseback.' The private residence of Crosby Hall that once stood in Bishopsgate in the City now stands at a new location in Chelsea (*Figure 25*). And the Hoop and Grapes still stands on Aldgate High Street.

8. Jewel Tower, Palace of Westminster (1366).

9. Remains of Edward III's manor house, King's Stairs Gardens, Rotherhithe (1353).

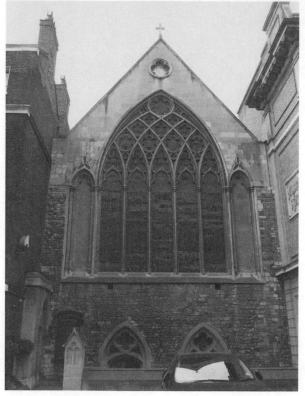

Above: 10. Church of
St Helen Bishopsgate
(1210). Early Gothic.

Left: 11. St Etheldreda,
Ely Place (1294).
Decorated Gothic.

12. Southwark Cathedral from Borough High Street (essentially late fourteenth century). This is the same view that pilgrims on their way to Canterbury would have had in Chaucer's time.

13. Late Medieval Wall-Painting, church of St Martin, Ruislip (probably fifteenth century). Depicting the Seven Deadly Sins in the form of a dragon-like creature emerging from the mouth of Hell. The deadliest Sin, Pride, sits on a throne in the creature's mouth, where Death thrusts at it with a lance. Gluttony, Lust and Avarice are represented in turn to the right, when viewed clockwise; Sloth, Envy and Anger to the left.

14. Remaining fragment of Blackfriars Priory, Ireland Yard (originally founded in 1278). This is believed to be part of the prior's lodgings.

Right: 15. Door to
Cell B, Charterhouse
(1371). Note the
guichet (left).

Below: 16. Surviving
stone arch,
Holy Trinity
Priory (probably
fifteenth-century).

Above: 17. Gate-House, Priory of St John, Clerkenwell (*c.* 1504).

Below: 18. Effigy of Prior William Weston, crypt of former priory church, Priory of St John, Clerkenwell (d. 1540). It is said that Weston died on the very day of the Dissolution, of a broken heart.

Above: 19. Crypt-cum-Charnel House, Priory of St Mary Spital, Spital Square. This is where many of the victims of the famine of 1258 were buried.

Below left: 20. Remaining fragment of Whitefriars Priory, Ashentree Court/ Magpie Alley (originally founded in 1253).

Below right: 21. Substantially surviving Great Hall, Winchester Palace, Southwark, twelfth century; rose window, fourteenth-century.

Above: 22. Westminster Hall (essentially late fourteenth to early fifteenth century).

Below: 23. Guildhall (early fifteenth century, with eighteenth-century porch in Hindoo Gothic style). A slate oval in the courtyard describes the outline of the Roman amphitheatre, which lies some 20 ft beneath.

24. Barnard's Inn Hall (late fourteenth to early fifteenth century).

25. Crosby Hall in its new location, Cheyne Walk, Chelsea (1475).

Archaeological Finds

The more important archaeological finds from Medieval London are on exhibition in the City's principal museums, including the Museum of London, which houses an extensive collection. A series of Museum of London and other publications either describe in detail or summarise the findings of archaeological excavations at various Medieval sites around the City. The commonest Medieval finds on the foreshore of the Thames are everyday items such as discarded animal bones, oyster shells, sherds of pottery, coins and *jetons*, or trading tokens.

Further Reading

Ackroyd, 2000, 2004, 2011; Anonymous, 1827, 1932, 1938; Aston, 2000; Bard, 2013; Barron, 1974, 2004; Barty-King, 1994; Beadle, 1994; Benham, 1902; Birch, 1887; Bird, 1949; Boulton, 1901; P. Boyd, 1928; Brereton, 1978; Brooke, 2003; Burford, 1973, 1977, 1990, 1993; Butler & Given-Wilson, 1979; Byrne & Bush, 2007; Chambers & Daunt, 1931; Clark, 1989, 2007; Daniell, 1971; G. Davies, 1921; Dockray, 2002; Ditchfield, 1926; Dudley, 1999; Egan, 2010; Ekwall, 1951, 1956; Fincham, 1933; FitzStephen, 1183; Girtin, 1958; Glover, 1991; Graves, 1947; Green, 2015; Hahn, 2003; Hanawalt, 1993, 2017; Harrison, 2004; Harvey, 1944, 1947; Heath, 1869; Herber, 1999; Herbert, 1884; Hibbert, 1969; Hooper, 1935; A. Hope, 1990; W. Hope, 1925; Impey, 2008; Johnson, 1914-22; D. Jones, 2009, 2014a, b; F. Jones, 2014; N. Jones, 2011; Jones & Smith, 1951; Keay, 2001; Kohl, 1960; J. Lang, 1975, 1984; R. Lang, 1993; Littlehales, 1898; Longman, 1873; Lucas & Russell, 2018; Macy, 2007; Matthews, 2008; McDonnell, 1909; McIlwain, 1994; McInnes, 1963; Moore, 1918; Mortimer, 2008; Mount, 2015; Myers, 2009; Nichols, 1952; Nicoll, 1964; O'Donoghue, 1914; Orridge, 1867; Parnell, 1999, 2009; Parsons, 1932-36; Pearson, 2011; Porter, 2010, 2012, 2018; Prest, 1972; Rappaport, 1989; Rees, 1923; Reid & Bowen, 2015; Riley, 1861, 1863; Robertson, 1968; Rosewell, 2012; Ross, 2016; Ross & Clark, 2008; Rowse, 1972; Rumbelow, 1982; Sayle, 1945; Schofield, 1984, 1994, 1995, 2011b, 2016. 2018; Seward, 2000; Sharpe, 1899-1912; Shepherd, 1971; Somerville, 1960; Spencer, 2010; Stanhope, 1887; Stone, 2017; Stow, 1598; Sutton, 2005; Sutton, 2016; Tames, 2012; Tatlock, 1906; A. Taylor, 1999; W. Taylor, 1912; Temple, 2010; The Clothworkers' Company, 2005; Thomas, 2002; Tudor-Craig, 2004; Unwin, 1963; Wadmore, 1902; Watney, 1914; Watson, 2004; Watson et al., 2001; Webb, 1921; Weir, 1999; West, 2014; Whipp, 2006; White, 2010; E. Williams, 1927; G. Williams, 1970; Wilson, 1978; Wright, 2017.

CHAPTER SIX

Post-Medieval (Tudor and Stuart) London (1485-1666)

The Medieval period ended and the post-Medieval, or early Modern period, began when the last Plantagenet or Yorkist King, Richard III, was killed at the Battle of Bosworth Field and the first Tudor King, Henry VII, came to the throne in 1485. The post-Medieval was a time of continuing political, religious and social turmoil, over two hundred years, and under two royal houses and a Parliamentarian Protectorate. It was also a time of continuing war: between the English and the Scots and the Irish; between the English and the French, and the Spanish, and the Dutch; and war among the English, in the Civil War of the seventeenth century.

There are sufficient surviving records of one kind or another to enable us to undertake a reasonably accurate reconstruction not only of the history of but also of the social history of post-Medieval London (see also 'Further Reading'). These include court, corporation and ward records, and also parish registers of 'every wedding, christening and burying', the keeping of which was mandated in 1538, by Henry VIII's Vicar-General Thomas Cromwell. Personal contemporary eye-witness accounts include those of Andreas Franciscus, writing in 1497; Henry Machyn, writing 1550-63; Charles Wriothesley, writing around 1558 and not later than 1562; Grenade, writing in 1578; John Chamberlain, writing between 1597-1626; John Stow, writing in 1598; John Manningham, writing 1601-3; John Evelyn, writing between 1631-1706; James Howell, writing in 1657); John Reresby, writing sometime after 1658; and Samuel Pepys, writing continuously between 1660-9, and sporadically between 1670-86 after his eyesight had begun to fail him. Contemporary biographical sketches of some of the key historical figures of the period are given by John Aubrey in his *Brief Lives* (1696). The Venetian Franciscus wrote of London in 1497, in early Tudor times:

> The town itself stretches from East to West, and is three miles in circumference. However, its suburbs are so large that they greatly increase its circuit. ... Throughout the town are to be seen many workshops of craftsmen... This makes the town look exceedingly prosperous and well-stocked... The working in wrought silver, tin or white lead is very expert here, and perhaps the finest I have ever seen. There are many mansions, which do not ... seem very large from the outside, but inside ... are quite considerable... All the streets are so badly paved that they get wet at the slightest quantity of water, and this happens very frequently... A vast amount of evil-smelling mud is formed, which does not disappear ... but lasts ... nearly the whole year round. The citizens, therefore, in order to remove mud and filth from their boots, are accustomed to spread ... rushes on the floors of all houses... Merchants not only from Venice but also Florence and Lucca, and many from Genoa and Pisa, from Spain, Germany ... and other countries meet here to handle business with the utmost keenness... Londoners have such fierce tempers and wicked dispositions that they not only despise the way ... Italians live, but actually pursue them with uncontrollable hatred, and whereas at Bruges foreigners are hospitably received ... by everybody, here the Englishmen use them with the utmost contempt and arrogance, and make them the object of insults. They eat very frequently, at times more than is suitable.

It is interesting to note how closely Franciscus's description follows the Venetian senate's written instructions to its ambassadors on intelligence-gathering! The Frenchman Grenade wrote in 1578 that the city 'is wondrously pleasing on the eye, and in its shape and situation alongside the river, describes an arc of very beautiful form. ... This river conveys large vessels of between two and 300 tons burden ... by which means all manner of goods from all countries abound here. ... She is encompassed on all sides by beautiful meadows ... gardens and cultivable lands, which, on account of their fertility, yield much produce each year. The villages (of which there is a great number in the environs) are ... only about two harquebus shots distant from the city.'

Machyn was a merchant taylor or clothier. His chronicles cover the Reformation, and the conversion of the country to Protestantism under Henry VIII, and the Counter-Reformation and reversion to Catholicism under his daughter Mary. Judging from his actions, as well as from the tone of his chronicle, Machyn would appear to have been at least a closet Catholic. In 1561, he committed the sinful act of 'spyking serten [slanderous] words against Veron the [Protestant] preacher', for which he paid penance at (St) Paul's Cross. Stow (*Figure 15c*) was another merchant taylor but also an amateur antiquarian, and the author of *A Survay of London* (the famous last words of which were 'And so I end, wanting time to travel further in this work'). His *Survay* describes in rich detail the changing social history of Elizabethan London. His memorial in the church of St Andrew Undershaft shows him with a quill-pen in his hand. Every third year, on or around the anniversary of his death on 5 April, as part of a special service in the church in his memory he is ceremonially presented with a new quill (and his old one is given to the winner of an essay competition for local children, with London as its subject).

Chamberlain is best known now as the author of a large number of letters that, collectively, 'constitute the first considerable body ... in English history and literature that the modern reader can easily follow'. His letters cover such events in late Tudor to early Stuart times as the trial of the Earls of Essex and Southampton, the Gunpowder Plot, and the execution of Walter Ralegh. Most of the nearly 500 that still survive were written to Sir Dudley Carleton while he was serving as an ambassador in Venice and The Hague, and were evidently intended to keep the ambitious diplomat abroad informed of events – especially those befalling 'the better sort of people' – at home. They contain much court and City tittle-tattle (who's in, who's out), picked up, no doubt, in St Paul's Cathedral, which at the time had a reputation as the fount of all such knowledge – it appears that Chamberlain was an inveterate 'Paul's walker'!

Evelyn was a gentleman of independent means, closely connected to court circles, a keen gardener, an author (of, for example, *Fumifugium* and *Sylva*); and also, like his friend Samuel Pepys, a diarist. His diary covers the Civil War and Commonwealth, the Restoration, the Great Plague, the Great Fire and much besides. The striking portrait of him painted by Robert Walker in 1648, and now in the National Portrait Gallery, shows a still youthful man with fine slender features wearing a melancholy expression as he meditates on death, symbolised by a skull at his left hand. From 1653 onwards, Evelyn lived at Sayes Court in Deptford. On 6 February 1698, he noted in his diary that he had leased his estate out to 'The Czar Emp: of Moscovy [Peter the Great], [his] having a mind to see the Building of Ships [in the nearby royal dockyard]'. Perhaps not surprisingly, the Czar, who had a reputation for drunken, riotous living, proved far from a model guest. He proceeded to trash Evelyn's house – knocking a hole in the wall to allow easier access to the shipyard, breaking over three hundred windows, twenty pictures and fifty chairs, ruining all the paintwork, curtains and bedding, covering all the floors with ink and grease, and in all causing something like £350 of damage – in today's terms several tens of thousands of pounds! Worst of all, he destroyed Evelyn's pride and joy, the impregnable hedge in his garden, 'four hundred foot in length, nine foot high, and five in diameter ... [that] mocks at the rudest assaults of the Weather, Beasts or Hedge-breakers', insisting on being repeatedly pushed through it in a wheelbarrow – of the £162 7s compensation eventually paid to Evelyn by the Office of Works, £1 was specifically to cover the damage to his wheelbarrows! Perhaps as an act of atonement, the Czar planted a mulberry tree in Evelyn's garden, which still stands, now ancient and gnarled, in what is now Sayes Court Park.

The best known of the chroniclers is of course Pepys, a high-ranking civil servant in the Navy Office, and eventual Secretary to the Admiralty. Pepys's diary covers such momentous events in late Stuart times as the Restoration of the Monarchy in 1660, the Great Plague of 1665 and the Great Fire of 1666. Pepys was an Establishment figure, well known in official and court circles; and, as such, less an everyman caught up in events than one very much of his time and particularly his place; that is to say, his place in the prevailing social and class hierarchy. His thoughts and deeds were often to greater or lesser degrees self-serving: he obsessed over his wealth ('To my accounts, wherein ... I ... to my great discontent, do find that my gettings this year have been less than last'). He employed sycophancy and deceitfulness to increase the same, or otherwise to get his way and was not beyond resorting to emotional cruelty, especially towards his wife, Elizabeth, and even to physical violence. However, his written words were almost always honest and true, unsparingly and disarmingly so when describing his own shortcomings. There was something of a child-like quality to the man, characteristically beautifully described by Robert Louis Stevenson:

'Pepys was a young man for his age, came slowly to himself in the world, sowed his wild oats late, took late to industry and preserved till nearly forty the headlong gusto of a boy. So, to come rightly at the spirit in which the Diary was written, we must recall a class of sentiments which with most of us are over and done before the age of twelve.' His accomplishments were many and varied, especially those at the Navy Office (it has been said that without Pepys, there could have been no Horatio Nelson).

Tudor History

The Tudor era was above all a time of religious reformation and counter-reformation, and of religious war – not to mention cold war and espionage. The Protestant Reformation may be said to have begun in Germany in 1517, with the publication by Martin Luther of the *Ninety-Five Theses* or *Disputation on the Power of Indulgences*, which, among other things, roundly attacked the established practice of the sale of indulgences ('When a penny in the coffer rings,/A soul from Purgatory springs'). Protestantism was to spread through much of northern Europe over the succeeding thirty years.

Henry Tudor was crowned King Henry VII of England in 1485. In 1497, around 10,000 lightly armed Cornish rebels gathered on Blackheath preparatory to marching on London to protest against oppressive royal rule and punitive taxation (suspension of the privileges of the Stannary Charter of 1305). Unfortunately for them, they failed to rally any support there from the Kentish, who were rightly fearful of a reprisal of the sort that had been meted out to them for their support of the Peasants' Revolt in 1381 and Jack Cade's Rebellion in 1450 (see above). It was thus a comparatively weak force, further diluted by desertion, that eventually lighted out for London, and certainly one that was easily crushed by the King's 20,000-strong professional army at the Battle of Deptford Bridge (also known as the Battle of Blackheath). Contemporary records indicate that between two hundred and two thousand Cornishmen were killed in the battle. The principal rebel leaders Michael Joseph the Smith (*An Gof*) and Thomas Flamank were captured at the battle and later hanged, drawn and quartered at Tyburn, whereupon their heads were put up on pike-staffs on London Bridge. Flamank was quoted as saying 'Speak the truth and only then can you be free of your chains.' The persecution and pauperisation of the Cornish continued for many years to come.

Henry VIII was crowned in 1512, while still in his early twenties. According to Hall's *Annals*, on May Day in 1515:

> The King and the Queen [Catherine of Aragon] accompanied with many lords and ladies rode [from the Palace of Placentia in Greenwich] to the high ground of Shooters Hill to take the open air, and as they passed by the way, they espied a company of tall yeomen, clothed all in green with green hoods and bows and arrows, to the number of two hundred. Then one of them which called himself Robin Hood came to the King desiring him to see his men shoot, and the King was content. Then he whistled, and all the 200 archers shot and loosed at once, and then he whistled again, and they likewise shot again; their arrows whistled by craft of the head, so that the noise was strange and great and much pleased the King, the Queen and all the company. Then Robin Hood desired the King and Queen to come into the greenwood and see how the outlaws lived. ... Then the horns blew till they came to the wood under Shooters Hill, and there was an arber made of boughs with a hall and a great chamber and an inner chamber very well made and covered with flowers and sweet herbs, which the King much praised. Then said Robin Hood: 'Sir, outlaws' breakfast is venison, and thereafter you must be content with such fare as we use.' Then the King and Queen sat down and were served with venison and wine by Robin Hood and his men, to their great contentation.

One of Henry VIII's less-well-known contributions to English history was his consolidation of the country's armed forces both at sea and on land – his construction of an island-fortress (Moorhouse, 2005). The Royal Naval Dockyard in Woolwich was opened early in his reign, in 1512, and prospered in the later sixteenth and seventeenth centuries, before eventually closing down in the nineteenth (the Royal Arsenal here became operational in 1671 and was decommissioned in 1967). A number of historically important ships were built here, including the carvel-built *Henry Grace a Dieu* or *Great Harry* in 1514; the *Prince Royal*, in 1610; the *Sovereign of the Seas*, in 1637; and the *Royal Charles* in 1655 (not to mention the *Beagle* in 1820). The Dockyard in Deptford was opened in 1513 and like the one in Woolwich prospered in the later sixteenth and seventeenth centuries, before eventually closing down in the nineteenth. Documentary evidence indicates that a number of naval vessels were brought to a specially constructed 'pond(e)' or wet dock here in 1520, possibly for repairs, among them the recently salvaged flagship, the *Mary Rose* (now in the Royal Naval Dockyard in Portsmouth, where it was built), the *Peter Pomegarnet* or *Peter Pomegranate*, the *Great Bark* and the *Lesser Bark*. The Dockyard in Erith was opened in 1514 and closed in 1521 due to persistent flooding. That in Chatham in Kent was opened in 1567, early in the reign of Elizabeth I, and prospered in the late sixteenth to nineteenth centuries before eventually closing in the twentieth. Chatham enjoyed the considerable advantage over the London dockyards of being located twenty-five miles downriver, at the point at which the Thames is met by the Medway, and obviously that much closer to the open sea.

The so-called 'Gresham Ship', an armed merchantman, recently (re) discovered, wrecked in – and recovered from – the Thames Estuary, is an example of the sort built in the aforementioned dockyards in the Tudor period. Dendrochronological analysis of the ship's timbers has yielded a construction date of around 1574, during the reign of Elizabeth I. Partial reconstruction indicates that the intact vessel would have measured a little over 80 ft from bow to stern, and a little under 25 ft from side to side, and weighed some 160 tons, making it similar in size to Drake's *Golden Hind(e)*, built in 1577. It was carvel-built of robust construction and fitted with gun ports. Significantly, one of the four cannon recovered from the ship bears the initials T.G., together with the grasshopper insignia of the City merchant Thomas Gresham, which is how she came to be known as 'The Gresham Ship'. (Thomas Gresham lived from 1519-79, founding what was to become known as the Royal Exchange in 1570, and, by bequest, Gresham College in 1597.) It is possible that the ship might actually be the *Cherabin*, which surviving historical records indicate was owned by the Levant Company 1590-1600. She served under Thomas Howard as a privateer in the Azores in 1591, capturing prize cargoes of sugar, ginger, and suchlike valued at £2000 (at least £400,000 today) and sank in the Kentish Flats in 1603 (after losing her rudder in a storm and striking a sandbank).

Tilbury Fort in Essex was originally built by Henry VIII in 1536 and was later extended and reinforced by Elizabeth I in 1588, to counter the threat from the Spanish Armada. What is now known as the Honourable Artillery Company had its origins in the 'Fraternity or Guild of Artillery of Longbows, Crossbows and Handgonnes', incorporated by a Royal Charter of Henry VIII in 1537 (and also known – although probably not to his face – as 'Fat Hal's Militia'). The original roles of the unit were 'the maintenance of the science of artillery' and 'the better increase of the defence of this our realm'. From 1572 onwards it also assumed responsibility for training the City of London's part-time militia, the so-called 'trained bands'. It remains the oldest unit still serving in the Regular – if not the Territorial – Army (the Grenadier Guards were formed from its ranks in 1656 and the Royal Marines in 1664). From around the time of its formation in the middle of the sixteenth century up until the end of the seventeenth the company trained in the Artillery Yard in Tasel Close in Spitalfields. The remains of the Master Gunner's House, dating to 1581, have recently been unearthed in an archaeological excavation in Spital Square, together with the remains of firing platforms (Harward *et al.*, 2015). Nearby are Artillery Lane and Artillery Passage.

In 1527, with Henry VIII's first wife, Catherine of Aragon, after nearly twenty years of marriage having borne him a daughter (Mary) but not a longed-for son and heir, Henry decided to petition Pope Clement VII to seek an annulment that would allow him to marry Anne Boleyn. This quest was to become known as 'The King's Great Matter'. In 1529, the Legatine Court convened in the Parliament Hall in Blackfriars Priory under the Papal Legate, Cardinal Lorenzo Campeggio, and the King's representative, the Archbishop of York, Lord Chancellor and, in practice, *alter rex*, or other king, Cardinal Thomas Wolsey, ruled against any such action. Wolsey died in 1530, *en route* from York to London, where he had been due to face a trial for treason over his failure to secure the annulment that Henry sought. Among his last words were the following: 'Had I but served my God with but half the zeal as I served my king [in his 'Great Matter'], He would not in mine age have left me naked to mine enemies.' The most impressive of his many notable earlier services to the state included arranging the Anglo-French Treaty in 1514, and the Treaty of London – essentially a pan-European non-aggression pact – in 1518, as well as the 'Field of the Cloth-of-Gold' (*Camp du Drap d'Or*) in 1520.

In the event, in January 1533 Henry proceeded to marry Anne in spite of the Legatine Court's ruling, albeit in secret, and in the June had her formally crowned Queen. Three short years later, in 1536, he was to order her execution in the Tower for treason. Henry also ordered the executions of Anne's brother George, on trumped-up charges of an adulterous and incestuous relationship with her; and of William Brereton, Henry Norris, Mark Smeaton, and Francis Weston, also on charges of adultery. Accused alongside the aforementioned, but ultimately spared the axe, was the courtier Thomas Wyatt the Elder (incidentally, also a fine poet, widely credited with introducing the Petrarchan sonnet into English literature). Wyatt the Younger would enjoy no such good fortune under Queen Mary (see below). On the scaffold, Anne gave a short speech to the assembled crowd, recorded in Foxe's *Actes and Monuments*:

> Good Christian people, I am come hither to die, for according to the law, and by the law I am judged to die, and therefore I will speak nothing against it. I am come hither to accuse no man, nor to speak anything of that, whereof I am accused and condemned to die, but I pray God save the king and send him long to reign over you, for a gentler nor a more merciful prince was there never: and to me he was ever a good, a gentle and sovereign lord. And if any person will meddle of my cause, I require them to judge the best. And thus I take my leave of the world and of you all, and I heartily desire you all to pray for me. O Lord have mercy on me, to God I commend my soul.

The King made himself, rather than the Pope, the Supreme Head of the Church in England, through the Act of Supremacy of 1534, whereafter his subjects were made to swear oaths acknowledging not only his supremacy (the Oath of Supremacy), but also that of his children and successors to the throne (the Oath of Succession). Even after the break with Rome and despite his excommunication by Pope Paul III in 1538, the King – the erstwhile *Fidei Defensor* or Defender of the Faith – appears to have remained theologically essentially Catholic. At the same time, though, the Church in England, and the country at large, became increasingly Protestant. Among those primarily responsible for the rise of Protestantism were Thomas Cranmer, the Archbishop of Canterbury and Thomas Cromwell, the King's Chief Minister from 1534 and Vicar-General, and Vice-Gerent in Spirituals from 1535. The spread of the word was facilitated by the publication of an English translation of the Bible by Miles Coverdale in 1535, and by the availability of copies thereof in every parish church in the land by 1541. It was Cranmer who established the doctrines and liturgies of the Protestant Church and suppressed – certain – Catholic sacraments, the practices of veneration of images and relics, and the belief in Purgatory, through the *Ten Articles* of 1536, the *Bishop's Book* of 1537, the *Six Articles* of 1539, and the *Forty-Two Articles* of 1553 (and also through his input into the *King's Book*, attributed to Henry himself, of 1543). The enforcer Cromwell was beheaded on Tower Hill in 1540, having been attainted, or in other words found guilty without trial, of a range of charges almost certainly trumped up by his enemies, including the Duke of Norfolk and Bishop Stephen Gardiner (King Henry is said later to have regretted his execution). He had finally fallen out of favour, and victim to the sort of court intrigue that to that date he had himself customarily been behind, over his ill-advised choice of Anne of Cleves as the new wife for the King. The lawyer, politician and chronicler Edward Hall recorded that '[H]e ... committed his soule into the handes of God, and so paciently suffered the stroke of the axe, by a ragged and Boocherly miser, whiche very ungoodly perfourmed the Office'. Cranmer would be burned at the stake in Oxford in 1556 during the then Catholic Queen Mary's Counter-Reformation, for Protestant heresy. At the stake, he thrust into the rising flames the 'unworthy' right hand with which he had signed the earlier coerced recantation of his Protestant faith, and retracted the recantation with the words: 'as for the Pope, I refuse him, as Christ's enemy, and Antichrist with all his false doctrine.' Coverdale would be exiled under Mary between 1553 and 1558, eventually to return to London in 1559 and die there in 1569. His body would be buried in the church of St Bartholomew by the Exchange, and later, when that church was demolished, moved to St Magnus the Martyr.

Any Catholic threat to the Protestant Reformation, whether actual or interpreted, was dealt with without mercy. By way of an example, in 1534, Elizabeth Barton, known as the Holy Maid of Kent, was hanged and beheaded at Tyburn for treason for having prophesied that if the Henry were to break from the Church in Rome he would die and be sent to Hell. In 1535, John Houghton, the Prior of the London Charterhouse, two further Carthusian Priors, a Bridgettine Monk from Syon Abbey, and a parish priest from Isleworth, were hanged, drawn and quartered at Tyburn for refusing to take the Oath of Supremacy (later, another six monks from the Charterhouse were executed and nine allowed to die of starvation in Newgate). The Bridgettine monk, Richard Reynolds, famously encouraged those who suffered alongside him by promising them that after their 'sharp breakfast' they would enjoy a 'heavenly supper'. Also in 1535, John Fisher, the Bishop of Rochester and a Cardinal and Sir Thomas More, the lawyer, humanist, social philosopher, author (of *Utopia*) and 'the King's good servant, but God's first', were beheaded at Tower Hill, also for refusing to take the Oath of Supremacy (interestingly, both Fisher and More are honoured as saints by both the Catholic Church and the Church of England). More had earlier witnessed, through the window of his prison cell in the Tower, Houghton and his co-condemned being taken to Tyburn to be executed and had commented to his daughter, Meg Roper: 'These blessed Fathers be now as cheerfully going to their deaths as bridegrooms to their marriage.' His son-in-law William Roper wrote of More's execution:

> And soe was he brought by Mr Lievetenaunt out of the Towre, and thence led towards the place of execution, where goinge upp the Scaffold, ... he sayde ... 'I pray you, I pray you, Mr Lievetenaunt, see me safe upp, and for my cominge downe let mee shift for my selfe.' Then desired he all the people thereaboutes to pray for him, and to beare witnesse with him, that he should suffer death in and for the faith of the holie Catholique Church, which done hee kneeled downe, and after his prayers sayed, hee turned to the executioner, and with a cheerful Countenance spake unto him, 'Plucke up thy spirittes, man, and be not affrayed to do thine office ...'. Soe passed Sir Thomas Moore out of this world to God.

In 1538, John Forest, a Franciscan friar and confessor to Catherine of Aragon, was burned at the stake in West Smithfield for heresy, for refusing to recant his faith; fuel for the fire, according to folk-legend, being provided by a statue of St Derfel from the pilgrimage site of Llandderfel in North Wales, which it had been prophesied would 'one day set a forest on fire'.

Neither were heterodox Protestants immune from persecution (Rounding, 2017). In 1546, the last full year of Henry's reign, Anne Askew, gentlewoman, was burned at the stake in West Smithfield for heresy, for preaching against the then still orthodox belief in transubstantiation. She had previously been racked by the Lord Chancelllor, Thomas Wriothesley, and his henchman, Richard Rich, in the Tower of London, and she had to be carried from there to, and seated at, the stake. The Protestant martyrologist John Foxe, in his *Book of Martyrs* of 1563, gives the following as Anne Askew's own account:

> They said to me there, that I was a heretic, and condemned by the law, if I would stand in my opinion. I answered, that I was no heretic, neither yet deserved I any death by the law of God. But, as concerning the faith which I uttered and wrote to the council, I would not, I said, deny it, because I knew it true. Then would they needs know, if I would deny the sacrament to be Christ's body and blood. I said, 'Yea: for the same Son of God that was born of the Virgin Mary, is now glorious in heaven, and will come again from thence at the latter day like as he went up. And as for that ye call your God ... a piece of bread ... let it but lie in the box three months, and it will be mouldy, and so turn to nothing that is good. Whereupon I am persuaded that it cannot be God.

The Reformation was followed by the Dissolution of the Monasteries 1536-40, which essentially resulted in the appropriation by the Crown of all the monastic houses in England, Wales and Ireland, of which there were several hundred, and of all of their assets (monastic houses in Scotland were annexed by the Scottish King, James VI, in 1587). The smaller houses, with incomes of less than £200 per year as evaluated by the *Valor Ecclesiacus*, were dissolved under The Act for the Dissolution of the Lesser Monasteries of 1536; the larger ones, by The Act for the Dissolution of the Greater Monasteries of 1539. Corresponding orders were given to 'pull down to the grounds all the walls of the churches, stepulls, cloysters, fraterys, dorters [and] chapterhowsys'. After the Dissolution, the assets of the monastic houses were disbursed under the auspices of Thomas Cromwell and his Court of Augmentations.

In London, the change in land ownership and usage is evident in the marked contrast between the *British Atlas of Historic Towns* map of 1520, from before the event), and the Copper Plate map of *c.* 1559, the 'Agas' one of *c.* 1570, and the Braun and Hogenberg one of 1572 (*Figure 14c*). Many of the former monastic properties evidently became parish churches, hospitals, orphanages or schools, or combinations thereof, or playhouses, while others passed into private ownership. For example, the priory church of St Mary Overie became the parish church of St Saviour, and eventually the collegiate church of St Mary Overie and St Saviour, or Southwark Cathedral; and that part of the priory church of St Bartholomew that was spared demolition became the parish church of St Bartholomew the Great, the associated hospital remaining in use and growing in importance. The Charterhouse, founded in 1371 by Sir Walter Manny, 'a stranger born, lord of the town of Manny, in the diocese of Cambray, beyond the seas, who for service done to Edward III was made Knight of the Garter', became initially a private residence in turn occupied by Sir Edward North, the Chancellor of the Court of Augmentations, from 1545; and eventually a charitable alms-house and school founded by a bequest from Thomas Sutton, the one-time Master of the Ordnance of the Northern Parts and the richest man in England, from 1611 (the school relocated to Godalming in Surrey in 1872).

Parts of the precincts of Holywell, Blackfriars and Whitefriars Priories became playhouses. For a while, Blackfriars priory church housed the 'Office of the Revels', where plays were either approved or censored and then licensed, and also where theatrical sets and costumes were procured, under the Master of the Revels Thomas Cawarden, who held the post 1544-59. After Cawarden's death, the Office relocated to either the Gate-House or the Great Chamber – sources differ – of the Priory of St John in Clerkenwell in 1560 and later still, in 1608, to Whitefriars. Incidentally, Whitefriars Priory was not dissolved immediately and its precinct served initially as a temporary sanctuary for its friars, and eventually as a semi-permanent one for the population at large. Indeed, the right of sanctuary, and exemption from local law, was upheld by Elizabeth I in 1580 and James I in 1608. In consequence, the area was to become notorious for its fugitive criminals and criminality, and, eventually to be known as 'Alsatia', after the – literally – lawless territory lying between France and Germany and outside the jurisdiction of either. As to the former monks, nuns and priors of the dissolved monastic houses, of whom there were several hundred city-wide, and several thousand countrywide, most went to work in the newly created parish churches, although a substantial number were forced to seek out entirely new ways of life. Most were at least offered more or less generous pensions. Some monks were executed during the Reformation (see above).

Henry VIII died in 1547 and was buried in Windsor Castle (it is said that while his body was being transported there for burial, it was temporarily accommodated at the former Syon Abbey where it burst open in its coffin and dogs lapped at the liquid that seeped out). On his death-bed, he handed over his kingly power, and with it the responsibility for the defence of the Protestant faith, to his only son, Edward, borne to him by his third wife, Jane Seymour (who died in the process). There is an extraordinary at least broadly contemporary anonymous painting of the scene, entitled 'An Allegory of Reformation' (now in the National Portrait Gallery). It depicts Edward with a defeated Catholic Pope at his feet. Lying to Edward's right is his dying father Henry. Standing to his left is his uncle, Edward Seymour, the 1st Duke of Somerset and Lord Protector. Seated round a table, under a painting of iconoclasm, are Thomas Cranmer, Archbishop of Canterbury, John Russell, the 1st Earl of Bedford and Lord Privy Seal; and five further gentlemen whose identities are either disputed or altogether unknown.

Edward duly became the boy-king Edward VI on his coronation. There was a painting of his coronation procession, of which copies survive (the original having been lost). It is noteworthy for featuring a fine bird's-eye view of the City of London (*Figure 26*). Edward became a hard-line Protestant and a literal iconoclast. According to *The Chronicle of the Grey Friars*:

Item the 5th day ... in September [1547] began the King's visitation at Paul's and all the images pulled down: and the 9th day of the same month the said visitation was at St. Bride's, and after that in divers

26. Edward VI's coronation procession (1547). The foreground shows, left to right, the Tower of London, London Bridge, Cheapside, Old St Paul's with its spire intact, and Westminster. The background shows, left, St Saviour's (Southwark Cathedral), and right, the white-washed stews or brothels of Bankside.

other parish churches... Item at this same time was pulled up all the tomes ... altars ... and walls of the quire ... in the church that was at some time the Gray friars and sold, and the quire made smaller... Item ... following [1548] ... was Barking chapel at the Tower hill pulled down, and Saint Martin's [le Grand] ... Saint Nicholas in the chambulles [Shambles], and Saint [Audouen, Ewen or] Ewyns, and within the Gatte of Newgate these were put with the church that was at some time the Gray Friars: and also [St Mary] Strand church was pulled down to make the protector duke of Somerset's place larger.

There was a statesman-like side to the boy-king as well. In 1551, he wrote in his diary of how he had, amid much pomp, accommodated and entertained the Catholic Queen Dowager (and mother of Mary Queen of Scots) Mary of Guise at Westminster, after her ship had been forced ashore by bad weather *en route* from France to Scotland:

[D]ivers ... lords and gentlemen ... ladies and gentlewomen went to her, and brought her through London to Westminster. At the gate there received her the Duke of Northumberland, Great Master, and the Treasurer, and Comptroller, and the Earl of Pembroke, with all the sewers [messieurs], and carvers, and cup-bearers, to the number of thirty. In the hall I met he, with all the rest of the Lords of my Council, as the Lord Treasurer ... etc., and from the outer gate up to the presence chamber, on both sides, stood the guard. And so having brought her to her chamber, I retired to mine. I went to her at dinner; she dined under the same cloth of state, at my left hand; at her rearward dined my cousin Francis, and my cousin Margaret; at mine sat the French Ambassador. We were served by two services, two sewers, cupbearers, and gentlemen. Her master hostel [Maitre d'Hotel] came before her service, and my officers before mine... After dinner, when she had heard some music, I brought her into the hall, and she went away.

Edward had stipulated in his will that he wished to be succeeded not by his half-sister, Mary, Henry's daughter by his first wife Catherine of Aragon, who was a Catholic, but by Lady Jane Grey, a fellow Protestant. Jane was indeed duly proclaimed Queen on 10 June, 1553, but was overthrown by Mary only nine days later, on 19 June. She was later tried and convicted on a charge of treason in November 1553 and eventually executed in February 1554. Her father, Henry Grey, was executed a few days after her for his role in Wyatt's Rebellion (see below). Mary was proclaimed Queen on 19 June 1553. Stow wrote:

> In the year 1553 the 19. of July, the Counsell partlie moved with the right of the Lady Maries cause, partly considering that the most of the Realme was wholly bent on her side, changing their mind from Lady Jane lately proclaimed Queene, assembled themselves at this Baynardes Castle, where they communed with the Earle of Pembrooke and the Earl of Shrewsbury and Sir John Mason Clearke of the Counsell, sent for the Lord Mayor, and then riding into Cheape to the Crosse, where Gartar King at Armes, Trumpet being sounded, proclaimed the Lady Daughter to King Henry the eighth and Queene Katharen Queene of England.

As intimated above, she evidently enjoyed a measure of popular support, at least initially. Henry Machyn described how her coronation was accompanied by 'song, and ... belles ryngyng thrugh London, and bone-fyres, and tabuls in evere strett, and wyne and beer and alle'.

Under Mary's reign, the country reverted to Catholicism. Under her Counter-Reformation, a number of Protestants were executed for heresy – hence her nickname, 'Bloody Mary', and that of one of her most enthusiastic supporters, Bishop Edmund Bonner, 'Bloody Bonner'. The total number of persons executed under Mary has been estimated to have been 290. In this context, though, the numbers of those executed under her Protestant predecessors Henry VIII and Edward VI have been estimated to have between 37,000 and 72,000 and 5,500 respectively; and the number executed under her Protestant successor Elizabeth I, 600.

In late 1553 to early 1554, Thomas Wyatt the Younger plotted a rebellion against Mary, and in particular her plan to marry the Catholic King of Spain, Philip. The aims of the rebellion were to overthrow Mary and to put in her place her half-sister Elizabeth (and also to have Elizabeth marry the Protestant Earl of Devon, Edward Courtenay). These aims were to be achieved by force of arms, with each of the four main rebel leaders responsible for assembling an army in his respective corner of the country before marching on London: Wyatt in Kent; Henry Grey (the father of Lady Jane Grey), the Duke of Suffolk, in Leicestershire; Sir James Croft in Herefordshire; and Sir Peter Carew in Devon. In the event, only Wyatt succeeded in raising much of a rebel army, which grew on its march to London through desertions from forces sent to oppose it, and eventually became some four thousand strong. The army arrived in Southwark in February 1554 to find its way into the City of London blocked at London Bridge by forces responding to Mary's stirring rallying-call at the Guildhall two days earlier (the army was also threatened by cannon in the Tower of London, commanded by the Lieutenant of the Tower, John Bruges or Brydges, who intimated that he was prepared to put them to use). It then withdrew, wheeled west to Kingston to cross the river there, marched back east and attempted to enter the City again at Ludgate, where it was again faced down, and where it broke up. After the failure of his rebellion, Wyatt was tortured at the Tower before being tried, convicted and eventually executed in April. His torturers had evidently hoped that he would somehow implicate Elizabeth, but he did not. Elizabeth was herself temporarily imprisoned in the Tower while her supposed complicity was further investigated, but none was ever proven.

In February 1555, John Rogers, the vicar of the church of St Sepulchre-without-Newgate, was burned at the stake in West Smithfield (*Figure 27*), becoming the first of the 'Marian martyrs'. John Foxe in his *Book of Martyrs* gives the following account of Rogers's execution:

[He] was brought ... toward Smithfield, saying the psalm 'Miserere' by the way, all the people wonderfully rejoicing at his constancy, with great praises and thanks to God for the same. And there, in the presence of ... a wonderful number of people, the fire was put unto him; and when it had taken hold both upon his legs and shoulders, he, as one feeling no smart, washed his hands in the flame, as though it had been in cold water. And, after lifting up his hands unto heaven, not removing the same until such time as the devouring fire had consumed them – most mildly this happy martyr yielded up his spirit into the hands of his heavenly Father. A little before his burning at the stake, his pardon was brought, if he would have recanted, but he utterly refused. He was the first proto-martyr of all the blessed company that suffered in Queen Mary's time, that gave the first adventure upon the fire. His wife and children, being eleven in number, and ten able to go, and one sucking on her breast, met him by the way as he went towards Smithfield. This sorrowful sight

27. The execution of John Rogers, West Smithfield (1555). Rogers was the vicar of St Sepulchre Newgate Street.

of his own flesh and blood could nothing move him; but that he constantly and cheerfully took his death, with wonderful patience, in the defence and quarrel of Christ's gospel.

A plaque in West Smithfield marks the site of Rogers's execution, and another in the parish church of St James, Clerkenwell, the site of his burial. Later in 1555, John Bradford and John Philpot were also burned in West Smithfield. In this instance, Foxe gives this account:

When Bradford and Leaf came to the Stake … they lay flat on their faces, praying to themselves the space of a minute of an hour. Then one of the Sheriffs said … Arise and make an end… At that word they both stood [and] Bradford took a Fagot in his hand, and kissed it, and so likewise the Stake… And so … Bradford went to the Stake: and holding up his hands, and casting his countenance to Heaven, he said thus, O England, England, repent thee of thy sins, repent thee of thy sins. Beware of Idolatry, beware of false Antichrists, take heed they do not deceive you… Bradford … asked all the world forgiveness, and forgave all the world, and prayed the people to pray with him, and turned ... unto the young man that suffered with him, and said, Be of good comfort Brother; for we shall have a merry Supper with the Lord this night: And so spake no more words that any man did hear.

As in the case of Rogers, a plaque in West Smithfield marks the site of Bradford and Leaf(e)'s execution, and another in the parish church of St James, Clerkenwell, the site of their burial. In 1556, eleven men and two women were burned in Stratford in front of a crowd of 20,000.

When Mary died in 1558, her half-sister Elizabeth I, Henry's daughter by his second wife Anne Boleyn, became Queen, and the country reverted once more to Protestantism. The 'Recusancy Acts', intended to enforce participation in Protestant religious activities, were passed in the first year of Elizabeth's reign, in 1558. Breaches were punished by fines, property confiscations or even imprisonment (the fine for missing a church service was 1s – half a week's wages for an unskilled labourer). Elizabeth's accession was extremely popular and, as Henry Machyn put it: 'All London did eat and drink and made merry'. Her coronation procession in 1559 paused on its way to Westminster Abbey for the staging of various pageants in her honour (the date having been chosen as a particularly auspicious one by her astrologer John Dee). The first of these symbolised her genealogy, and emphasised her 'Englishness' and Protestantism (in contrast to her late sister Mary's 'Spanishness' and Catholicism) and her descent from Henry Tudor and Elizabeth of York, whose marriage had unified the country after the Wars of the Roses. The second was her government and its virtues of true religion, love of subjects, wisdom and justice. The third, during which the Mayor presented her with a gift of gold, was the interdependence of the Crown and the City. During the fourth, a figure representing Truth presented her with a copy of the Bible bearing the English inscription 'The Word of Truth', the thriving – English, Protestant – commonwealth. The fifth portrayed Elizabeth as Deborah, the prophetess of the Old Testament who rescued the House of Israel and went on to rule for forty years. Elizabeth's reign was widely, although by no means universally, regarded as some sort of 'Golden Age' of – comparative – stability, peace and prosperity; of exploration and discovery (see below), and of the arts, in particular the performing arts (see 'Entertainment and Culture' below). It brought 'melody and joy and comfort to all true Englishmen and women'.

The merchant-adventurer, privateer and naval commander Martin Frobisher set sail on board the *Gabriel* from Ratcliff in 1576 on the second of his three ultimately unsucceful voyages in search of the North-West Passage through the Arctic to Cathay (China) in the Pacific, returning from Canada with a cargo of what turned out to be worthless 'fool's gold' (Hakluyt, 1600; Bicheno, 2012). The site in Ratcliff is marked by a London County Council plaque of 1922 in King Edward Memorial Park. Incidentally, the plaque also commemorates another merchant-adventurer, Hugh Willoughby, who had even earlier, in 1553, set sail on board the *Bona Esparanza* from Ratcliff in search of the North-East Passage through the Arctic to the Pacific, getting as far as Novaya Zemlya before having to turn back, and dying on the remote Kola Peninsula east of Murmansk, on what was supposed to have been an overwintering stop. Frobisher went on to be knighted for his services in seeing off the Spanish Armada in 1588. He died in 1594 of wounds sustained in another action against the Spanish. His organs were buried in the church of St Andrew in Plymouth, and the rest of his body in the church of St Giles Cripplegate in London, where there is a memorial to him. There is a portrait of Frobisher, commissioned by the Cathay Company, and painted by the Dutch artist Cornelis Ketel in 1577, in the Bodleian Library in Oxford. It depicts a man of action, an 'uncultured' man, with an 'acutely violent temperament', wearing a bosun's whistle round his neck, with a scabbarded rapier on his left hip and brandishing a wheel-lock pistol in his right hand. Frobisher also wears a particularly splendid pair of baggy knee-length breeches called 'Venetians', and a matching jerkin over a plain white doublet.

The Devonian explorer, privateer and naval commander Francis Drake set sail from Plymouth on board the *Golden Hind(e)* in 1577 on a voyage of circumnavigation of the globe (*Figure 28*). On his return to England in 1581, his ship was 'drawn into a creek … at Deptford as a perpetual memorial for having circuited round about the whole earth', and consecrated 'with great ceremonie, pompe and magnificence eternally to be remembered'. Drake was knighted by the Queen. The ship remained at Deptford for about 100 years until it started to disintegrate and had to be broken up. A plaque on the waterfront there marks the site. There is a replica of the ship in St Mary Overie Dock in Southwark, a couple of miles upstream from Deptford. There is a fine miniature portrait of Drake on the reverse of a playing card in the National Portrait Gallery, painted by Nicholas Hilliard in 1581.

28. Replica of *Golden Hind*, St Mary Overie Dock, Southwark. The original ship, captained by Francis Drake, completed a circumnavigation of the world between 1577 and 1580.

The Devonian landed gentleman, writer, poet, court favourite, politician, soldier, spy and explorer Sir Walter Ralegh was granted a Royal Charter by Elizabeth I in 1584 to explore, colonise and rule any 'remote, heathen and barbarous lands, countries and territories, not actually possessed of any Christian Prince or inhabited by Christian People [in the New World]', in return for one-fifth of all the gold and silver that might be mined there. He first organised, although did not himself participate in, two voyages to Roanoke in Virginia in the 1580s, in an ultimately unsuccessful attempt to establish an English colony in North America under the governorship of John White (it was not until 1607 that a successful colony was to become established, at Jamestown in Virginia: see 'Trading Colonies in the Americas' in 'Trade and Commerce' below). White first went out to Roanoke in 1587 but returned to England shortly afterwards in order to pick up further supplies. He had intended to go back again within the year, but for various reasons was not actually able to do so until three years later than planned. When he finally did arrive back in Roanoke, he found no trace of the colony or of the colonists, other than the word 'CROATOAN' carved into tree trunks.

Ralegh then himself participated in a voyage in 1595 in search of 'El Dorado', the fabled city of gold in South America, again, unsurprisingly, with no success. In between times, in 1591, he had been temporarily imprisoned in the Tower of London for having married Elizabeth Throckmorton, one of Elizabeth I's ladies-in-waiting, without first having sought the Queen's permission. After Elizabeth I died and James I succeeded her to the throne Ralegh was imprisoned again, this time on the altogether more serious charge of complicity in the so-called 'Main Plot' against the new King in 1603 (which sought to remove him and replace him with his cousin Arbella Stuart). He was eventually pardoned and released in 1616, in order to undertake a second voyage in search of 'El Dorado'. This time, he did find gold, albeit by ransacking a Spanish outpost, in violation of the terms not only of his pardon but also of the Treaty of London of 1604 that had brought to an end the long-running Anglo-Spanish War. On his eventual return to England in 1618, he was arrested and executed in Westminster Palace Yard, essentially to appease the Spanish. There is a portrait of Ralegh, by an unknown artist of the English School, in the National Portrait Gallery, depicting him in the Queen's colours of black and white. Ralegh is of course remembered for supposedly once having made the chivalrous gesture of casting one of his cloaks upon a puddle so as to allow the Queen to walk over it without getting her feet wet. He is also widely credited with having supposedly introduced the potato, and tobacco, to England. The potato introduction is almost certainly false.

The Anglo-Spanish War between Protestant England and Catholic Spain broke out in 1585 after a prolonged period of escalating tension with the seizure of English ships moored in Spanish and Netherlandish ports. The war would only finally be ended in 1604, that is, during the first full year of the reign of Elizabeth's successor, James I, with the signature of the Treaty of London in Somerset House, an event commemorated by a painting now in the Queen's House in Greenwich. At its height, the threat of a Spanish invasion of England was very real, never more so than at the time of the ill-fated Spanish Armada in 1588. In February 1587 Elizabeth I had had the Catholic Pretender, Mary, Queen of Scots, executed. The Catholic King of Spain, Philip II, vowed revenge and in July 1587 obtained Papal authority to overthrow Elizabeth by force of arms and place whoever he chose on the throne in her stead. To that end, he assembled an armada of 130 ships and in 1588 despatched it under the Duke of Medina Sidonia to the Netherlands to 'join hands' with an army under the Duke of Parma, the intention being that the two forces then cross the Channel together and sail up the Thames to take London. In the event, the armada arrived early at the rendezvous, harried by the English fleet under Howard and Drake, and the Duke of Parma's men were not ready to embark. Later, in attempting to escape English fireships, the armada was dispersed to the four winds and many of its ships were wrecked, with great loss of life. Elizabeth, who had been in Richmond Palace or St James's Palace in London throughout the crisis, and in consultation with Burleigh and Walsingham, addressed her armed forces at Tilbury Fort:

My loving people, We have been persuaded by some that are careful of our safety, to take heed how we commit our selves to armed multitudes, for fear of treachery; but I assure you I do not desire to live to distrust my faithful and loving people. Let tyrants fear. I have always so behaved myself that, under God, I have placed my chiefest strength and safeguard in the loyal hearts and good-will of my subjects; and therefore I am come amongst you, as you see, at this time, not for my recreation and disport, but being resolved, in the midst and heat of the battle, to live and die amongst you all; to lay down for my God, and for my Kingdom, and my people, my honour and my blood, even in the dust. I know I have the body of a weak, feeble woman; but I have the heart and stomach of a King, and of a King of England too, and think foul scorn that Parma or Spain, or any prince of Europe, should dare to invade the borders of my realm; to which rather than any dishonour shall grow by me, I myself will take up arms, I myself will be your general, judge, and rewarder of every one of your virtues in the field. I know already, for your forwardness you have deserved rewards and crowns; and We do assure you on a word of a prince, they shall be duly paid. In the mean time, my lieutenant general shall be in my stead, than whom never prince commanded a more noble or worthy subject; not doubting but by your obedience to my general, by your concord in the camp, and your valour in the field, we shall shortly have a famous victory over these enemies of my God, of my Kingdom, and of my people.

Towards the end of Elizabeth's reign, in 1601, Robert Devereux, the 2nd Earl of Essex, led an unsuccessful attempt to overthrow her and her court, a treasonous act for which he was later tried, convicted, and beheaded at the Tower of London. Some of his supporters were also executed, although some others, including the Earl of Southampton, were spared. Essex had earlier been publicly disgraced and politically and financially ruined by being placed under house arrest and removed from his office as Lord Lieutenant of Ireland for failing to execute Elizabeth's orders to him to suppress an insurrection in that country (the so-called 'Tyrone's Rebellion' or 'Nine Year's War'). His overthrow plan was once widely believed to have involved taking a taking a boat from Essex Steps to the 'Globe' in Southwark on 7 February 1601, to bribe the 'Lord Chamberlain's Men' to overplay the scene in that day's performance of Shakespeare's *Richard II* in which the King is deposed, with a view to encouraging support among the watching crowd. Sadly, like all too many good stories, this one has since been conclusively demonstrated to have had no basis in fact (Hammer, 2008). Essex's actual plan, such as it was, simply to march from Essex House to the City of London, began to backfire on the morning of the fateful following day, 8 February, when four of the Queen's men arrived at the house to arrest him and he was forced to take them hostage. He recklessly decided to carry on regardless, but when he and his followers, numbering some two hundred, arrived at the City, they were met with a hostile reception, having by that time already been denounced as traitors (by Robert Cecil, the 1st Earl of Salisbury, the Secretary of State). At this, most of his followers deserted him, and he was forced to return to Essex House, where after a short siege, during which he attempted to destroy any evidence that might incriminate him, he found himself forced to surrender to the Queen's men (under the Earl of Nottingham).

Stuart History

The Stuart era was a time of War and Plague and purifying Fire; of a bloody Civil War between Royalist and Parliamentarian; and of a peculiarly English revolution under the Parliamentarian Commonwealth and Protectorate of Oliver and Richard Cromwell, which ended with the Restoration of the Monarchy – albeit, importantly, a monarchy that could thenceforth only rule with the consent of Parliament. It was also, though, the time not only of a continuing renaissance in the arts, but also of the birth of science, or 'natural philosophy', as it was known. The Royal Society of London for Improving Natural Knowledge, nowadays generally known as the Royal Society, was founded in 1660, the founding members being William Ball, William Brouncker, 2nd Viscount Brouncker, Jonathan Goddard, Abraham Hill, Robert Moray, Paul Neile, William Petty and Lawrence Rooke. The purpose of the Society, according to its Charter, was 'To improve the knowledge of all natural things, and all useful Arts, manufactures, Mechanick practises, Engines and Inventions by Experiments – (not meddling with Divinity, Metaphysics, Moralls, Politicks, Grammar [or spelling, presumably], Rhetorick or Logick)'. Its first meetings were held at Gresham College. Perhaps the most famous seventeenth-century collection of Naturalia, or 'Cabinet of Curiosities', was the *Musaeum Tradescantianum*, founded in around 1634 by the gentleman-travellers and collectors John Tradescant the Elder (c. 1580-1638), and his son John Tradescant the Younger (1608-62), and housed in a building called 'The Ark' in Vauxhall, which was the first such in England to be open to the general public – albeit at a cost of 6d. In time, the Tradescants' collection was acquired by Elias Ashmole, and in 1691 donated by him to Oxford University, to form the nucleus of the Ashmolean Museum. The Tradescants, who were employed as gardeners – John the Elder by Robert Cecil, the 1st Earl of Salisbury, and by William Cecil, the 2nd Earl and John the Younger by Charles II – are both buried in the church of St Mary-at-Lambeth, which now incorporates a Garden Museum. John the Younger created the gardens designed by Inigo Jones at the Queen's House, Greenwich. (Both men are worthy subjects of study in Vanessa Berridge's excellent *Great British Gardeners*.)

On 24 March 1603, John Manningham wrote: 'This morning about three at clock her Majesty departed this life, mildly like a lamb, easily like a ripe apple from the tree ... About ten at clock the Council and divers noblemen having been awhile in consultation, proclaimed James VI, King of Scots, the King of England, France and Ireland.' On 15 March 1604, James made a triumphal entry into the City of London, and thence processed to Westminster to attend his first parliament, amid much pomp and pageant. A number of contemporary accounts of the event still survive, including that of the King himself, who wrote, with characteristic bombast: 'The people of all sorts rode and ran, nay, rather flew to meet me, their eyes flaming nothing but sparkles of affection, their mouths and tongues uttering nothing but sounds of joy, their hands, feet, and all the rest of their members in their gestures discovering a passionate longing and earnestness to meet and embrace their new sovereign.' On its way through the City, the procession passed beneath a series of allegorical triumphal arches designed by Stephen Harrison that formed the backdrops for entertainments by some of the finest writers of the day, including Dekker, Jonson, Middleton and Webster.

James, like Elizabeth, was a Protestant, although one widely suspected of harbouring Catholic sympathies. In 1605, he saw off the Catholic Gunpowder Plot, 'a most horrible conspiracy of the Papish' to blow up the Houses of Parliament in the Palace of Westminster, and had Guy Fawkes and the other ringleaders executed, and their remains exhibited as a deterrent to others (*Figure 29*). Sir Edward Hoby, the son-in-law of Elizabeth I's cousin Henry Carey, the 1st Baron Brunsdon, and the nephew of her chief advisor William Cecil, the 1st Baron Burghley or Burleigh, a courtier during the reigns of Elizabeth I and James I, wrote of the event:

> On the 5th of November we began our Parliament, to which the King should have come in person, but refrained, through a practice but that morning discovered' [the discoverer, one Thomas Knyvet(t), the Keeper of Whitehall Palace, was rewarded by the granting of an extension of the lease on his house in what was to become Downing Street]. The plot was to have blown up the King at such time as he should have been set in his royal throne, accompanied by his children, Nobility and Commons and … Bishops, Judges and Doctors, at one instant and blast and to have ruined the whole estate and Kingdom of England. And for the effecting of this there was placed under the

29. A famous depiction of the Gunpowder Plot conspirators by Dutchman Crispijn van de Passe (*c.* 1605). He never saw any of them.

Parliament house, where the King should sit, some 30 barrels of gunpowder... In a vault under the parliament chamber before spoken of one Johnson [Guy Fawkes's assumed name] was found ... who, after being brought into ... the court, and there demanded if he were not sorry for his so foul and heinous a treason, answered he was sorry for nothing but that the act was not performed. Being replied unto him that no doubt there had been a number in that place of his own religion, how in conscience he could do them hurt, he answered a few might well perish to have the rest taken away... When he was brought into the King's presence, the King asked him how he could conspire so hideous a treason against his children and so many innocent souls which never offended him? He answered that ... a dangerous disease required a desperate remedy.

Popular suspicion of James's supposed Catholic sympathies remained, even after the Gunpowder Plot, and in 1622, on the seventeenth anniversary thereof, the Dean of St Paul's, John Donne, felt compelled to give a sermon reassuring the congregation as to his commitment to Protestantism. In his sermon, Donne described the King as 'in his heart, as farre from submitting us to that Idolatry, and Superstition, which did heretofore oppresse us, as his immediate Predecessor, whose memory is justly precious to you, was'.

When James I died in 1625, his son Charles I came to the throne and so abused his supposed 'divine rights' as a King in the eyes of Parliament, and of much of the population at large, as ultimately to trigger the Civil War in 1642. In 1641, Thomas Wentworth, Earl of Strafford and Lord Deputy of Ireland, an ardent supporter of the King in his power-struggle with Parliament in the period leading up to the Civil War, was executed on Tower Hill for high treason (specifically, for allegedly saying to the King 'You have an army in Ireland you may employ here to reduce this Kingdom'). His last words, taken from the Psalms, were: 'O put not your trust in Princes, nor in any child of man; for there is no help in them.' A not particularly oblique reference to the sense of betrayal he felt toward the King, who had promised him that he 'should not suffer in his person, honour or fortune'; and then, when expedient, signed his death warrant. In January of 1642 the King and his henchmen entered the Houses of Parliament and attempted to arrest five Members of Parliament, namely, John Hampden, Arthur Haselrig, Denzil Holles, John Pym and William Strode (Hampden was

Cromwell's cousin, and one of his ablest military commanders during the early part of the war, dying of wounds sustained at the Battle of Chalgrove Field in 1643). It is said that when the King demanded to be told the whereabouts of the MPs, the Speaker of the House, William Lenthall, retorted: 'May it please your Majesty, I have neither eyes to see nor tongue to speak in this place but as the House is pleased to direct me, whose servant I am here.' The attempted arrest, which is ceremonially re-enacted each year during the State Opening of Parliament, when the Crown's representative, 'Black Rod', is despatched from the Lords to the Commons, there to have the doors slammed shut in his face, was essentially the last in the series that eventually led to the outbreak of war in the August.

The City of London remained largely Parliamentarian in its sympathies throughout the course of the Civil War (Rowles, 2018). On 7 November 1642 Giovanni Giustiniani, the Venetian ambassador to the court of Charles I, wrote in a letter to the Doge and Senate of Venice:

They do not cease to provide with energy for the defence of London... They have sent a number of parliamentarians to the surrounding provinces with instructions to get together the largest numbers they can of their trained bands, with the intention of despatching these subsequently to where the remains of the parliamentary army are quartered. They have brought a number of the companies of these trained bands ... into this city. All the troops are kept constantly at arms. There is no street, however little frequented, that is not barricaded ... and every post is guarded... At the approaches to London, they are putting up trenches and small forts of earthwork, at which a great number of people are at work, including the women and children. They have issued a new manifesto to the people full of the usual representations against the ... King, for the purpose of arousing their enthusiasm still more in the support of this cause.

In 1643, William Lithgow wrote:

I found the ... court before Whitehall Gate guarded, and what was more rarer, I found the grass growing deep in the ... king's house. The daily musters and shows of all sorts of Londoners here are wondrous and commendable in marching to the fields and outworks ... carrying ... iron mattocks and wooden shovels, with roaring drums, flying colours and girded swords; most companies being interlarded with ladies, women and girls ... carrying baskets to advance the labour... I saluted ... two forts upon Tyburn Way and Marylebone Fields ... both pallisaded, double-ditched and barricaded with iron pikes, the one clad with eight demi-culverins and the other ... with four ... , both wondrous defensible.

At the time of the outbreak of the war, the City of London's militia, the so-called 'trained bands', comprised around 6,000 men organised into twenty companies and four regiments (North, South, East and West). Subsequently, it grew to 8,000 men in forty companies and six regiments (Red, Blue, Green, White, Orange and Yellow) and eventually to 20,000 men in fourteen regiments (five of them 'auxiliary'). The militia was at least partly under the command of the Mayor and Aldermen. Its primary role was the defence of London, although it also contributed brigades of foot to Parliament's armies in the field. Its importance waned after the establishment of the New Model Army in 1645. The Honourable Artillery Company was unusual in that it, or rather elements of it, fought on both sides! The City's civilian population, including large numbers of Puritans, broke its rule against working on the Sabbath in order to construct a ring of defence, eleven miles in circumference, known as the 'Lines of Communication', of which there is now little trace. Though the remains of one of the star forts that once formed part of the defences have recently been unearthed in an archaeological excavation in Spital Square in Spitalfields (Harward *et al.*, 2015).

The Battle of Brentford took place on 12 November 1642. The site of the battle is marked by a granite memorial and by a series of informative plaques. According to the plaques, what happened here was as follows:

Parliamentarians had arrived in the prosperous market town on Friday 11 November. The following day the royalists marched from Hampstead Heath and in the early afternoon broke through a parliamentary barricade at the bridge over the Brent... [T] he royalists were delayed, fighting two or three hours until the parliamentarian soldiers fled. This position was defended by about 480 of Lord Brooke's regiment and survivors of the earlier fighting, with two small pieces of artillery. The royalists soon gained the upper hand. There seem to have been no civilian dead despite the capture of the town. About 20 royalists were killed, and perhaps 50 parliamentarians died in the fighting with more drowning in the Thames. Parliamentary Captain John Lilburne was amongst those captured... Later that afternoon the royalists pressed on towards London. There were more parliamentary troops in a large open area, probably Turnham Green and Chiswick's Common Field. These green-coated men of John Hampden's regiment of foot charged five times, holding the royalists back. But with night coming and the royalists exhausted from fighting both sides disengaged. The royalist soldiers who had captured Brentford ransacked the town.

John Gwyn, a royalist soldier, wrote: 'We beat them from one Brainford to the other, and from thence to the open field, with ... resolute and expeditious fighting, ... push of pike and the butt-end of muskets, which proved so fatal to Holles' butchers and dyers that day.'

The Battle of Turnham Green took place the following day, on 13 November. After losing the Battle of Brentford, the Parliamentarians took up a strategic defensive position at Turnham Green, with their left flank protected by the river, and their right by a series of enclosures. It was here that they essentially faced down the Royalists, who found themselves unable to manoeuvre past, in one of the largest ever confrontations on English soil (albeit a substantially bloodless one), involving some 40,000 troops. This was a decisive moment in the history of the war, the country, and its capital.

On 2 May 1643, John Evelyn wrote in his diary: 'I went from Wotton to London, where I saw the furious and zealous people demolish that stately Cross in Cheapside' (*Figure 30*). The so-called Eleanor Crosses on Cheapside and at Charing Cross in Westminster, originally put up in the late thirteenth century by King Edward I in memory of his late wife, Eleanor of Castile, were both demolished in the Civil War as symbols of Royal oppression. The closest surviving one to London is in Waltham Cross in Hertfordshire. In 1645, William Laud, sometime Bishop of London and Archbishop of Canterbury, and a man well known for his 'High Church' views and his fierce opposition to and persecution of Puritans, was executed as a traitor on Tower Hill. Among the charges levelled against him were that

...by false erroneous doctrines, and other sinister ways and means, he went about to subvert religion, established in this Kingdom, and to

The 2 of May. 1643. y' Crosse in Cheapeside was pulled downe, a Troope of Horse & 2 Companies of foote wayted to garde it & at y' fall of y' tope Crosse dromes beat trū pets blew & multitudes of Capes wayre throwne in y'Ayre. & a greate Shoute of People with ioy, y' 2 of May the Almana: he sayeth, was y' invention of the Crosse. & 6 day at night was the Leaden Popes burnt, in the pla: ce where it stood with ringinge c'Bells, & a greate Acclamation & no hurt done in all these actions.

30. The Demolition of the Cheapside Cross (1643).

set up popery and superstition in the church ... to save and preserve himself from being questioned and sentenced from these and other his traiterous designs, from the first year of his now Majesty's reign, until now, he hath laboured to subvert the rights of parliamentary proceedings, and to incense his Majesty against parliaments.

In 1647, with the war virtually won, the Parliamentarian leadership gathered in the church of St Mary in Putney for the 'Putney Debates'. The debates, chaired by Cromwell and attended by officers and men of his New Model Army, many of whom were 'Levellers', addressed no less than the post-Civil War future and constitution of England. Among the issues debated were whether power should be vested in the King and House of Lords or in the Commons, and whether there should be universal – male – suffrage. Colonel Thomas Rainsborough, personifying the radical contingent, famously argued that: '[T]he poorest hee that is in England hath a life to live, as the greatest hee.' Among the outcomes was a declaration of 'native rights' for all Englishmen, including freedom of conscience, and equality before the law. Rainsborough went on to be killed during the siege of Pontefract and was buried in the church of St John in Wapping in November

1648. (For a fuller account of his extraordinary life, the reader is referred to *The Rainborowes* by Adrian Tinniswood.)

On 6 December 1648, the Parliamentarian Colonel Thomas Pride expelled over a hundred Presbyterian Members of the 'Long Parliament' from the Houses of Parliament, in what became known as 'Pride's Purge'. At this time, the King and supporting Royalists were Episcopalians (who believed in the supremacy of the bishops), and opposing Parliamentarians were divided among two factions, Independents who also supported the pre-eminence of the bishops, and Presbyterians, who did not. The Independents mistrusted the English Presbyterians because their Scottish counterparts had earlier entered into an alliance with the King, hence the purge. The Independent Members who remained after the purge, constituting the 'Rump Parliament', then instigated the legal proceedings against Charles that led to his trial for treason and eventually to his execution.

The Interregnum

On 30 January 1649, having bid a heartbreaking goodbye to his young children, Charles was executed for treason outside the Banqueting House in Whitehall (*Figure 17c*). It was a freezing cold day, so he put on an extra shirt, that no-one might see him shiver ('the season is so sharp as probably may make me shake, which some observers may imagine proceeds from fear [and] I would have no such imputation'). Eventually, after what must have been a harrowing wait, at 2pm he delivered an almost inaudible address to the crowd, at the end proclaiming 'I go from a corruptible to an incorruptible crown, where no disturbance can be, no disturbance in the world.' He then made a silent prayer, laid his head upon the block, and had it stricken from his body. Whereupon, according to an eye-witness account by one Philip Henry, 'there was such a Grone given by the Thousands there present, as I never heard before & desire I may never hear again.' The usually ubiquitous John Evelyn was pointedly not among those who bore witness to the event, writing in his diary: 'The Villanie of the Rebells proceeding now so far as to Trie, Condemne, & Murder our excellent King ... struck me with such horror that I kept the day of his Martyrdom a fast, & would not be present, at that execrable wickednesse.'

On 19 May 1649, at what was effectively the end of the Civil War (although skirmishing was to continue for a further two years), the Long Parliament passed an Act making England a Commonwealth and Free State 'where Parliament would constitute the officers and ministers of the people without any Kings or lords'. The authoritianism of the Commonwealth – and later Protectorate – made it increasingly unpopular. On 25 December 1657 John Evelyn wrote in his diary:

I went to London with my wife, to celebrate Christmas day, Mr Gunning preaching in Exeter chapel... Sermon ended, as he was giving us the Holy Sacrament, the chapel was surrounded with soldiers, and all the communicants and assembly surprised and kept prisoner by them... In the afternoon came Colonel Whalley, Goffe, and others ... to examine us one by one; some they committed to the marshal, some to prison. When I came before them, they took my name and abode, examined me why, contrary to the ordinance made, that none should any longer observe the superstitious time of the nativity (so esteemed by them), I durst offend ... and ... pray for Charles Stuart... I told them we did not pray for Charles Stuart, but for all Kings, princes, and governors. They replied ... with other frivolous and ensnaring questions, and much threatening; and, finding no color to detain me, they dismissed me with much pity of my ignorance. These were men of high flight and above ordinances, and spake spiteful things of our Lord's Nativity.

And in 1658, John Reresby wrote in his diary:

The citizens and common people of London had then soe far imbibed the custome and manners of a Commonwealth that they could scarce endure the sight of a gentleman, soe that the common salutation to a man well dressed was 'French dog,' or the like. Walkeing one day in the street with my valet de chambre, who did wear a feather in his hatt, some workemen that were mending the street abused him and threw sand upon his cloaths, at which he drew his sword, thinkeing to follow the custome of France in the like cases. This made the rabble fall upon him and me, that had drawn too in his defence, till we gott shelter in a hous, not without injury to our bravery and some blowes to ourselves.

The Restoration of the Monarchy

On 25 April 1660, which would have been Oliver Cromwell's 61st birthday (he had died in 1658), the 'Convention Parliament' was convened for the first time, in theory as a 'free parliament', with no allegiance to either the Commonwealth or the Monarchy, although in practice as one with overwhelmingly Monarchist sympathies. Indeed, according to Trevelyan, it was 'by the letter of the law no true Parliament, because the King did not summon it, on the contrary, it summoned the King.' On 8 May it restored the monarchy to Prince Charles, making him King Charles II. On 29 May Charles entered the City of London. According to an unnamed source:

> On Tuesday, May the 29th (which happily fell out to be the anniversary of his majesty's birth-day), he set forth of Rochester in his coach; but afterwards he took horse on the farther side of Black-heath... In magnificent fashion his majesty entered the borough of Southwark, about half an hour past three of the clock ... and, within an hour after, the city of London at the bridge; where he found the windows and streets exceedingly thronged with people to behold him; and the walls adorned with hangings ... and in many places ... loud musick; all the conduits ... running claret wine; and the companies in their liveries ... as also the trained bands ... standing along the streets ... welcoming him with joyful acclamations... His majesty entered Whitehall ... the people making loud shouts, and the horse and foot several vollies of shot, at this his happy arrival. Where ... parliament received him, and kissed his royal hand. At the same time ... the Reverend Bishops ... with divers of the long oppressed orthodox clergy, met in that royal chapel of King Henry the Seventh, at Westminster [Abbey], there also sang Te Deum, & c. in praise and thanks to Almighty God, for his deliverance of his majesty from many dangers, and ... restoring him to rule these Kingdoms, according to his just and undoubted right.

On 22 April 1661 Charles ceremonially processed on horseback through the City of London to Westminster, as portrayed by the Dutch artist Dir(c)k Stoop in a painting now in the Museum of London. The route passed through four specially constructed allegorical triumphal arches: one on Leadenhall Street; one at the Royal Exchange on Cornhill; one on Cheapside; and one in Whitefriars (the arches are thought to have been inspired by those designed by Rubens for the triumphal entry of Cardinal-Infante Ferdinand of Austria into Antwerp in 1635). The associated lavish entertainments were described in detail in print by the Scots stage-manager John Ogilby, in a book entitled, in part(!), *The entertainment of His Most Excellent Majestie Charles II, in his passage through the city of London to his coronation containing an exact accompt of the whole solemnity, the triumphal arches, and cavalcade...* The following day, 23 April, Charles was formally crowned King at Westminster Abbey. Samuel Pepys wrote:

> About 4 I rose and got to the Abbey [and] with a great deal of patience I sat ... till 11 before the King came in... At last comes in the Dean and Prebends of Westminster, with the Bishops (many of them in cloth of gold copes), and after them the Nobility, all in their Parliament robes, which was a most magnificent sight. Then the Duke, and the King with a scepter (carried by my Lord Sandwich) and sword and mond before him, and the crown too. The King in his robes, bare-headed (that is, without his customarily-affected wig), which was very fine. And after all had placed themselves, there was a sermon and the service; and then in the Quire at the high altar, the King passed through all the ceremonies of the Coronacon, which to my great grief I and most in the Abbey could not see. The crown being put upon his head, a great shout begun.

Before he had even been formally crowned, Charles set about arresting and executing the surviving regicides who had signed his father's death warrant, thereby violating the terms of his own 'Declaration of Breda', which had promised a pardon for all crimes committed during the Civil War and interregnum (Jordan, 2017). On 13 October 1660, Major-General Thomas Harrison was hanged, drawn and quartered at Tyburn ('he looking as cheerful as any man could do in that condition' as Pepys drily noted); on 14 October Thomas Scot, Adrian Scroop, John Cook and John Jones at Charing Cross; and on 15 October John Carew, also at Charing Cross. John Cook had been the chief prosecutor at Charles I's trial. Shortly before his execution, he wrote: 'We fought for the public good and would have enfranchised the people and secured the welfare of the whole groaning creation if the nation had not more delighted in servitude than in freedom.' On 14 June 1662 Sir Harry Vane was beheaded at Tower Hill. Pepys wrote on this occasion:

> [A]bout eleven o'clock we all went out to the Tower-hill; and there, over against the scaffold, made on purpose this day, saw Sir Harry

Vane brought. A very great press of people. He made a long speech, many times interrupted by the Sheriff and others there; and they would have taken the paper out of his hand, but he would not let it go. ... trumpets were brought that he might not be heard. Then he prayed, and so fitted himself, and received the blow.

The composure and courage with which the regicides met their fate elicited much sympathy from the watching masses – far from the reaction that the authorities had wanted!

On 19 January 1661, the cooper Thomas Venner was hanged, drawn and quartered for high treason for attempting with fifty or so following so-called 'Fifth Monarchists' to overthrow the recently restored King Charles II and seize London in the name of 'King Jesus'. (They believed that the Saviour about to return, in fulfilment of a prophecy in the Book of Daniel that Four Monarchies would precede the Kingdom of Christ – the Babylonian, Persian, Macedonian and Roman). Venner and his men, many of whom were veterans of the Parliamentarian New Model Army of the Civil War, had earlier in the month congregated in Swan Alley, descended upon and occupied St Paul's, accosted passers-by and asked them who they were for, and shot dead one man who answered that he was for Charles. They had then gone on the run and on the rampage for several days, with Venner personally responsible for three murders committed with a halberd on Threadneedle Street (a number of people killed in the rebellion were buried in the Bedlam Burial Ground). The men were finally surrounded by an overwhelmingly superior force of troops, according to one colourful account, in the Helmet Tavern on Threadneedle Street and the Blue Anchor on Coleman Street, where they made a last stand, and were either killed or captured (after troops broke in from roof level, smashing aside the roof tiles with the butts of their muskets). Venner himself was captured, after being wounded no fewer than nineteen times, and then tried and convicted at the Old Bailey for his crimes.

The Second Anglo-Dutch War broke out in 1665, as England and the Netherlands continued to vie for control of the seas and lucrative maritime trade (Rideal, 2016). The early exchanges mainly went England's way. In August 1666 the English Vice-Admiral Robert Holmes launched a raid on the Vlie estuary, razing the town of West-Terschellling on the island of Terschelling and destroying around 130 Dutch merchantmen in what was to become known as 'Holmes's

Bonfire'. The following month, the Great Fire destroyed the City of London, and came to be widely interpreted by the Dutch as an act of divine retribution for 'Holmes's Bonfire', and by the English as an act of Dutch sabotage. The war's later exchanges went the way of the Netherlands, as England's economy and war effort suffered during and after the Great Plague in 1665 and the Great Fire. In 1667, the Dutch Admiral de Ruyter launched a raid on the English naval base on the Medway, a tributary of the Thames, a short distance downstream from London, capturing the fort at Sheerness and destroying eighteen naval ships, including the *Loyal London*, *Royal James* and *Royal Oak*, and capturing another, the flagship, the *Royal Charles*. It was an ignominious defeat for the Royal Navy and effectively forced the English to sue for peace. The war ended in 1667, with the Dutch ascendant in the field. In accordance with the terms of the Treaty of Breda, the Dutch were allowed to retain control of the spice island of Pulau Run in the Moluccas in the East Indies and the sugar plantations in Suriname in South America. In exchange, the English were able to keep paper possession of the perceived less valuable New Netherland in North America, the capital of which, New Amsterdam, they renamed New York, after James, Duke of York (the future James II).

The 1665 'Great Plague' (*Figure 18c*) killed at least 70,000 people, and possibly as many as 100,000 – far more than the 'Black Death' of 1348-9, although far fewer in proportion to the overall population (Porter, 2018). There had also been outbreaks in 1563, 1578-9, 1582, 1592-3, 1603, 1625, 1636 and 1647. One John Harvard of the Queen's Head Inn in Southwark decided to sail to America to seek his fortune after the rest of his family died in the outbreak in 1636. The university that he helped found there, in Cambridge, Massachuetts, still bears his name. The Worshipful Company of Parish Clerks' 'Bills of Mortality' – now in the London Metropolitan Archives – show that of the 70,000 *recorded* plague deaths in London in 1665, only 10,000 were in the 97 parishes within the walls of the City – possibly because a significant proportion of those inhabitants who could afford to do so had fled to the country. The remaining 60,000 plague deaths were in the sixteen parishes without the walls, the five in Westminster and the twelve in Middlesex and Surrey. St Giles Cripplegate, St Giles-in-the-Fields, St Margaret Westminster, St Martin-in-the-Fields, and Stepney, where there were 'pest-houses', were among the worst affected, with a total of well over 20,000 deaths – 6,500 of them in

Stepney alone. The bodies of the plague victims were buried either in parish churchyards or in emergency 'plague pits', the latter including those of Tothill Fields in Westminster to the west; Bedlam, Bunhill Fields and Holywell Mount to the north; Aldgate and the Stepney pest-fields to the east; and Crossbones Graveyard and Deadman's Place to the south.

In his diary, Samuel Pepys wrote with mounting horror of the advance of the disease across Europe from October 1663, of the vain attempts to stem it by the quarantining of incoming ships, of its eventual arrival in London in June 1665 and then of its devastating spread over the succeeding summer and autumn. On 31 August 1665 he wrote:

[T]he plague having a great increase this week, beyond all expectation of almost 2,000, making the general Bill [of Mortality] 7,000, odd 100; and the plague above 6,000. [14 September] '[T]he Bill ... in the City ... is increased and likely to continue so, and is close to our house there. My meeting dead corpses of the plague, carried to be buried close to me at noon-day ... in Fenchurch Street. To see a person sick of the sores carried close by me by Grace-church in a hackney-coach. My finding the Angell tavern, at the lower end of Tower-hill, shut up; and more than that, the alehouse at the Tower Stairs; and more than that, that the person was then dying of the plague when I was last there, a little while ago at night. To hear that poor Payne, my waiter, hath buried a child, and is dying himself. To hear that a labourer I sent but the other day to Dagenhams, to know how they did there, is dead of the plague; and that one of my own watermen, that carried me daily, fell sick as soon as he had landed me on Friday morning last, when I had been all night upon the water ... is now dead of the plague. ... To hear that Mr. Lewes hath another daughter sick. And, lastly, that both my servants, W. Hewers and Tom Edwards, have lost their fathers, both in St. Sepulchre's parish, of the plague this week, do put me into great apprehensions of melancholy, and with good reason. [20 September] But, Lord! What a sad time it is to see no boats upon the river; and grass grows all up and down White Hall court, and nobody but poor wretches in the streets! And, which is worst of all, the Duke [of Albemarle] showed us the number of the plague this week ... that it is encreased ... more than the last, which is quite contrary to our hopes and expectations, from the coldness of the late season. For the whole general number is 8297, and of them of the plague 7165; which is more in the whole ... than the biggest Bill [of Mortality] yet: which is very grievous to us all.

On the same day, one John Tillison wrote:

Death stares us continually in the face in every infected person that passeth by us; in every coffin which is ... carried along the streets... The custom was to bury the dead in the night only; now, both night and day will hardly be time enough to do it... [L]ast week ... the dead was piled in heaps above ground ... before either time could be gained or place to bury them. The Quakers ... have buried in their piece of ground [Bunhill Row] a thousand... Many are [also] dead in ... other places about the town which are not included in the bill of mortality.

The Great Plague was now at its peak, killing over a thousand people a day. It had grown so deathly quiet in London that throughout the City the river could be heard flowing under the nineteen arches of the old bridge. My distant ancestor Frances West's first husband, citizen and clothworker Robert Mickell, died of the plague on 17 September 1665, having written in his will only days earlier, evidently only too aware of his own mortality, 'I ... being well in body ... praised bee God for the same but considering the frailty of man's life and not knowing how soon it may please Almighty God my creator to call me out of this transitory world doe make and ordayne this my last will and testament.'

Pepys later wrote with heartfelt relief of the its ultimate departure in the winter of 1665 (it is commonly thought that the plague was only killed off by the Great Fire of September 1666, but the 'Bills of Mortality' confirm Pepys's observation that it died out at the beginning of the winter of 1665). On 5 October, 'The Bill, blessed be God! is less this week by 740 of what is was the last'. And on 26 October: 'The 'Change pretty full, and the town begins to be lively again'. The plague was now well past its peak, and some semblance of normality was beginning to return to a stricken city. The heroic physician Nathaniel Hodges, the only one, it is thought, who had remained in London throughout the plague year to treat the afflicted, could finally rest. Twice he thought he felt himself succumbing to the symptoms of the disease, and twice he kept it at bay by drinking increased draughts of sack (he also took a preventive electuary – some kind of medicinal concoction usually sweetened with honey – as large as a nutmeg each day). He went on write an account of his experiences entitled *Loimologia, sive Pestis nuperæ apud Populum Londinensem grassantis Narratio Historica* in 1672, lamenting therein the uselessness of bezoar stone, unicorn horn and dried toad as anti-pestilential treatments. Tragically, he died a pauper in Ludgate Prison in 1688 and was buried in the church of St Stephen Walbrook.

Social History

The social history of post-Medieval London is discussed by, among others, R. Porter (2000) and S. Porter (2016) (see also 'Further Reading'). The role of women in post-Medieval society – in London and elsewhere – is discussed by Laurence (1994). For most, life continued to revolve around the 'daily grind'. For some, there would have been opportunities for advancement in education, in paid employment or self-employment, albeit in the trades rather than in the professions, and in public office. However, as the anonymously authored *The Lawes Resolutions of Women's Rights* pithily put it in 1632, 'Women have no voice in Parliament, they make no laws, they consent to none, they abrogate none.'

Religion

The predominant religion of the period before the Reformation was Catholicism; and after the Reformation, either Protestantism – or a hard-line form known as Puritanism – or Catholicism, depending upon Royal patronage. Sadly, if not entirely atypically of human history, there was much persecution of the one sect by the other, such that the fortune and fate of a man could be determined by his faith and allegiance, or by scheme and intrigue, as by the toss of a coin. In 1597, the Jesuit priest Father John Gerard was imprisoned and tortured in the Tower of London, in an ultimately unsuccessful attempt to get him to reveal the whereabouts of Fr Henry Garnet (who eventually went on to be executed in the aftermath of the Gunpowder Plot of 1605). There was also persecution of believers in other faiths, and of non-believers.

Jews, who had been expelled from the City and country in 1290, and for the next nearly four hundred years lived there only as converts or coverts ('Marranos'), were finally readmitted under the Protectorate of Oliver Cromwell following a personal approach to Cromwell by one Menasseh ben Israel, in 1656. The first to arrive were Sephardim, escaping religious persecution in Portugal, Spain and elsewhere in western Europe. Slightly later came the Ashkenazim from central and eastern Europe. A Sephardic Synagogue was built on Creechurch Lane, on the eastern fringe of the City, in 1657, and later relocated to an adjacent site on Bevis Marks in 1701, where it still stands (Barnett, 1940). The Bevis Marks Synagogue was built by Joseph Avis, a Quaker, who refunded to the congregation the difference between the final cost of the construction and his original – higher – estimate, not wanting to profit from working on a House of God. The Ashkenazi Great Synagogue was built on nearby Duke's Place in 1690. Sadly, it was destroyed during the Blitz. The old Jewish cemetery in Cripplegate, until 1177 the only one in all England, to which bodies would be brought for burial from as far afield as Exeter and York, was also destroyed in the War. New cemeteries were opened in Mile End in the East End of London in the late seventeenth century (Beyahayim Velho), and in the early eighteenth (Betahayim Novo). The latter lies in what is now the Mile End campus of Queen Mary College.

Some Londoners were curious as to Jewish observances; others suspicious, mistrustful or fearful. In 1662, one Joseph Greenhalgh wrote in a letter:

> I lighted upon a learned Jew with a mighty bush beard, with whom ... I fell into conference ... at which time he told me that he had special relation as Scribe and Rabbi to a private Synagogue ... in London, and that if I had a desire to see their manner of worship ... he would give me such a ticket, as, upon sight thereof, their porter would let me in... When Saturday came ... I was let ... in ... , but there being no Englishman but myself, ... I was at first a little abashed to venture alone amongst all them Jews, but my innate curiosity to see things strange ... made me confident... . I ... went in and sate me down among them; but Lord what a strange sight was there ... [as] would have frightened a novice... Every man had a large white ... covering ... cast over the high crown of his hat, which from thence hung down on all sides ... nothing to be seen but a little of the face; this, my Rabbi told me, was their ancient garb, used in divine worship in Jerusalem ... and though to me at first it made altogether a strange show, yet me thought it had in its kind, I know not how, a face and aspect of venerable antiquity.

In 1663, Samuel Pepys wrote:

> [A]fter dinner my wife and I, by Mr. Rawlinson's conduct, to the Jewish Synagogue [on Creechurch Lane]... Their service all in a singing way, and in Hebrew. And anon their Laws that they take out of the press are carried by several men, four or five several burthens in all, and they do relieve one another; and whether it is that every one desires to have the carrying of it, I cannot tell, thus they carried it round about the room while such a service is singing. And in the end they had a prayer for the King, which they pronounced his name in Portugall; but the prayer, like the rest, in Hebrew. But, Lord! to see the disorder, laughing, sporting, and no attention, but confusion in all their service ... would make a man forswear ever seeing them more and indeed I never did see so much, or could have imagined there had been any religion in the whole world so absurdly performed as this.

Unbeknownst to him, he had witnessed the service of *Simchat Torah* ('Rejoicing in the Torah'), marking the end of the *Sukkot(h)*, the annual cycle of readings from the *Torah*, which is always a celebratory rather than a solemn event. The associated activity that most bewildered him was the *Hakafo*t (dancing with the *Torah*). There would almost certainly also have been drinking of ritual wine (symbolising life), although he does not mention it. Indeed, a traditional source recommends performing the priestly blessing earlier than usual in the service, to make sure that the priests are still sober when the time comes!

The earliest records of Muslims ('Mahometans') visiting if not living in London are from the Tudor period (Brotton, 2016). There were a number of important emissary visits by Muslims to London during the reign of Elizabeth I, as she sought to build an alliance between the Islamic World and Protestant England against Catholic Spain. The alliance essentially ended when the Anglo-Spanish War ended in 1604 (the first full year of the Stuart King James I's rule).

Food and Drink

The rich continued to gorge themselves on meat, and the poor, whose wages were still only 2s a week or less, to subsist on potage, as in the Medieval period. According to surviving records, the guests at a banquet in the Great Hall in Ely Palace in 1531, who included Henry VIII and Catherine of Aragon, managed over the course of five days to work their way through 24 oxen, 51 cows, 91 pigs, 100 sheep, 168 swans, 444 pigeons and 720 chickens – not to mention 340 *dozen*, that is, 4080, larks! The lack of fibre in the diet of the wealthy evidently led to widespread constipation. In Pepys's time, it was common practice to take purges to relieve the condition – and days off work to recover from the consequences!

By the sixteenth century, the water supply system had become inadequate to meet the demands of the rising population (it had also become subject to much abuse and over-use by individuals and by commercial and industrial concerns). A short-term solution to this problem was provided by the construction by the Dutchman Pieter Maritz in 1582 of a – rather rickety – apparatus under one of the arches of London Bridge that allowed water to be pumped from the Thames into the heart of the City, or, in the case of the original demonstration to City officials, over the spire of the church of St Magnus the Martyr! The apparatus was destroyed in the Great Fire, but thereafter replaced by Maritz's grandson, and continued in use, after a fashion, until the early nineteenth century.

A longer-term solution was provided by the construction by the Welshman and wealthy merchant, goldsmith, banker and Member of Parliament Sir Hugh Myddelton or Myddleton in 1609-13 of a 10-ft wide and 4-ft deep canal, or 'New River', all the way from springs at Amwell and Chadwell in Hertfordshire into the City, an incredible 37 miles away, parts of which may still be seen along the 'New River Walk', for example in Canonbury Grove in Islington (*Figure 31*). The 'New River' was formally opened on 29 September 1613 by Myddelton's older brother Thomas, the Mayor of London. The playwright, poet and writer of pageants Thomas Middleton (no relation) wrote in 'The manner of His Lordships entertainment ... at that most famous and admired worke of the running streame from Amwell head, into the cesterne neere Islington':

Long have we laboured, long cherished and prayed
For this great work's perfection, and by th'aid
Of heaven and good men's wishes 'tis at length
Happily conquered by cost, art and strength.
And after five years' dear expense in days,

31. Surviving section of New River, Canonbury Grove, Islington (originally built in 1613). My elder son Wynn for scale.

> Travail, and pains, besides the infinite ways
> Of malice, envy, false suggestions,
> Able to daunt the spirits of mighty ones
> In wealth and courage, this, a work so rare,
> Only by one man's industry, cost and care
> Is brought to blest effect...

Myddelton had to overcome any number of technological obstacles and land-owner and political opposition to see this major civil engineering project through to completion. The 'New River' relied on gravity to allow flow, and hence had to be constructed on a gradient, of as little as two inches per mile, or 1:31,680. He did so with a mixture of drive and determination, the financial support of twenty-nine investors or 'adventurers', and the tacit backing of the King. His backers had to wait some time until they profited from the enterprise (actually, until 1633, although by 1695 the New River Company ranked behind only the East India Company and the then newly constituted Bank of England in terms of its capital value). The public health benefits of Myddelton's project were immediate, though, and immeasurable, and indeed it has been described as 'An immortal work – since men cannot more nearly imitate the Deity than in bestowing health.' Myddelton died in 1631, and was buried in the church of St Matthew Friday Street, where he had served as a warden. Fittingly, there is a statue to the great man on Islington Green. Some of the fittings from the New River Company's offices, including the 'Oak Room', possibly by Grinling Gibbons, may still be seen in the London Metropolitan Water Board building, also in Islington.

Ale and beer continued to be staples. By 1656, there were a quite literally staggering 1153 drinking establishments in the City, ranging from basic ale-houses through middling taverns, where wine could also be had, to up-market inns, where there would be food and drink of the finest, accommodation and often also entertainment. Among them were the Bell Savage of 1452 on Ludgate Hill; the Olde Mitre of 1546 in Ely Court; the Devil and St Dunstan of 1563, the Olde Cheshire Cheese of 1584, the Cock of 1600, and the 'Mitre of 1602/3, all on Fleet Street; the Seven Stars of 1602 on Carey Street; the Wig and Pen of 1625 on the Strand; and the Olde Wine Shades of 1663 on Martin Lane. Perhaps unsurprisingly, drunkenness became something of a social problem. So did the so-called 'dry-drunkenness' caused by smoking tobacco, first introduced from the Americas in the 1570s. In the post-Medieval period, tobacco was smoked in clay pipes, the remains of which came to litter the City like the cigarette ends of today, and are common finds on the foreshore of the Thames.

More socially acceptable was the consumption of equally addictive, although less harmful, coffee and tea, first imported from Arabia and China respectively in the 1650s (*Figure 32*). Coffee and tea were expensive commodities in the later seventeenth century, and consumed exclusively by the rich. The coffee- and teahouses that began to spring up all over London at this time became places where respectable wealthy gentlemen, who would not be seen dead in ale-houses, might congregate to converse and to transact business: one, Lloyd's, eventually evolved into an entirely separate business enterprise, and another, Jonathan's, into the Stock Exchange (Green, 2013). The very first of the coffee-houses to open was at the sign of 'Pasqua Rosee's Head', just off Cornhill, in 1652. The eponymous Pasqua Rosee was employed as a man-servant by one Daniel Edwards, a London merchant, member of the Levant Company and trader in Turkish goods. He appears to have run the coffee-shop as a sideline, in partnership with one Christopher Bowman, a freeman of the City

32. 'Coffee-House Jests' (1664).

and former coachman of Edwards's father-in-law, Alderman Thomas Hodges. It is thought that Rosee and Edwards met in Smyrna in Anatolia, although Rosee was of ethnic Greek extraction. The 'Coffee House', also just off Cornhill, the 'Globe' and 'Morat's', in Exchange Alley, and an unnamed coffee-house in St Paul's Churchyard, were also all open by the early 1660s, and all referred to by Pepys, as was an unnamed teahouse, where in 1660 he 'did send for a cup of tee, a China drink, of which I had never drunk before'. A contemporary advertising handbill described the 'Vertue of the *Coffee* Drink First publiquely made and sold in England by *Pasqua Rosee*' as follows:

The Grain or Berry called *Coffee*, groweth upon little Trees, only in the *Deserts of Arabia*. It is brought from thence, and drunk generally throughout all the Grand Seigniors Dominions. It is a simple innocent thing, composed into a Drink, by being dryed in an Oven, and ground to Powder, and boild up with Spring water, and about half a pint of it to be drunk, fasting an hour before, and not Eating an hour after, and to be taken as hot as possibly can be endured... The quality of the Drink is cold and Dry ... It quickens the *Spirits*, and makes the Heart *Lightsome*... It suppresseth Fumes exceedingly, and ... will very much ... help *Consumption* and the *Cough of the Lungs*... It will prevent Drowsiness, and make one fit for business ... and therefore you are not toe Drink it *after Supper*, unless you intend to be *watchful*, for it will hinder sleep for 3 or 4 hours.

One George Sandys described the coffee of the time as 'black as soote, and tasting not much unlike it'. The first chocolate-house opened in a Frenchman's house in Queen's Head Alley, off Bishopsgate, in 1657, and 'Mr Bland's' in 1664, the latter also referred to in Pepys's diary, as the place where he went to drink his 'morning's draft in chocolate'. Chocolate was a very considerable luxury in the mid 1600s, costing as much as 13s/lb (£50/lb today).

Sanitation
Myddelton 's New River triumph not withstanding (see above), the systems and standards of sanitation remained as in the Medieval. Samuel Pepys wrote in his diary one day in 1660 of how he had gone down into his cellar and 'stepped into a great heap of ****', by which he found that his neighbour Mr Turner's 'house of office' was full to bursting! The open sewer that the River Fleet had become by the fourteenth century was only finally enclosed in the eighteenth. The line of the river is followed by that of Farringdon Road, Farringdon Street and New Bridge Street.

Medical Matters
The diagnosis and treatment of disease continued to be based essentially on Galenic principles. Treatments remained largely plant-based, with medicinal herbs being widely grown both at monastic sites, for example at Syon Abbey, and commercially, for example in the herbalist and apothecary John Parkinson's garden in Long Acre in Covent Garden. Parkinson (1567-1650) made his living preparing and dispensing plant-based and other medicines from a shop on Ludgate Hill, a short walk from the Apothecaries' Hall. He was one of the founder-members of the Apothecaries' Company, and apothecary to

James I and Royal Botanist to Charles I. He wrote *A Garden of All Sorts of Pleasant Flowers* in 1629, and *The Theatre of Plants* in 1640. Another herbalist, Nicholas Culpeper, of Spitalfields, died in 1654 of consumption, or possibly of some other lung disease caused by his excessive smoking (and was buried in Bedlam). He, was the author of *The Complete Herbal*. Sad to say, the herbal treatments remained largely ineffectual against the diseases of the day, including not only plague and consumption, but also Sweating Sickness.

Sweating Sickness was diagnosed by 'a ... burnyng sweate ... by the tormentyng and vexation of which ... men ... being not hable to suffre the importunate heat, they cast away the sheets & all the clothes', leading to delirium, and in almost all cases, after a matter of hours, death ('all ... yelded up their ghost'). The disease is now thought to have been either Hantavirus Pulmonary Syndrome (HPS) or Pulmonary Anthrax (the latter caused by inhaling spores of the bacterium *Bacillus anthracis*, perhaps contained in contaminated wool). The boy-king Edward VI wrote of an outbreak in 1551: 'At this time came the sweat into London, which was more vehement than the old sweat. For if one took cold he died within 3 hours, and if he escaped it held him but 9 hours, or 10 at the most. Also if he slept ... as he should be very desirous to do, then he raved, and should die raving.' This outbreak 'carried off many people both noble and commoners', as Henry Machyn put it. There were notable outbreaks in England in 1485, 1507, 1517 and 1528-9, as well as 1551, after which last date the disease disappeared as suddenly and mysteriously as it had appeared, never to return. It is possible that the disease killed Arthur Tudor at Ludlow Castle in 1502, while sparing his wife, Catherine of Aragon, who went on to marry his brother, by then King Henry VIII, in 1509.

Surgical operations continued to be performed by Barber-Surgeons. Against the odds, Samuel Pepys survived having a gallstone the size of a billard ball removed, without anaesthetic, by the skilled surgeon Thomas Hollier on 26 March 1658. Each year thereafter, he celebrated the anniversary of the event rather like a second birthday, writing in his diary on 26 March 1660: 'This day it is two years since it pleased God that I was cut of the stone at Mrs Turner's in Salisbury Court; and did resolve while I live to keep it a festival, as I did last year at my house, and for ever to have Mrs Turner and her company with me. ... I can and do rejoice, and bless God, being at this time, blessed be his holy name, in as good health as ever I was in my life.'

Some of the hospitals that had been attached to monastic houses in the Medieval period survived the Dissolution and into the post-Medieval (Barnett & Jay, 2008). The mental hospital at the Priory of St Mary of Bethlehem was depicted as a mad-house even on the Jacobean stage. In 1669, Samuel Pepys wrote: 'I to the Office, while the young people went to see Bedlam' (to view the antics of the inmates, as a form of entertainment). It was subsequently rebuilt by Robert Hooke in Moorfields in 1676, relocated to the junction of Kennington Road and Lambeth Road in the Borough of Southwark in 1815, and relocated again to the site of a former country house estate in Beckenham in the Borough of Bromley in Kent in 1930. The Danish sculptor Caius Gabriel Cibber's (1630-1700) extraordinary statues of figures representing 'Raving and Melancholy Madness' that used to stand outside the old hospital in Moorfields, may now be seen inside the museum of the new one in Beckenham. Inside the museum may be seen a padded cell, a strait-jacket and other restraints, and an Electro-Convulsive Therapy Kit from the hospital's later days.

Population

From various accounts, it appears that the population of London was of the order of 60,000 in the 1520s; 80,000 in 1550; 120,000 in 1583; 200,000 in 1630; 460,000 in 1665; and 360,000 in 1666, after the 'Great Plague' (Rappaport, 1989). It is evident that it took until 1550 for the population to recover following the Black Death of 1348-9. The death rate among native Londoners continued to exceed the birth rate, significantly so during outbreaks of plague (life expectancy in the city's poorer parishes was only 20–25, around half the national average, and even that in the wealthier parishes was only 30–35). The city's population could only be maintained and grown by immigration. In 1541, 652 out of 3,433 assessments for tax purposes were of 'aliens' or 'strangers' (equating to 19% of the total); in 1582, 1,358 out of 5,900 (23%) (Lang, 1993). Interestingly, persons of colour were present in some numbers in London by Tudor times. Among them were John Blanke, a court-musician to Prince Arthur's – and later King Henry VIII's – wife Catherine of Aragon, possibly originally from Moorish Spain; Reasonable Blackman, a silk-weaver of Southwark during the reign of Elizabeth I, possibly a refugee from the former Spanish Netherlands; Mary Fillis, a maid-servant to the Barker family of Mark Lane also in Elizabethan times, originally from

Morocco, a Muslim who converted to Christianity; and later Anne Cobbie, a 'Tawny Moor with Soft Skin', and courtesan of Westminster, in the Jacobean era. Rather remarkably, there is a surviving portrayal of the aforementioned John Blanke – in a turban, trumpeting – on the *Westminster Tournament Roll* of 1511, which resides in the Royal College of Arms.

The unprecedented rise in population in the late Tudor and Stuart periods made London one of the first true world-cities, alongside Madrid, Lisbon and Amsterdam, and was accompanied for the first time by significant growth beyond the old City wall, especially westward along the Thames towards Westminster. The growth beyond the City wall took place even despite the issuing of the 'Proclamation of Queen Elizabeth against new buildings in and about London', in 1580, and of further such attempts on limitation by the succeeding Stuart kings. The area between the Cities of London and Westminster became a particularly fashionable one in which to live in the post-Medieval period. Also at this time, the many high-status Bishops' Inns in the area were appropriated by the Crown and either became Royal residences or else were disbursed among the aristocracy. These included those of the Bishops of Ely and Lincoln on Holborn; those of the Bishops of Salisbury, Exeter, Bath & Wells, Llandaff, Chester and Worcester on the Strand; and that of the Archbishops of York on Whitehall, which became Whitehall Palace.

Administration and Governance

The City of London remained at least in part self-governing, under the Corporation and its officials, the Mayor, Sheriffs, Aldermen and Common Councilmen. The Corporation continued to be responsible for the education of the populace, and the maintenance of the law. Benefactors continued to found educational establishments. Christ's Hospital School was originally founded by Edward VI in 1552 on the site of the former conventual buildings of the Greyfriars Priory, subsequently burned down in the Great Fire and rebuilt, and eventually relocated to Horsham in Sussex in 1902. The Merchant Taylors' School was originally founded by the Merchant Taylors' Company in 1561 on the site of the former estate of the Dukes of Suffolk and subsequently relocated to Northwood. Gresham College was founded in 1597 through the benefaction of the financier Thomas Gresham on the site of his house on Bishopsgate, relocated initially to Gresham Street and eventually to Barnard's Inn. The College of Physicians was founded in 1518 at Amen Corner, subsequently burned down in the Great Fire and rebuilt, and eventually relocated to Regent's Park. The Choir School attached to Westminster Abbey was founded in the sixteenth century.

The law of the land continued to be maintained locally and legal training, to be provided by the Inns of Court. 'Revels' are known to have been held on a number of occasions for the entertainment of the lawyers and student-lawyers in the Inns, for example in 1561, 1594/5, 1616 and 1617/8, the famous lawyer, statesman, philosopher, 'natural philosopher', writer, and all-round Renaissance Man Francis Bacon (1561-1626) being involved with the organisation of the 1594/5 ones. Shakespeare's plays were performed in his lifetime in certain of the Inns' Halls; *Twelfth Night* premiered in Middle Temple Hall in 1602. The Inns of Court, incidentally, played a formative role in the founding of the United States of America. Francis Bacon, who was instrumental in the creation of the first English colonies in the Americas in the seventeenth century and is widely regarded as one of the 'founding fathers' of the United States, received his legal training in Gray's Inn. Later, many of the court officers who worked on the establishment of the legal infrastructure in the colonies in the period prior to the Revolutionary War in the eighteenth century also received their initial training in the Inns (as noted by William Taft, the sometime Chief Justice and President). Others have even suggested that the principles of secession originated in the Inns. Certainly, Peyton Randolph trained in Middle Temple before going on to become the first President of the Continental Congress in 1774; as did John Dickinson, before going on to help draft the Declaration of Independence in 1776; and John Rutledge, before chairing the committee that drafted the Constitution in 1787. A number of Templars were signatories to one or or both of the aforementioned documents.

The law continued to be upheld through a judicial system that placed particular emphasis on punishment as a deterrent. The least serious or petty crimes continued to be punishable by fines or corporal punishment; more serious ones by deportation to the colonies in the Americas, once founded, in the early seventeenth century (deportation to Australia did not begin until after the loss of the colonies in the Americas in the late eighteenth century); and the perceived most serious by capital punishment. Imprisonment continued to be used essentially as an expedient rather than as a punishment *per se*.

Corporal punishment might include the use of the pillories and stocks, which restrained convicted criminals and allowed them to be harangued or to have missiles thrown at them by the general public (Daniel Defoe, who was perceived to have been unjustly convicted, was garlanded with flowers). It also might include the nailing of one's ears to the pillory, as in the cases of John Daye and of an unnamed surgeon, who had been convicted of 'seditious words', the former 'speaking of the Queen's Highness', and the latter 'speaking of the preacher at the sermon at Paul's Cross', in 1553 ('and when they had stood onn the pillory 3 houres the nails were pulled out with a pair of pincers'). Whipping was sometimes 'at a cartes arse', as in the case of Hugh Weaver, who had been convicted of 'misusing the mayor ... and strykinge his officer', in 1545.

Capital punishment might include hanging, burning, or hanging, drawing and quartering. Executions were carried out in various parts of the city, most famously at Tower Hill and West Smithfield, and also at Tyburn. Among those executed at Tower Hill were John Fisher, Thomas More, Thomas Cromwell, Thomas Wyatt the Younger, Robert Devereux and Harry Vane; and among those executed at West Smithfield, John Forest, Anne Askew and John Rogers. Among those executed at Tyburn were not only Elizabeth Barton, John Houghton and Thomas Harrison (see above) but also, in 1499, Perkin Warbeck, for pretending to the throne. In 1541, Thomas Culpeper and Francis Dereham, were executed for treason against the King's majesty in misdemeanour with the Queen (Catherine Howard); Rafe Egerton and Thomas Herman for counterfeiting the King's Great Seal; in 1564, three unnamed persons, for 'ye stelynge and receyvynge of ye Queens lypott [chamber pot] and ... other small ware out of hir chambar in her progresse'; and in 1610, John Roberts, a Catholic priest, for contravening the 'Act Forbidding Priests to Minister in England'. (The watching crowd, who revered Roberts for the work he had done among them during an outbreak of the plague in 1603, saw to it that he died by hanging and was spared the suffering of drawing and quartering: one of his finger bones is preserved as a holy relic in Tyburn Convent). In 1660, the disinterred corpse of Oliver Cromwell was ritually hanged and beheaded there. Capital sentences could be commuted in the cases of those who could claim the 'benefit of clergy', by reciting a psalm that came to be known as the 'neck verse' (*Miserere mei Deus secundum misericordiam tuam iuxta multitudinem miserationum tuarum dele iniquitates meas*). One such case was that of the playwright, poet, actor and bricklayer Ben Jonson, who had killed a man – a fellow actor named Gabriel Spencer – in a duel in Hoxton, and was able to get off scot free.

Newgate Prison remained in use, rebuilt in 1672 after having been burned down in the Great Fire, and yet again in 1782 after having been destroyed during the Gordon Riots of 1780. Until 1783, condemned prisoners continued to be taken from Newgate to Tyburn to be executed. On the day of the execution, the sexton from the nearby church of St Sepulchre would ring his handbell and recite a brief prayer, ending with the words 'And when St Sepulchre's bell in the morning tolls, The Lord above have mercy on your soul.' The handbell of 1605 may still be seen in the church. From 1783 onwards, the condemned were executed in the prison itself, at first in public, and then, from 1868, in private. The last execution there was in 1902, the year the prison was decommissioned, of George Woolfe, who had beaten and stabbed his girlfriend to death. Newgate was demolished in 1904, whereupon the present Central Criminal Court –the 'Old Bailey' – was built in its place.

Trade and Commerce

Trade continued to prosper and the port to remain central to it. The Royal Exchange in the City was built by Thomas Gresham 1566-9 and officially opened by Elizabeth I in 1570/1 (*Figure 33*). It was modelled on the Bourse in Antwerp, itself built in 1513. By Stuart times, the port extended as far east as Wapping, Shadwell, Ratcliff, Limehouse, Poplar and Blackwall on the north side of the Thames, and as far east as Bermondsey and Rotherhithe on the south side. Perhaps my favourite tombstone in all of London is the crudely fashioned and poignantly inscribed one in the church of St Dunstan and All Saints in Stepney to 'Honist Abraham Zouch of Wappin, Rope Maker', who died in 1684. In Shadwell, there were docks, wharves, roperies, and smithics. Here, a survey of 1650 revealed four docks and thirty-two wharves along a 400-yard section of river, and that 53% of the working population were mariners, 10% ship-builders and 7% lightermen (there were also carpenters, smiths, rope-makers and other ancillary tradesmen, tanners and, of course, brewers). In Poplar, there were more docks, and sail-makers' warehouses. In Tudor times, Sir Thomas Spert and 54 mariners lodged here while sails were made for Henry VIII's

33. The Royal Exchange.

great ship *Henri Grace a Dieu* (which would see action against the French at the Battle of the Solent, in which the *Mary Rose* sank; and later transport the King to the peace summit with the French at the Field of the Cloth-of-Gold). In Blackwall, there were more docks. In Rotherhithe there were docks, wharves, and ship-building and timber-yards, where artisan mast-makers, anchor-smiths, coopers and others plied their trades. Annual exports – even excluding 'shortcloth' – were valued at approximately £700,000 at the turn of the sixteenth and seventeenth centuries (Corfield & Harte, 1990This equates to approximately £100,000,000 today.

The trades guilds, or Livery Companies, continued to make money. Interestingly, they also played an important role in the Protestant Plantation of Northern Ireland (the 'Ulster Plantation'), and the subjugation of the native Catholic population in the early seventeenth century, which is how Derry came to be known as Londonderry. The Livery Companies' involvement in the plantation began under James I in 1609 shortly after Tyrone's and O'Doherty's rebellions and continued under Charles I, who at one point was evidently forced to take action against the companies to ensure their continuing, by then unwilling co-operation. The Goldsmith's Company became so wealthy it even lent money to Charles II in the 1660s, in exchange for promissory notes, in effect becoming the first national bank (the Bank of England was not founded until 1694). Of the total of 77 Livery Companies in existence in London at the time of the Great Fire of 1666, 13 (17%)

were involved in the cloth and clothing sectors of the economy; 12 (16%) in food and drink; 10 (13%) in construction and interior design; 10 (13%) in metal-working; 5 (7%) in wood-working (including shipwrighting); 4 (5%) in leather-working; 3 (4%) in arms manufacture; 3 in equestrian accoutrement manufacture; 3 in the medical profession; 2 (3%) in chandlery; 2 in the clerical profession; 2 in entertainment; 2 in transport; and the remaining 6 (8%) in sundry trades (analysis of data in Melling, 2003). London's economy was evidently still dominated by the manufacture of goods, rather than by services.

The Hanseatic League continued to control overseas trade with the ports on the coasts of the North Sea and Baltic, although the former privileges extended to the German merchants of the Steelyard were revoked by Edward VI in 1551, and those who stayed on after that date were expelled – albeit only temporarily – in 1598. The Steelyard burned down in the Great Fire and was rebuilt, only to be demolished in 1855 to make way for Cannon Street Station. It was in the Steelyard in 1532 that Holbein painted his portrait of the Hanse merchant Georg Gisze, from Danzig [Gdansk], which now hangs in the Staatliche Museen zu Berlin. The painting depicts a self-confident – possibly even self-important – man posing in a fine white shirt, ruched pink silk doublet, and black velvet three-quarter-length overgown and matching cap. Surrounding him in his wood-panelled office are some of the tools of his evidently lucrative trade: on the shelves in the background, a wooden box and chest, a bunch of impressive-looking keys hanging from a hook, weighing-scales, an account-book, and various papers, perhaps including shipping contracts, bills of lading and cargo manifests. On the table in the foreground is a gold ring bearing his seal, a pewter desk-set comprising a low circular storage box *cum* ink-pot, a pounce-pot, and two matching stands holding quills and a rod of sealing-wax, a letter-opener, a clock, and a pestle, all on a section of geometrically patterned Anatolian carpet. Also on the table is a Venetian glass vase of carnations, symbolising his recent engagement to Christine Kruger (the couple married in 1535, and would have ten children).

Other ultimately immensely important overseas trade links became forged through the establishment by charter of the Muscovy, or Russia Company, an outgrowth of the even more venerable 'Company of Merchant Adventurers to New Lands' (or, in full, the 'Mystery and Company of Merchant Adventurers for the Discovery of Regions, Dominions, Islands, and Places Unknown'), in 1555, the Virginia

Company (of London), in 1606, and the Royal African Company, originally the 'Company of Royal Adventurers Trading to Africa', in 1660 (*Figure 19c*). The Muscovy Company, and later its semi-independent subsidiary the Greenland Company, dominated the lucrative whaling industry until the turn of the seventeenth and eighteenth centuries. At this time, whale-oil was used for lighting and for lubrication (and whale-bone for stiffening garments). By the middle of the seventeenth century, goods were being brought in from all over the New World as well as the old. The so-called Cheapside Hoard, believed to have been buried on the eve of the Civil War, includes not only various types of jewel and jewelry from continental Europe and Sinai, Iran, Afghanistan, India and Sri Lanka but also heliodors from Brazil and emeralds from Colombia (Forsyth, 2013). The hoard includes a carnelian *intaglio* bearing the arms of William Howard, First Viscount Stafford, and therefore must date to some time after his ennoblement in 1640.

In 1606, the merchant-adventurer, Citizen of London and Cordwainer Captain John Smith set sail aboard the *Susan Constant* from Blackwall to found Jamestown in Virginia, the first successful English colony in the Americas, from which began the overseas expansion of the English-speaking peoples. Smith later returned to London and died there in 1631. He is buried in the church of St Sepulchre Newgate Street. There is a statue of him in nearby Bow Churchyard on Cheapside, and a memorial to all the 'Virginia Settlers' on what is now Virginia Quay in Blackwall. The Algonquin princess Pocahontas, who famously saved Smith's life in the Americas in 1607, visited London in 1616-7, with her by-then husband the tobacco planter John Rolfe, staying at the 'Bell Savage' off Ludgate Hill. She died in Gravesend in 1617. Francis Bacon set out his utopian vision of how life might be in the English colonies in the Americas in his novelised book, *New Atlantis*, published in 1627, a year after his death.

To the City's – and indeed the country's – eternal shame, from as long ago as the late sixteenth century onwards it traded in slaves. In 1562, John Hawkins took three ships from London or Plymouth (sources differ) to Sierra Leone, where he seized 300 Africans 'by the sword' (Hazelwood, 2004). Then, in the 'Middle Passage', he transported them across the Atlantic to the Spanish West Indies, where he sold them in order to purchase sugar, ginger and other goods. He returned to London and sold his cargo to City merchants for a fortune, completing the infamous triangle. Hawkins's venture was backed by the Mayor of

London, Thomas Lodge. It was also supported by the Queen, Elizabeth I, although apparently only after she had been – falsely – assured that the enslavement was *unforced*. She actually described *forced* enslavement as 'detestable', as something that would 'call down the vengeance of Heaven upon the undertakers'. In 1567, Hawkins wrote to the Queen, requesting her permission for another slaving voyage: 'The voyage I pretend is to lade negroes in Guinea and sell them in the West Indies in truck of gold, pearls and emeralds, whereof I doubt not but to bring home great abundance for the contentation of your Highness ... Thus I ... do most humbly pray your Highness to signify your pleasure by this bearer, which I shall most willingly accomplish.' In 1619, under Elizabeth's successor James I, the trade in enslaved Africans spread to the English Americas for the first time, with 'twenty and odd Negroes' being transported to Jamestown in Virginia, presumably to work on the tobacco plantations there (see above). Many more would soon be sent to back-breaking toil in the sugar plantations on Barbados, St Kitts, Jamaica and elsewhere in the West Indies, under an unforgiving tropical sun. In the late 1640s and 1650s, one London merchant, John Paige, made a fortune transporting enslaved persons from Guinea in West Africa to Tenerife in the Canary Islands, which at that time was technically illegal. Even when the captain of one of his ships, the *Swan*, died in the Bight of Biafra, and the ship, under the command of the mate, became 'staved upon the seas' and 'was utterly lost' at Rio del Rey, he was able to keep his losses within acceptable bounds by selling the nineteen enslaved persons who survived.

The slavery trade was to continue to grow further, and faster, after the end of the War of the Spanish Succession in 1713, when Spain was compelled under the terms of the Treaty of Utrecht to grant to Britain the *Asiento*, or – exclusive – 'Contract ... Allowing ... the Liberty of Importing Negroes into the Spanish America'. The trade was only finally abolished throughout the British Empire in 1843. By this time, 3351 slaving voyages had begun in London, which had become the fourth largest centre involved in the trade in the world, after Rio de Janeiro, Bahia and Liverpool. Shockingly, given that each vessel could accommodate anywhere between 250 to 600 enslaved persons, those 3351 voyages beginning in London would have transported, in round numbers, between 850,000 and 2,000,000 persons; of whom, again in round numbers, between 100,000 and 250,000 would have died *en route* (assuming an average mortality rate of 13%).

Wealth and Poverty

The rich remained rich, and the poor, poor, and deprived of any opportunity of social advancement. If anything, the divide between the classes widened during the 'price revolution' of the sixteenth century, which witnessed a four-fold increase in the cost of living (Rappaport, 1989). There was never an equitable distribution or redistribution of wealth, although there continued to be an informal system of charitable patronage and donation from the churches, other rich institutions such as the Livery Companies, and rich individuals. John Stow noted that: 'Sir Thomas Roe, Marchant Taylor, Mayor, 1568, gave to the Marchant Taylors lands or Tenements, out of them to bee given to ten poore men, Clothworkers, Carpentars, Tilars, Plasterers, and Armorers, 40 pounds yearely, viz., 4 pounds to each, also 200 pounds to bee lent to 8 poore men'. The rich and poor continued to live rather uneasily together, although there continued to be concentrations of wealth in the wards in the centre of the City, and of poverty in those around its margins and without the walls (Ross & Clark, 2008). In the sixteenth century, as indicated by the subsidy rolls of 1541 and 1582, the wards containing the highest number of householder tax assessments in the highest bracket were Bread Street, Broad Street, Cheap, Cordwainer, Cripplegate, Tower and Walbrook. The ones containing the highest number of assessments in the lowest bracket were Aldersgate, Aldgate, Castle Baynard, Cripplegate, Farringdon Within and Farringdon Without (Lang, 1993). It is interesting that Cripplegate falls into both categories, Cripplegate Without being 'where the noble, the rich and the famous lived ... because they wanted space, which had become scarce within the walls'; Cripplegate Within was home to a more mixed community (Gordon & Dewhurst, 1985).

After the passage of the 'Old Poor Law' in 1601, there was a formalised further charge on ratepayers to provide for relief at the level of the local parish. This saw the 'impotent poor' cared for in alms-houses; the 'able-bodied poor' either put to work in 'Houses of Industry' (the fore-runners of workhouses) in exchange for board and lodging, or else provided with 'out-relief' payments or payments-in-kind; and the 'idle poor' were sent to 'Houses of Correction' (essentially prisons). After the passage of the 'New Poor Law' in 1834, the – 'deserving' – impotent poor continued to be cared for in alms-houses, and the – 'undeserving' – idle poor to be sent to 'Houses of Correction'. However, the 'deserving' able poor were now refused 'out-relief', and made to work in workhouses, where conditions were quite deliberately made sufficiently inhumane as to deter extended stays. The workhouse system was only finally abolished as recently as 1930, and indeed many former workhouses remained in use until 1948.

It might seem incongruous to discuss poverty and poor relief in what is now the conspicuously wealthy City of Westminster. However, throughout much of its long history, including the Medieval and post-Medieval periods, Westminster was at the poverty-blighted ragged outer edge of the built-up area of London. Tothill Fields Bridewell was built here in 1618; the Palmer Almshouses, in 1656; and the St Margaret's Workhouse, in 1692.

Entertainment and Culture

There continued to be at West Smithfield archery, wrestling and cock-fighting, a weekly horse fair, and Bartholomew Fair every August, and regular jousting tournaments. At East Smithfield there was a fair, on Undershaft an annual May Fair and on Cheapside further tournaments. In the Tower of London, a menagerie; and on Bankside in Southwark, animal-baiting. In 1554, Henry Machyn wrote: 'The sam day at after-non was a bere-beyten on the Banke syde, and ther the grett blynd bere [whose name was Sackerson] broke losse, and in ronnyng away he chakt a servyng man by the calff of the lege, and bytt a gret pesse away, and after by the hokyll-bone, that with-in iii days after he ded.' And in 1599, the Swiss visitor Thomas Platter wrote:

> Every Sunday and Wednesday in London there are bear-baitings. ... The theatre is circular, with galleries for spectators [and] the space ... below, beneath the clear sky ... unoccupied. In the middle of this place a large bear on a long rope was bound to a stake, then a number of English mastiffs were brought in and first shown to the bear, which they afterwards baited... [N]ow the excellence ... of such mastiffs was evinced, for although they were much ... mauled by the bear, they did not give in, but had to be pulled off by sheer force... When the first mastiffs tired, fresh ones were brought in... When the bear was weary, another one was supplied... When this bear was tired, a ... bull was brought in... Then another powerful

bear... Lastly they brought in an old blind bear which the boys hit with ... sticks; but he knew how to untie his leash and ... ran back to his stall.

In 1623, John Chamberlain wrote: 'The Spanish Ambassador is much delighted in beare baiting: he was the last weeke at Paris garden [in Southwark], where they shewed him all the pleasure they could ... and then turned a white [polar] beare into the Thames, where the dogges baited him swimming, which was the best sport of all.' In 1666, Samuel Pepys wrote: '[A]fter dinner, with my wife and Mercer to the Beare-garden [in Southwark], where I have not been, I think, of many years, and saw some good sport of the bull's tossing of the dogs: one into the very boxes. But it is a very rude and nasty pleasure.' The old animal-baiting arenas on Bankside in Southwark eventually closed down in the later seventeeth century, although at the same time new ones opened up at Hockley-in-the-Hole in Clerkenwell, 'the home of low-caste sport' (Boulton, 1901). Animal-baiting was only finally outlawed, under the Cruelty to Animals Act in 1835. On the Thames, when it froze over, there continued to be 'frost fairs'. In 1683-84 an entire street of stalls was set up on the frozen river, together with a press printing souvenir papers, one of which, entitled 'A Winter Wonder of the Thames Frozen Over with Remarks on the Resort thereon' asked '[W]ho'd believe to see revived there in January, Bartholomew Fair?' The ice was so thick that it was even possible to roast an ox on it. Outside the compass of this bookk, in 1813-14 thousands attended the greatest fair of the nineteenth century, although only after navigating a gap in the ice created by temporarily unemployed watermen, who demanded a fee of twopence for their assistance! In 1831, the demolition of Old London Bridge, which had nineteen arches, and the construction of the new one, which only had five, allowed the rate of flow of the river to increase to the extent that it became much less susceptible to freezing over.

Everywhere, there continued to be drinking and gambling and whoring. A Royal Proclamation was issued by Henry VIII in 1546, with the intention of ending once and for all the 'toleration of such dissolute and miserable persons as have been suffered to dwell in common open places called the stews without punishment or correction (for) their abominable and detestable sin'. Its success was short-lived, and new stews appeared in Southwark in the later sixteenth and seventeenth centuries, including the infamous 'Holland's Leaguer'. The women who worked in the stews in Southwark were known as 'Winchester Geese', because the buildings belonged to the Bishops of Winchester. Many of them ended up being buried, alongside the other 'Outcast Dead' in the unconsecrated burial ground known as 'Crossbones Graveyard' on Redcross Way, which remained in use until the mid-nineteenth century. A Museum of London Archeology (MoLA) monograph describes in detail the findings of archaeological excavations at the site (Brickley *et al.*, 1999). Lesions in the bones of one of the excavated skeletons, of a nineteenth-century woman aged only around sixteen, indicated that she had been suffering from advanced syphilis, and chemical residues show that she had been treated with mercury. Research undertaken for an episode of the BBC television series 'History Cold Case' in 2010 indicated that this skeleton was likely to be that of one Elizabeth Mitchell, who is recorded as having been admitted to nearby St Thomas's Hospital suffering from the running sores all over the body symptomatic of the disease, and as having died there in 1851.

There also continued to be occasional royal spectacles, including increasingly lavish triumphal and coronation processions, not to mention private court masques, to which only the favoured few would be invited; as well as civic ceremonials such as the Lord Mayor's Show. In 1626 the visiting Alsatian Chevalier de Bassompierre wrote in his journal:

November 9th, which is the election of the Mayor, I came in the morning to Sommerset [House] to meet the Queen [Henrietta Maria], who had come to see him go on the Thames on his way to Westminster to be sworn in, with a magnificent display of boats. Then the Queen dined, and afterwards got into her coach and placed me at the same door with her. The Duke of Boukinham also by her commands got into her coach, and we went into the street called Shipside to see the ceremony, which is the greatest that is made for the reception of any officer in the world. While waiting for it to pass, the Queen played at primero with the Duke, the Earl of Dorchit and me; and afterwards the Duke took me to dine with the Lord mayor, who that day gave a dinner to more than 800 persons.

There were enormously popular history plays, tragedies and comedies performed initially in inns, or in Inns of Court, and eventually in purpose- built or adapted playhouses. Inns where plays were performed included the Bell Savage, Bell, Bull and Cross Keys; and Inns of Court, Middle Temple, in whose Hall, as noted above, *Twelfth Night* premiered in 1602 (and was staged again in 2002, in celebration of the occasion of the 400th anniversary of the event, with an authentic all-male cast, hand-made costumes, and period music and instruments). Open-air playhouses and indoor theatres included the Red Lion in Whitechapel, purpose-built by John Brayne in 1567; an unnamed building in Newington Butts, adapted by Jerome Savage in 1576; the 'Theatre' in Shoreditch, built – on the site of the dissolved Holywell Priory – by James Burbage in 1576; the 'First Blackfriars' in the City, adapted – on the site of the dissolved Blackfriars Priory – by Richard Farrant in 1576; the 'Curtain' in Shoreditch (*Figure 34*), built by Henry Lanman in 1577; the 'Rose' in Southwark, built by Philip Henslowe in 1587; the 'Swan' in Southwark, built by Francis Langley in 1596; the 'Boar's Head' in Whitechapel, built by Oliver Woodliffe in 1598; the 'Globe' in Southwark, originally built by Cuthbert Burbage in 1599 and subsequently rebuilt following a fire in 1613; the 'Second

34. Site of the Curtain playhouse, Curtain Road, Shoreditch (originally built in 1577). Recent archaeological excavation showed the performing space to have been rectangular rather than circular, as had been anticipated The stage is to the rear on the right.

Blackfriars' in the City, adapted by James and Richard Burbage in 1596-1600; the 'Fortune' in Cripplegate, built by Edward Alleyn, in 1600; the 'Red Bull' in Clerkenwell, built by Aaron Holland in 1606/7; the 'Hope' in Southwark, built by Philip Henslowe in 1613, after the 'Globe' was burned down and before it was rebuilt; the 'Whitefriars', just off Fleet Street, by Thomas Woodford, in 1606; the 'Cockpit' on Drury Lane in the West End, originally built by John Best, Cockmaster to the Prince of Wales, in 1616, and subsequently rebuilt, and renamed the 'Phoenix', in 1617; the Salisbury Court, just off Fleet Street, built by William Blagrave and Richard Gunnell, in 1629; and the 'Theatre Royal', on Bridges Street, just off Drury Lane, built by Thomas Killigrew in 1663, where the favourite of the restored King's thirteen mistresses, 'pretty, witty' Nell Gwynne, performed from 1665-71. Ben Jonson's lost play *Isle of Dogs* was performed at the Swan in 1597, drawing such criticism for its 'seditious and slanderous' content that the author was temporarily thrown into the – first – Marshalsea prison. Henry Wotton wrote in a letter to Sir Edmund Bacon (reproduced in *Reliquiae Wottoniae*) of the fire at the Globe in 1613, which took place during a performance of Shakespeare's *Henry VIII*:

> Now, King Henry making a Masque at the Cardinal Wolsey's House, and certain Cannons being shot off at his entry, some of the Paper, or other stuff, wherewith one of them was stopped, did light on the Thatch [and] kindled inwardly, and ran round like a train, consuming within less than an hour the whole House to the very ground. This was the fatal period .... wherein yet nothing did perish but wood and straw ... one man had his breeches set on fire, that would perhaps have broiled him, if he had not by the benefit of a provident wit put it out with bottle ale.

And John Chamberlain wrote: '[I]t was a great marvaile and fair grace of God, that the people had so little harm, having but two narrow doors to get out.'

A modern replica of the Elizabethan Globe open-air playhouse, the brainchild of the American film director Sam Wanamaker, stands on Bankside in Southwark, a stone's throw from the site of the original, which stood opposite the Rose, on what was once Maiden Lane and is now Park Street (*Figure 20c*). Here it is possible to experience performances as the common man would have at the

35. Exterior of the replica Jacobean theatre, Bankside, Southwark.

turn of the sixteenth and seventeenth centuries, standing in the open as a 'groundling'– and surrounded by 'penny stinkards'! On a plot adjoining the reconstructed Globe is a modern replica of a Jacobean indoor theatre, fittingly named the 'Wanamaker' (*Figure 35*). Its design was in part based on a set of plans once – although no longer – thought to have been of the Phoenix, and its interior conveys a real sense of what an indoor theatre such as the Phoenix or the 'Second Blackfriars' would have been like (Tosh, 2018); a sense of enclosed space, of intimacy, of proximity to the players, of exclusiveness perhaps, of being surrounded by the shadowy light of dancing candles and the reflecting costumes and jewellery of the actors and audience, 'So Glisterd in the Torchy Fryers'. And, perhaps even more particularly, one is surrounded by sound, and in interludes in which the wicks of the candles are trimmed, by the sound of music.

The theatre was enormously popular with the citizens of London and with visitors alike in Elizabethan, Jacobean and Restoration times. In 1599, Thomas Platter wrote:

After dinner I went with my companions over the water [to Southwark], and in the strewn roof-house [possibly the newly-built Globe] saw the tragedy of the first Emperor Julius with at least fifteen characters very well acted. At the end ... they danced according to their custom with extreme elegance. Two in men's clothes and two in women's gave this performance, in wonderful combination with each other. [On another occasion] I saw a comedy; if I remember right, in Bishopsgate. Here they represented various nations, with whom ... an Englishman fought ... and overcame them all except the German... [H]e outwitted the German... [E]very day at two o'clock ... two and sometimes three comedies are performed, at separate places, wherewith folk make merry together, and whichever does best gets the greatest audience.

In 1662, Samuel Pepys wrote: 'Thence into Covent Garden to an alehouse [and] to see an Italian Puppet Play, that is within the rayles there, which is very pretty, the best that ever I saw... So to the Temple and by water home, and ... in the dark there played upon my flageolette [a type of flute], it being a fine still evening.' Pepys was evidently also proficient on the five-stringed seventeenth-century guitar.

The theatre was equally as unpopular with the City authorities, who objected to its 'profane fables, lascivious matters, cozening devices, and scurrilous behaviours [that] give opportunity to evil-disposed and ungodly people ... to assemble themselves'. As mentioned earlier, during the post-Medieval period, plays were vetted by the 'Office of the Revels' (the most famous 'Master of the Revels' was Edmund Tilney, who held the post for essentially the entirety of Shakespeare's time in the London theatre. In 1564, Edmund Grindal (then Bishop of London and later Archbishop of Canterbury) wrote in a letter to William Cecil: '[[I]n my judgement, ye should do very well to ... inhibit all plays for one whole year (and if it were for ever, it were not amiss) within the City or three miles' compass, upon pains as well to the players as to the owners of the houses where they play their lewd interludes.' And in 1594, even such a figure as Henry Carey, the 1st Baron Brunsdon, the son of Anne Boleyn's sister Mary (possibly by Henry VIII), and the cousin of the Queen, Elizabeth I, a patron of Shakespeare's acting troupe, the 'Lord Chamberlain's Men', was forced to write in a letter to the Mayor of London:

Where my now company of players have been accustomed ... for the service of her majesty ... to play at the Cross Keys in Gracious [Gracechurch] Street; these are to require and pray your lordship ...

to permit and suffer them to do so. The which I pray you rather to do for that they have undertaken to me that ... they will now ... have done between four and five and will not use any drums or trumpets at all for the calling of people together and shall be contributories to the poor of the parish where they play, according to their abilities.

In the late sixteenth to early seventeenth centuries there were numerous actual attacks on playhouses and bawdy-houses by bands of apprentices and others, on Shrove Tuesdays (the so-called 'Shrove Tuesday Riots'). John Chamberlain wrote in a letter to Dudley Carleton in 1617:

On ... Shrove Tuesday, the 'prentices, or rather the unruly people of the suburbs, played their parts in divers places, as Finsbury Fields, about Wapping, by St Catherine's, and in Lincoln's Inn Fields, ... in pulling down of houses, and beating of guards that were set to keep rule, specially at a new playhouse, some time a cockpit, in Drury Lane, where the queen's players used to play. Though the fellows defended themselves as well as they could, and slew three of them with shot, and hurt divers, yet they entered the house and defaced it, cutting the players' apparel into pieces, and all their furniture, and burnt their playbooks, and did what other mischief they could... There be divers of them taken since and clapped up, and I make no question but we shall see some of them hanged next week, as it is more than time they were.

The performance of plays was indeed temporarily banned by the Puritans in 1642, under an Act of Parliament forced through by them: 'while these sad Times ... do continue, Public Stage Plays shall cease ... instead of which are recommended ... the profitable and seasonable considerations of Repentance, Reconciliation, and Peace with God, which probably may ... bring again Times of Joy and Gladness to these Nations.' There is some evidence to suggest that plays continued to be performed illegally at this time, for example, at the Red Bull in Clerkenwell. The theatres only officially re-opened after the Restoration of the Monarchy in 1660. After the Restoration, the audience's tastes were mainly for bawdy comedies (the court at this time was notoriously dissolute).

London was the home of William Shakespeare (1564-1616). It was also the home of an exraordinary company of other Renaissance men and women:

The playwrights and/or poets Edward de Vere, 17th Earl of Oxford (1550-1614), Edmund Spenser (1552-1599), John Lyly (1553-1606), Philip Sidney (1554-86), Anthony Munday (1560-1633), Christopher Marlowe (1564-1593), John Donne (1572-1631), Thomas Dekker (1572-1632), Ben Jonson (1572-1637), John Fletcher (1579-1625), Thomas Middleton (1580-1627), John Webster (1580-1634), Francis Beaumont (1584-1616), Mary Wroth (1587-1651), William Davenant (1606-68), John Milton (1608-1674), Thomas Killigrew (1612-83), Andrew Marvell (1621-78), John Bunyan (1628-1688), John Dryden (1631-1700), George Etherege (1636-92), Aphra Behn (1640-89); the painters Hans Holbein (1497-1543), Nicholas Hilliard (1547-1619), John Bettes the Younger (c. 1550-1616), Anthony van Dyck (1599-1641), and Peter Lely (1618-80); the philosophers Thomas More (1478-1535) and Francis Bacon (1561-1626); the composers John Taverner (1490-1545), Thomas Tallis (1505-1585), William Byrd (1543-1623), John Dowland (1563-1626), Orlando Gibbons (1583-1625), and Henry Purcell (1659-95); and the architects Inigo Jones (1573-1652), Christopher Wren (1632-1723) and Nicholas Hawksmoor (1661-1736).

Shakespeare was born and died in Stratford-upon-Avon, but spent almost the entirety of his productive working life in London, and in truth is much more a London than a Stratford figure. He is known to have arrived in London sometime between 1585 and 1592, and to have lived in the parish of St Helen, near 'The Theatre' and the 'Curtain' in Shoreditch in 1596; in the Liberty of the Clink in Southwark, near the Globe in 1599; and in the parish of St Olave Silver Street, a short walk and ferry-ride from the Globe, in 1604; and also to have purchased a property in Ireland Yard, near the 'Second Blackfriars', in 1613 (according to the Deed of Conveyance in the London Metropolitan Archives, which incidentally bears one of the few surviving examples of his signature, it cost him £140, at a time when the average annual salary for a professional person was £20). At least some of his early plays are known to have been performed in the Rose by 'Lord Strange's Men', in around 1592; in the 'Theatre', by the Lord Chamberlain's Men, a troupe he both acted and wrote for, from 1594; and in the 'Curtain', also by the Lord Chamberlain's Men, from 1597 (after the twenty-one year lease on the 'Theatre' had expired). His later plays are known to have been performed in the Globe, by the Lord Chamberlain's Men and their successors the 'King's Men', who owned it, from 1599; and in the 'Second Blackfriars', by the King's

Men, who owned it as well, from 1609. The musical content of certain of his later plays, such as *Cymbeline*, *The Winter's Tale* and *The Tempest* is sufficient as to suggest that they were specifically written to be performed in the indoor arena of the 'Second Blackfriars'.

As Ackroyd (2005) put it, in his marvellous *Shakespeare – The Biography*: 'Shakespeare did not need to address London directly … it is the rough cradle of all his drama.' However, as Crawforth *et al.* (2014) have suggested, in their thoughtful and thought-provoking *Shakespeare in London*, he may have indirectly referenced the violence of Tyburn in *Titus Andronicus*; the political machination of Whitehall in *Richard II*; the class distinction of the Strand in *Romeo and Juliet*; the legal machination of the Inns of Court in *The Merchant of Venice*; the religiosity of St Paul's Cathedral in *Hamlet*; the madness of Bedlam in *King Lear*; the misery of imprisonment for debt in the King's Bench Prison in Southwark in *Timon of Athens*; the strange new world of the 'cabinet of curiosity' on Lime Street in *The Tempest*; and the rich variety and cosmopolitanism of one of the first true world-cities in the form of an ever-present backdrop. Moreover, he did set one of his most famous scenes here, in Ely Palace: in *Richard II*, in which John of Gaunt utters the immortal words: 'This royal throne of Kings, this sceptr'd isle,/This earth of majesty, this seat of Mars,/This other Eden, demi-paradise,/This fortress built by Nature for herself/Against infection and the hand of war,/This happy breed of men, this little world,/This precious stone set in the silver sea,/Which serves it in the office of a wall,/Or as a moat defensive to a house,/Against the envy of less happier lands,/This blessed plot, this earth, this realm, this England'.

Shakespeare's sometime mentor Christopher or Kit Marlowe was a poet and playwright best known for the 'mighty line' of his blank verse, and for his plays *Dido, Queen of Carthage*, *Tamburlaine the Great*, *The Jew of Malta*, *Doctor Faustus*, *Edward II* and *The Massacre at Paris*, many of which premiered at the Rose. Indeed, all are still performed on the site to this day. Marlowe was a colourful character, an avowed lover of tobacco and boys, a supposed spy, and a sometime resident of the Liberty of Norton Folgate, where a warrant was once issued for his arrest. In 1593, he was fatally stabbed in a tavern in Deptford, apparently in a dispute over the bill, and is buried in the nearby church of St Nicholas. His death is alluded to in his friend Shakespeare's *As You Like It* as 'a great reckoning in a little room'.

Above: 1. Iron Age hill-fort, Ambresbury Banks, Epping Forest.

Below: 2. Iron Age earthwork, Grim's Dyke, Harrow Weald.

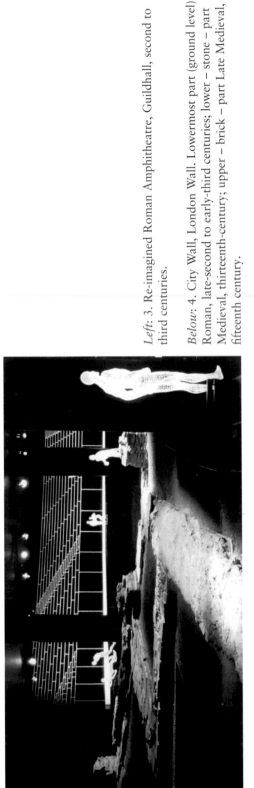

Left: 3. Re-imagined Roman Amphitheatre, Guildhall, second to third centuries.

Below: 4. City Wall, London Wall. Lowermost part (ground level) Roman, late-second to early-third centuries; lower – stone – part Medieval, thirteenth-century; upper – brick – part Late Medieval, fifteenth century.

Right: 5. Detail of Saxon cross, Church of All Hallows Barking *c.* 1000.

Below: 6. Saxon Westminster Abbey, as depicted in the Bayeux Tapestry. The body of Edward the Confessor is brought to the abbey for burial.

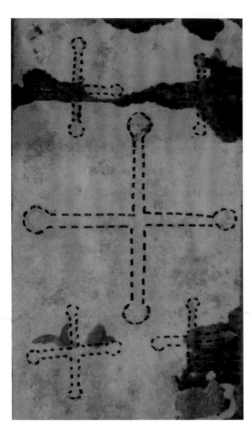

Left: 7. Detail of Saxon altar table,
St Pancras Old Church.

Below: 8. Saxon church of St Andrew,
Greensted. Note the 'eag-thyrel' or
eye-hole, left-hand side of image,
and niche, right.

Above: 9. The culmination of the Peasants' Revolt, West Smithfield, 1381, as depicted in Froissart's *Chroniques*. The ringleader Wat Tyler is attacked by the Mayor William Walworth, left. The boy-king Richard II looks on.

Right: 10. Replica of a pilgrim souvenir depicting the murder of St Thomas Becket in Canterbury Cathedral in 1170. This is the one I treated myself to after completing my pilgrimage from London to Canterbury in 2017. The original was found in Thames-side deposits in Dowgate in the City of London.

Above: 11. Tower of London, late fifteenth century. The figure looking wistfully out of the window in the Tower is Charles, Duc d'Orleans, imprisoned there for twenty-five years after having been captured at the Battle of Agincourt in 1415. While imprisoned he began work on a book of poems, which, when completed, included this illuminated frontispiece.

Below: 12. The Tower today under a suitably wintry patina.

Right: 13. Chapel of St John, Tower of London, late eleventh century.

Below: 14. Braun and Hogenberg map of London, 1572. This was the first true map of London, as opposed to earlier panoramic views.

Left: 15. Memorial to John Stow, church of St Andrew Undershaft, 1605.

Below: 16. The Visscher panorama, published in Amsterdam in 1616.

Above: 17. The execution of Charles I outside the Banqueting House, Whitehall, 1649.

Below: 18. The 'Bills of Mortality' for the 'Plague Year', 1665.

HET HUIS VAN DEN
OOST INDISCHE COMPAGNIE IN
LON DEN

THE OLD EAST INDIA HOUSE IN LEADENHALL STREET 1648 TO 1726
FROM A PAINTING IN THE POSSESSION OF Mr PELHAM OF THE INDIA HOUSE. IS INCHES BY 8

Left: 19. East India House,
Leadenhall Street, 1648.

Below: 20. Replica of the
Elizabethan Globe playhouse,
Bankside, Southwark.
The original was built nearby
in 1599.

21. Statue of Elizabeth I,
St Dunstan-in-the-West, 1586.
The statue formerly stood above
Ludgate.

22. Le Sueur's equestrian statue of
Charles I, Charing Cross, 1633.

Above: 23. Henry VII Lady Chapel, Westminster Abbey, 1508.

Below: 24. Interior, Sutton House, Hackney, 1535.

Above: 25. The Banqueting House, Whitehall Palace, 1622.

Right: 26. Inner Temple Gate-House, 1611, also known as 'Prince Henry's Room'.

27. York House Water-Gate, 1626.

28. Photographic reconstruction of Old St Paul's.

Etiam periere Ruinæ

W. Hollar fecit. Aᵒ 1666

Above: 29. Old St Paul's blazes. A military engineer was brought in to mine and bring down the tower before the rebuild.

Below: 30. The Great Fire of London by an unknown artist viewed from a boat by Tower Wharf on the evening of 4 September.

Above: 31. Interior of St Paul's today.

Below: 32. St Paul's by George Thomson, 1897, held in the Tate; a reminder of just how dominant that dome was on the skyline.

Benjamin or Ben Jonson was a playwright and poet of the Elizabethan and Jacobean eras, best known for his satirical plays *Every Man In His Humour, Volpone, The Alchemist* and *Bartholomew Fair*, and for his associations with the 'Curtain' and 'Hope'. His so-called 'lost' play, *The Isle of Dogs*, performed at the Swan, earned him a brief spell in the Marshalsea Prison by way of its libellous and seditious content. He himself, though, wrote that his 'best piece of poetry' was his first son, also Benjamin, who died of the plague in 1603 aged just seven. Jonson senior is buried – famously, upright – in Westminster Abbey.

It seems that Jonson and his friends, possibly including Shakespeare and Marlowe, were wont of an evening to gather at the Mermaid Tavern in Bread Street, for what one might now call a 'bard-off'. Beaumont memorably wrote of the exchanges that took place there: 'What things have we seen/Done at the Mermaid! Heard words that have been/So nimble, and so full of subtle flames/if that every one from whence they came/Had meant to put his whole wit in a jest,/And had resolv'd to live a fool the rest/Of his dull life.'

Milton was a poet, man of letters and sometime statesman of the later Caroline, Civil War, Commonwealth and Restoration areas. He is best known now as the author of the epic poem *Paradise Lost*, published in 1667, which Samuel Johnson argued 'with respect to design may claim the first place ... among the productions of the human mind'. During the Civil War and Commonwealth, though, he was known as the author of a number of – non-fiction – prose works opposing the monarchy and episcopacy, and supporting Republican and Parliamentarian causes. These included the polemical *Tenure of Kings and Magistrates* and *Eikonoklastes* (a counter-blast to *Eikon Basilike*, popularly attributed to Charles I himself), both published in 1649; and *Defensio pro Populo Anglico*, published in 1652 (*First Defence*) and 1654 (*Second Defence*). His Republicanism led to his arrest and temporary imprisonment after the Restoration, his release being secured by, among others, Andrew Marvell (then a Member of Parliament). He is buried in the church of St Giles Cripplegate, half a mile from his birthplace on Bread Street.

London was also an important centre of publishing, of books, tracts, pamphlets, handbills and eventually newspapers. All reading matter had of course to be written out long-hand in the Middle Ages, the Gild of Writers of Court Hand and Text Hand, and the Limners (Illustrators), becoming incorporated in 1357, and the Scriveners in

1373. Printing, and hence mass production, only came into existence at the turn of the Medieval and post-Medieval periods. William Caxton set up the first printing press in Greater London at the sign of the 'Red Pale' in Westminster in 1476, publishing *The Canterbury Tales* there the same year. His apprentice Wynkyn de Worde, the first one in the City, set up at the sign of the 'Sun' on Shoe Lane, off Fleet Street, in 1500, publishing his first book there the following year. The industry boomed almost from the start, and by 1640 there were 837 separate publishing businesses in London, many of them in the areas around Fleet Street, Ludgate Hill and St Paul's. Foreign-language texts were published in French from the fifteenth century, in Greek from 1524, in Italian from 1553, in Spanish from 1594, and in Dutch from 1615; newspapers from 1621 and dailies from 1702. The Stationers' Company was incorporated by Royal Charter in 1557. Its second Hall, in Stationers' Hall Court, off Ludgate Hill, was burned down in the Great Fire, alongside a number of bookshops in nearby St Paul's Churchyard and surrounding areas, and a large number of books removed to the cathedral for supposedly safe keeping. The surviving third Hall was built on the same site in 1673 (and burned down during the Blitz alongside a number of bookshops in Paternoster Row, and up to six million books). Incidentally, one of my distant ancestors, Simon West (1614-79), was a stationer apprenticed to John Bull in 1629 and 'made free by servitude' in 1636/7. He owned a shop under the sign of the Blackamore's Head in Wood Street, off Cheapside, and was also a Warden of St Peter Westcheap, both of which were burned down in the Great Fire. In 1647, he wrote a book about short-hand, entitled *Arts improvement or short and swift writing*. London was the nourishing womb of the English Renaissance.

Dress

Dress underwent something of a revolution in the post-Medieval period. In Tudor times, during Henry VIII's reign, in imitation of the King, men began to wear elaborately embroidered and quilted 'doublets' over short 'breeches' and 'hose', and under short sleeveless 'jerkins' and fur-trimmed three-quarter-length overgowns, with feathered flat caps, and to attempt at least to convey an image of masculinity – emphasised by enormous cod-pieces (witness any of the many reproductions of Holbein's famous portrait of Henry of 1536 – the original of which, housed in Whitehall Palace, was lost in a fire in

1698). Women began to wear figure-hugging corsets. During Elizabeth I's reign, women began to wear hooped, crinoline-like devices called 'farthingales' under their gowns, which imparted flare and enabled flounce, and increasingly elaborate ruffs around their necks (see the statue of Elizabeth of 1585 on the church of St Dunstan-in-the-West, (*Figure 21c*). Men also attempted, almost entirely unsuccessfully, to rock the ruff look (see the memorial in the church of St Olave Hart Street to the Florentine merchant – and rumoured informant to Elizabeth's spymaster Walsingham – Piero Capponi, who died of the plague in 1582 (*Figure 36*). Puritan men and women dressed modestly and simply, and in sombre colours, although not always in black, as is often thought (black dye was expensive, and mainly used in the manufacture of legal and clerical garb). In Stuart times, during James I's reign, men began to wear buttoned tunics with high-standing collars in place of the previously fashionable ruffs, long boots in place of shoes, long coats, and high and pointed hats (see de Critz's portrait of James of 1609 in the National Portrait Gallery). Women also began to wear high-standing collars in place of ruffs. During Charles I's reign,

36. Memorial to Piero Capponi, church of St Olave Hart Street (1593).

men began to wear unbuttoned tunics with falling collars, shirts, long breeches, short boots and cloaks (see le Sueur's equestrian statue of Charles I of 1633 in Charing Cross (*Figure 22c*). Cavaliers dressed extravagantly and flamboyantly, with low hats with wide brims and with or without plumed trims. French-style wigs became *de rigueur* – among men – in fashionable circles after the Restoration (Charles II had spent some time in exile in France during the Republic). Pepys wrote in his diary in 1663 of one that his wig-maker Jervas had attempted to sell to him that had been 'full of nits'!

Building Works

New building activity continued in the City, and especially in Westminster and the West End beyond. In the Tudor period, Bridewell Palace, Lambeth Palace, St James's Palace, Somerset House, the Tower of London, and Whitehall Palace were built, rebuilt or extended in the Tudor style, as seats of power. Outside the continuously built-up area, although still within easy reach, were, among others, Elsyng Palace, Eltham Palace, Fulham Palace (the principal residence of the Bishops of London), Greenwich Palace (also known as the Palace of Placentia), Hampton Court Palace, Nonsuch Place, Richmond Palace, and William Cecil's 'prodigy-house' Theobalds. The site of the dissolved Charterhouse was redeveloped, becoming initially a private residence occupied by Sir Edward North from 1545. The site of the former Savoy Palace, which was burned down in the Peasants' Revolt, was also redeveloped, new buildings on the site including the Savoy Hospital, founded by a bequest from Henry VII, who died in 1509 (the hospital became a military one in 1642, and was used to treat some of the wounded from the Civil War, and parts of it later became a military barracks and prison).

Bridewell Palace was originally built by Henry VIII in 1520 and granted by Edward VI in 1553 to the City of London to house a hospital, hostel, work-house and prison, and burned down in the Great Fire. It was subsequently rebuilt in 1667 and eventually demolished between 1864 and 1871. It was in Bridewell Palace in 1533 that Holbein painted his portrait *The Ambassadors*, which now hangs in the National Gallery. The painting depicts, on the left, Jean de Dinteville, the French ambassador, posing in a shirt, ruched pink silk doublet, black hose, black velvet jerkin, and fur-trimmed black velvet three-quarter-length overgown; and on the right, Georges de

Selve, Bishop of Lavaur, and ambassador to the Emperor, the Holy See and the Venetian Republic, in a black shirt with a white clerical collar, and an expensive-looking dark brocaded and fur-trimmed full-length silk overgown. In the background behind them is a heavy emerald-green brocaded silk curtain. Between them, a wooden unit displaying on its top shelf a celestial globe and various state-of-the-art precision astronomical and navigational scientific instruments on a section of geometrically patterned Anatolian carpet, and on its bottom shelf a terrestrial globe, and a range of musical instruments, including a lyre with a broken string, and a box of flutes. In the foreground is an expanse of geometrically patterned tiled floor. Also in the foreground is a *memento mori* in the form of an anamorphic skull.

Lambeth Palace, the London residence of the Archbishop of Canterbury, was actually originally built in the thirteenth century, and subsequently extended in the late fifteenth and sixteenth, under Henry VII and Mary respectively. The Gate-House, built by Cardinal John Morton, dates to 1495 (the Chapel and the Lollard's Tower to the late Medieval). The Garden was probably also originally laid out in the late fifteenth or sixteenth century (Christiansson, 2005).

St James's Palace was originally built by Henry VIII between 1531 and 1536 on a site where, according to Stow: 'the citizens of London, time out of mind, founded an hospital … for leprous women.' It remained one of the principal residences of the Kings and Queens of England for the next three hundred years.

Somerset House was originally built for the Lord Protector Somerset in 1547-50, and after his execution in 1552 it was owned, occupied and modified in turn by the then-future Queen, Elizabeth I in 1553; by James I's wife, Anne of Denmark, in 1603; by the then-future King, Charles I in 1619; and by Charles I's wife, the Henrietta Maria, in 1626. It survived the Civil War and Commonwealth of 1642-60, during which time it was temporarily appropriated by Parliamentarian authorities, as well as the Great Fire. In 1669, Charles II's wife, the Portuguese Catherine of Braganza, acquired it and in 1692, shortly after Charles II had died and James II, who was a Catholic, had been deposed, she relinquished it, fearing for her safety there in the midst of what by that time had become a fiercely anti-Catholic populace. It was then allowed to fall into disrepair and mostly demolished to make way for the present building in 1775. Some Tudor foundation stones survive, in the 'Archaeology Room'; and some Stuart headstones from the former – Catholic – chapel, in the 'Dead House': those of Catherine Guilermet, French servant to Henrietta Maria (d. 1633), Jacques d'Angennes, French ambassador (d. 1637), Blasius Nunes Manhans, Portuguese doctor to Catherine of Braganza (d. 1673), Edmund Fortescue, usher to Henrietta Maria and Catherine of Braganza (d. 1674) and Fr Hyacint(h), priest (d. 1692).

The Tower of London was repaired, extended and extensively remodelled in the Tudor period, becoming, as Raphael Holinshed put it, in his *Chronicles* of 1577-87, 'an armouries and house of munition, and thereunto a place for the safekeeping of offenders [rather] than a palace roiall for a King or Queen to sojourne in'. A detailed plan of the precinct from around the end of the period was produced by Haiward & Gascoyne in 1597.

Whitehall Palace, formerly York Place, was acquired by Henry VIII from the then Archbishop of York, Cardinal Wolsey, in 1529, whence, from Shakespeare's *Henry VIII*, 'You must no more call it York Place: that is past; For since the Cardinal fell that title's lost. 'Tis now the King's, and called Whitehall.' It was later extended both by Henry and by James I, gaining wall hangings, traverses, curtains, furniture and sanitary apparatus, all of the finest quality. In 1598 the Moravian aristocrat and gentleman-traveller Baron Waldstein described his visit to the palace in his diary:

It is truly majestic, bounded on the one side by a park which adjoins another palace called St James's, and on the other side by the Thames, and it is a place which fills one with wonder, not so much because of its great size as because of the magnificence of its ... rooms which are furnished with the most gorgeous splendour. First you come to a vast hall which leads through into a very large walled garden where they keep deer and all kinds of other animals. We then went to see the rooms, every one of them furnished and arranged with perfect taste and elegance, with all sorts of statues and pictures to add to their beauty... There is a portrait of Edward VI in 1546 at the age of nine... Another room has ... some very rich hangings. A portrait here shows Queen Elizabeth when she was still young, in the dress which she wore when going to attend Parliament... we saw ... the Queen's couch which is woven with gold and silver thread... The Queen's bed-chamber has rich tapestries all around. The adjoining room is reserved for the Queen's bath: the water pours from oyster shells... In the next room there is an organ on which two persons can play duets... The next room to this was the one where the Queen keeps her books, some of which she wrote herself... From here we were taken into a large and lofty banqueting hall... In another room Henry VII and Henry VIII and their wives are painted.

Notable new religious building works of the Tudor period included the Henry VII Lady Chapel in Westminster Abbey, the parish church of St Margaret Westminster, rebuilt in 1523, and further afield, the parish church of St Mary in Stoke Newington, rebuilt by the local Lord of the Manor William Patten in 1563, and thus representing one of the earliest churches anywhere in the country specifically designed for Protestant rather than Catholic worship. The Henry VII Lady Chapel in Westminster Abbey, thought to have been designed and built by Robert Janyns the Younger (fl. 1499-1506), Robert Vertue (d. 1506), and William Vertue (d. 1527) between 1503 and 1508 is at the very pinnacle of the Perpendicular Gothic, with exceptional external flying buttresses and internal pendant vaults, and even known in its own time as *orbis miraculum*, or 'the wonder of the world'. Whittled away to a fine filigree of near-nothingness, the stone ceiling seems to hover like a second heaven high over the head of the worshipper. The magnificent effigial monuments of Henry VII and his Queen, Elizabeth of York, in what John Pope-Hennessy called 'the finest Renaissance tomb north of the Alps', were made by the Italian sculptor Torrigiano 1512-7. In 1540 Westminster Abbey was made a Cathedral with its own See and shortly afterwards was incorporated into the Diocese of London, at which time much of its estate was sold off to pay for repairs to Old St Paul's – hence the expression, 'robbing Peter to pay Paul' (the current status of the abbey is that of a Royal Peculiar). Old St Paul's lost its spire to a lightnng strike in 1561. A contemporary account of the event read as follows:

[B]etween one and two of the clock at afternoon was seen a marvellous great fiery lightning, and immediately ensued a most terrible hideous crack of thunder such as seldom hath been heard, and that by estimation of sense, directly over the City of London... Divers persons in time of the said tempest being on the river of Thames, and others being in the fields near adjoining to the City affirmed that they saw a long and spear-pointed flame of fire (as it were) run through the top of the broach or shaft of Paul's steeple, from the east westward. And some of the parish of St Martin's [Ludgate] being then in the street did feel a marvellous strong air or whirlwind with a smell like brimstone coming from Paul's Church... Between four and five of the clock a smoke was espied ... to break out under the bowl of the said shaft... But suddenly after, as it were in a moment, the flame broke forth in a circle like a garland round about the broach ... and increased in such wise that within a quarter of an hour or a little more, the cross and the eagle on the top fell down upon the south cross aisle... Some there were, pretending experience in wars, that counselled the remnants of the steeple to be shot down with cannons, which counsel was not liked... Others perceiving the steeple to be past all recovery, considering the hugeness of the fire and the dropping of the lead, thought best to get ladders and scale the church, and with axes to hew down a space of the roof of the church to stay the fire, at the least to save some part of the church: which was concluded.

New private buildings of the Tudor period included further Inns of Court and Livery Company Halls. New private residences of the period included that of the merchant trader and ambassador to the Ottoman court Paul Pindar on Bishopsgate, completed *c.* 1599, which would appear from surviving drawings, paintings and photographs – and the carved oak façade salvaged when the building was demolished in 1890, now in the Victoria and Albert Museum – to have been particularly extravagantly and flamboyantly appointed. And, further afield, Canonbury Tower in Islington was originally built sometime between 1509 and 1532 for the Prior of St Bartholomew's, William Bolton, and subsequently occupied by, among others, Francis Bacon, Oliver Goldsmith and Washington Irving. Sutton House in Hackney was built around 1535 for the courtier and sometime 'Keeper of the Great Wardrobe', Ralph Sadleir.

In the Stuart period the Banqueting House was built in Whitehall Palace for James I and the Queen's Chapel in St James's Palace for the future Charles I. The site of the dissolved Charterhouse was redeveloped again, becoming a charitable alms-house and school founded by a bequest from Thomas Sutton, from 1611 (the school relocated to Godalming in Surrey in 1872). The Banqueting House was built by the Palladian architect Inigo Jones in 1622 and was the first building in central London in the Renaissance style, with a ceiling by Rubens. Jones's Classical Queen's House in Greenwich was built between 1616 and 1635. The Queen's Chapel was built by Jones between 1623 and 1627. It was originally intended for the use of the Spanish Infanta, who was to have married the then Prince Charles. After that arrangement fell through and Charles instead married Henrietta Maria, the chapel came to be used by her. In 1642, during the Civil War, it was used by the Parliamentarian army as a barracks and, 1662 after the Restoration of the Monarchy it was restored to its original purpose by Charles II and his Queen, Catherine of Braganza, who established a friary in the grounds (whence, Friary Court).

Notable new religious building works of the Stuart period included the Renaissance renovations to Old St Paul's by Inigo Jones 1633-41, and by Christopher Wren in 1660; and the renovations to the churches of St Katharine Cree 1628-31; and St Helen in 1633 – the Medieval Gothic style had well and truly gone out of fashion by the time of Charles I. In the West End, the parish church of St Paul, Covent Garden, 'the handsomest barn in England', was built by Inigo Jones in 1624. Further afield, although still within the more-or-less continuously built-up area, the chapel that became the church of St John, Wapping, was built in 1617, Poplar Chapel, between 1642 and 1654, and the chapel that became the church of St Paul, Shadwell, in 1656. Poplar Chapel was built by the East India Company for its dock-workers during the Civil War and succeeding interregnum, the date of construction making it unique in London, and indeed unusual in the country as a whole. The design of the chapel was originally 'severely rectangular', and as such ideally suited to the form of worship practised by Puritans, which emphasised the importance of the word over that of the ceremony. The chapel became a parish church, dedicated to St Matthias, when the East India Company dissolved in the 1860s and the church became a community centre in the 1990s. The exterior of the building was rebuilt by William Milford Teulon, younger brother of the more famous Samuel Sanders Teulon, in the mid-nineteenth century, although, remarkably, the interior remains to this day essentially as it was in the mid-seventeenth.

New private buildings of the period included yet more Inns of Court and Livery Company Halls. New private residences included

41/42 Cloth Fair, completed in 1614; York House, completed in 1626; 59/60 Lincoln's Inn Fields, completed in 1640; and, further afield, Newington Green Terrace in Newington, completed in 1658. The town-houses of the men of wealth typically had cellars below ground, store-rooms for merchandise and well-appointed living quarters on the ground floor, bedrooms upstairs, and long galleries on the projecting uppermost, third or fourth, storey (they had to accommodate not only the owner and his extended family, but also his apprentices and his many servants). Dwellings of the common man, such as those on Bishopsgate occupied by Luke Clapham, Richard Plowman and Edward Walker, and surveyed by Ralph Treswell in 1607, typically had only two storeys, each of two rooms.

41/42 Cloth Fair, 'the oldest house in London', was first owned by one William Chapman, who was evidently a businessman of some means. It has been memorably described by the architectural critic Ian Nairn as 'an embodiment of the old London spirit. Chunky, cantankerous, breaking out all over in oriels and roof-lights, unconcerned with ... anything else other than shapes to live in'. York House was originally built for the Bishops of Norfolk sometime before 1237. It subsequently came to be owned by Henry VIII's brother-in-law Charles Brandon, the Duke of Suffolk, in 1536; by Queen Mary in 1556; by Francis Bacon, the Lord Keeper of the Great Seal, from 1617; by George Villiers Senior, the 1st Duke of Buckingham, from 1621; by General Sir Thomas, Lord Fairfax, during the Civil War; and eventually by George Villiers Junior, 2nd Duke of Buckingham, after the Restoration (by which time he had married Fairfax's daughter Mary). It survived the Great Fire but was substantially demolished in the 1670s, whereupon the site was developed by Nicholas Barbon, who in deference to its former owner set out new streets named George, Villiers, Duke and Buckingham – and even an alley named Of!

By the time of the Great Fire as recorded in the Worshipful Company of Parish Clerks' 'Bills of Mortality' there were 97 parish churches within the walls of the City, and 16 without, a total of 113. There was also one cathedral, Old St Paul's within the walls, and a number of conventual churches and private chapels within and without, including St Etheldreda and Temple Church. In addition, there were five parish churches in the City and Liberties of Westminster: St Clement Danes, St Paul Covent Garden, St Margaret Westminster, St Martin-in-the-Fields and St Mary Savoy. There were twelve in the out-parishes of Middlesex and Surrey, including St Giles-in-the-Fields. Many of the places of worship were lovingly embellished with bell towers, spires, churchyards and gardens by their parishioners, splashing colour onto an otherwise drab canvas. (The grounds of St Andrew Hubbard were sown with hemp, which would probably be an arrestable offence these days.) Numerous seats of power and Royal palaces, important secular public buildings, and private residences and places of business were similarly enlivened. Revealing drawings, paintings and panoramas ('pictorial surveys') of the City of the time include those of Bol, Briot, Hollar, de Jongh, Norden, Rembrandt, Smith, Visscher and Wyngaerde (*Figure 16c*). And important maps include the *British Atlas of Historic Towns* one of 1520 (Lobel, 1989), the 'Copper Plate' one of *c.* 1559, the 'Agas' one of *c.* 1569, the Braun and Hogenberg one of 1572, the Norden one of 1593, the Newcourt and Faithorne one of 1658, and the Moore one of 1662. The 'Copper Plate' map must have been published no later than 1559, as it shows the parish church of St Botolph Bishopsgate still with its cross, which was lost through fire in that year. The 'Agas' map must have been published no earlier than 1569, as it shows the Royal Exchange with its trademark grasshopper weather-vane, that was erected in that year. The Braun & Hogenberg map was published in 1572, although it still shows Old St Paul's with the spire it lost in 1561 (*Figure 14c*).

The post-Medieval street layout was still a maze or web. By the end of the period around a hundred yards of land had been reclaimed from the river and there was a dense network of quays, wharves, steps, alley-ways, passage-ways and lanes along the foreshore. As long ago as 1636, traffic congestion had become such a problem that it prompted one Henry Peacham to write:

It is most fit, and requisite, that princes, nobility, the more eminent and abler among the gentry should be allowed their coaches and carroches ... but what I pray you are the coaches of these few, to that multitude at this day in England? When in London ... and within four miles compass without, are reckoned to the number of six thousand and odd. ... [I]n certain places of the City ... I have never come but I have there the way barricado'd up with a coach, two, or three, that what haste, or business soever a man hath, he must wait my Lady's (I know not what) leisure (who is in the next shop, buying pendants for her ears: or a collar for her dog) ere he can find any passage. The most eminent places for stoppage are Paul's gate into Cheapside, Ludgate, and Ludgate Hill, especially when a play is done at the Friars, then Holborn ... Hosier Lane, Smithfield, and Cow Lane ... then about the Stocks and Poultry, Temple Bar, Fetter Lane and Shoe Lane ... but to see their multitude ... when there is a masque at Whitehall, a Lord Mayor's feast, a new play ... how close they stand together (like mutton-pies in a cook's oven) that hardly you can thrust a pole between.

'An Ordinance for the Regulation of Hackney-Coachmen in London and the places adjacent' had had to be issued in 1654.

Surviving Structures
Essentially nothing now remains of the majority of the post-Medieval seats of power, religious houses and secular buildings that stood within and without the walls of the City of London before the Great Fire. However, from Tudor London, of the seats of power, parts of the Whitehall Palace, Lambeth Palace (*Figure 37*), and St James's Palace (*Figure 38*), survive still, without the walls (as does the Savoy Chapel, part of the Savoy Hospital). Much of Tudor Whitehall Palace was destroyed in fires in 1512 and 1698 but Henry VIII's wine cellar in what is now the Ministry of Defence building in Horse Guards' Avenue still survives, as does the site of his tilt-yard in Horse Guards' Parade and part of his tennis court in the Cabinet Office at No. 70 Whitehall. The Holbein Gate, built in 1532, the probable location of the clandestine marriage of Henry and Anne Boleyn in 1533, survived both fires, but was demolished in 1759. Of the religious buildings, there is the Henry VII Lady Chapel in Westminster Abbey (*Figure 23c*), the parish church of St Margaret Westminster (*Figure 39*) and the parish church of St Mary, Stoke Newington. Of North's former Charterhouse, the Great Hall and the Great Chamber survive, where Queen Elizabeth I once held court, at great cost to her host. Of the Inns of Court, there is the Henrician Lincoln's Inn 'Old Hall' (*Figure 40*), Gate-House and 'Old Buildings', the Elizabethan Middle Temple Hall (*Figure 41*) and the Elizabethan Staple Inn Buildings (*Figure 42*). Lincoln's Inn 'Old Hall' was built on the site of the Medieval Bishop of Chichester's Inn, incorporating into its structure a Gothic arch from the old inn. Of the private residences, Canonbury Tower in Islington (*Figure 43*) and

Sutton House in Hackney (*Figures 44, 24c*) survive; and of the places of business, the 'Olde Mitre' in Ely Court.

From Stuart London, of the seats of power we have the Renaissance Banqueting House (*Figure 25c*), part of Whitehall Palace and the Queen's Chapel (*Figure 45*), part of St James's Palace both in Westminster. The surviving religious houses are the parish churches of St Helen and St Katharine Cree with their Renaissance additions, within the walls of the City; and St Paul, Covent Garden (*Figure 46*), Poplar Chapel (*Figure 47*), St Paul, Shadwell (*Figure 48*), and the Chapel of Sutton's former Charterhouse, without. Of the Inns of Court, without, the Jacobean Gate-House in Inner Temple, also known as 'Prince Henry's Room', survives (*Figure 26c*); and the Jacobean Chapel in Lincoln's Inn. Of the Livery Companies' Halls, within, parts of the Apothecaries'. Of the private residences, without, 41/42 Cloth Fair (1614) (*Figure 49*); Master Mason Nicholas Stone's York House Water-Gate (1626) (*Figure 27c*); 59/60 Lincoln's Inn Fields (1640) (*Figure 50*); and Newington Green Terrace (1658) (*Figure 51*). And of the places of business, within, parts of the 'Olde Wine Shades' on Martin Lane; and without, the Seven Stars on Carey Street, and the Wig and Pen on the Strand (*Figure 52*).

37. Lambeth Palace Gate-House (1495) and the church of St Mary-at-Lambeth.

Left: 38. St James's Palace Gate-House (1536).

Below: 39. St Margaret, Westminster (1523).

40. Lincoln's Inn
Old Hall (1491).

Right: 41. Middle Temple Hall (1571).

Below: 42. Staple Inn Buildings (1589).

Left: 43. Canonbury
Tower, Islington
(1532).

Below: 44. Exterior,
Sutton House,
Hackney (1535).

Above: 45. The Queen's Chapel, St James's Palace (1627).

Below: 46. St Paul, Covent Garden (1624).

Above: 47. Poplar Chapel (1654). The ceiling boss features the arms of the East India Company.

Below left: 48. St Paul, Shadwell (1656).

Below right: 49. 41/42 Cloth Fair (1614).

50. 59/60 Lincoln's Inn Fields (1640).

51. Newington Green Terrace (1658).

52. Wig and Pen, Strand (1625). It was originally built as the home of the gatekeeper of Temple Bar.

Archaeological Finds

The Museum of London houses an extensive collection. The Museum of London Docklands in West India Quay houses, among other things, a harrowing permanent exhibition on 'London, Sugar and Slavery', featuring a wide variety of associated artefacts. The National Maritime Museum in Greenwich has a newly opened permanent exhibition on 'Tudor and Stuart Seafarers', featuring artefacts associated with maritime exploration and trade, including the slave trade.

A series of Museum of London and other publications either describe in detail or summarise the findings of archaeological excavations at various post-Medieval sites around the City.

The commonest post-Medieval finds on the foreshore of the Thames are sherds of pottery, and clay pipes. Tobacco was expensive when it was first introduced in the late sixteenth century, but became cheaper over the course of the seventeenth, so early clay pipe bowls are typically small, and later ones larger.

Selected Further Reading

Ackroyd, 1998, 2000, 2012, 2014; Alford, 2017; Arber, 1890; Auer & Maarleveld, 2014; Barber, 2012; Barnett, 1940; Bergeron, 2017; Berry, 1978, 1986, 1989; Besant, 1894, 1903, 1904; Boyd, 1928; Brenner, 1993; Brett-James, 1935; Brown, 1921; Bruce, 1868; Burford, 1973, 1990, 1993; Campbell et al., 2013; Cartwright, 1875; Chaudhuri, 1965, 1968; Chute, 1949; Clayton, 2003; Cook, 1981; Craven, 1957, 1964; FK. Davies, 1957; P. Davies, 2009; Day, 2011; Dekker, 1603; de la Bedoyere, 1995, 2006; Dennis, 2004; Dick, 1949; Draper, 1962; Duff, 1906; Dutton, 2018; Epstein, 1908; Franciscus, 1497; Fraser, 1973; Fuller, 1981; Gair, 1982; Greg, 1956; Grueninger, 2017; Gurr, 2004, 2009; Hakluyt, 1600; Hanson, 2003; Hamilton, 1875; Hayward, 2004; Hibbert, 1969;Hodges, 1968; Holland, 1993; Hollyer, 2001, 2003; Holmes, 1969; Hotson, 1928, 1959; Howell, 1657; Inwood, 1998, 2008; Judges, 1930; Keene et al., 2004; Knighton, 2004; Lipscomb, 2012; Lucas & Russell, 2018; Mackinder, 2013; Mishra, 2018; Neill, 1869; Nichols, 1848; Nicoll, 1964; Nurse, 2017; Olusoga, 2016; Ormond, 1979; Panton, 2005; Parsons, 2005; E. Pearce, 1908; Picard, 1997, 2003; Polk, 2006; Pooley, 1945; Porter, 1996, 2011a, b, 2018; Rawley, 2003; Reed, 1952; Reid, 1967; Riches, 2011; Rideal, 2016; Robins, 2012; Rowles, 2018; Rudden, 1985; Rule, 2017; Rutter, 1984; Ryrie, 2017; Schofield, 1984, 1987, 2011b, 2016; Schuler, 2011; Shelley, 1909; Shrimplin, 2017; Sibun & Ponce, 2018; Simpson, 1928; Stone, 2002, 2017; Stow, 1598; Sutton, 1981; Taylor, 2002; Thomson, 1983; Thurley, 1998, 1999, 2009, 2017; Tomalin, 2002; Wallace, 1908; Walvin, 2011; Way & Chapman, 1902; Weinstein, 1994; Wellsman, 1973; Wilbur, 1965; A. Wilson, 1983; F. Wilson, 1925, 1927; Young & Young, 1956.

CHAPTER SEVEN

The Great Fire

On the evening of Saturday 1 September 1666, the King's baker Thomas Farriner, whose premises were on Pudding Lane, went to bed evidently leaving the fire that heated his oven still burning, in contravention of the curfew law passed six hundred years previously by William I (the word curfew deriving from the Norman French '*couvre-feu*', meaning, literally, 'cover fire'). In the early hours of the following morning, a spark from the fire settled on a pile of firewood stacked nearby for use on the following working day, and set it alight. Flames soon engulfed the house, and although Farriner and his family were able to escape by climbing through an upstairs window and along the outside of the building to a neighbouring one, his unfortunate maid-servant, being afraid of heights, stayed put and burned to death, becoming the first of – reportedly – mercifully few to die in what was about to become the Great Fire. According to some sources, her name was Rose.

The fire soon spread from Farriner's bakery to nearby Fish Street Hill, burning down the Star Inn, where flammable faggots and straw were stacked up in the yard, and the church of St Margaret Fish Street Hill; and thence on to Thames Street, where wood, cloth sails, rope, tar and coal were stacked up on the river-front. It went on to take a firm hold of the City, largely built of wooden houses, weatherproofed with pitch and separated by only a few feet at ground level, even less at roof level, on account of the'jettying' of successive storeys, allowing flames to leap from one to another with ease. The spread of the fire was further facilitated by the weather, with the strong easterly wind that had been creaking and rattling shop signs on their hinges now fanning it and carrying it towards the heart of the City; everything in its path tinder dry from the preceding exceptionally long, hot, dry summer, which also meant that the supply of water with which to fight it was short. (Most of the old signs of London were destroyed during the Great Fire, and the few that remained had to be taken down after a Proclamation of 1667 ordered that they not hang across the street, as had been the fashion, but instead that they be fixed to buildings: Meadows, 1957).

We are fortunate to have a number of vivid contemporary eye-witness accounts of what followed, the best-known being those of John Evelyn and Samuel Pepys. We also have a number of more or less contemporary paintings of the fire at its height, one of which, attributed to Waggoner, is in the Guildhall Art Gallery and another, by an anonymous artist, in the Museum of London. A significant number are by foreign artists, one of whom entitled his work *Sic Punit*, or 'Thus He Punishes' – remember that England was at war with the Netherlands and France at the time.

John Evelyn wrote of the spread of the fire:

[2 September] [W]ith my Wife and Son, took Coach & went to the bank side in Southwark, where we beheld that dismal speectaccle, the whole Citty in dreadful flames neere the Water side [and] consumed … from the bridge … towards Cheape side … (*Figure 30c*). [3 September] The fire having continud all this night (if I may call that night, which was as light as day for 10 miles round) when conspiring with a fierce Eastern Wind, in a very drie season, I went on foote to the same place, when I saw the whole of the … Citty burning … to Bainard Castle, and … taking hold of St Paule's Church, to which the Scaffalds contributed exceedingly. The Conflagration was so universal, & the people so astonish'd, that from the beginning … they hardly stirr'd to quench it, so … there was nothing heard or scene but crying out & lamentation, & running about like distracted creatures [the fire] leaping after a prodigious manner from house to house … at great distance one from the other, for the heate … had even ignited the aire [and] devoured after an incredible manner houses, furniture, & everything: Here we saw the Thames coverd with goods floating … barges & boates laden with what some had time & courage to save [and] Cartes &c. carrying out to the fields, which for many miles were strewed with movables of all sorts, & Tents … to shelter both people & what goods they could get away. O … miserable & calamitous spectacle... God grant mine eyes never behold the like [again], who now saw ten thousand houses all in one flame ... the fall of houses, towers & churche... Thus I left it ... burning, a resemblance of Sodome... London was, but is no more. [4 September] The burning still rages; now gotten as far as the Inner Temple, al Fleetestreete, old baily, Ludgate Hil, Warwick Lane, Newgate, Paules Chaine, Wattling-streete now flaming & ... the stones of Paules flew lie Granados, the Lead melting down the streets in a stream, & the very pavements ... glowing with a fiery rednesse, so as nor horse nor man was able to tread on them, ... the ... Wind still more impetuously driving the flames forewards: nothing but the almighty power of God ... able to stop them, for vaine was the help of man.

Fortunately, the spread of the fire across the river to Southwark was halted at a gap in the buildings on London Bridge that formed a natural firebreak – ironically, the result of another fire some thirty years previously. Samuel Pepys wrote [2 September]:

I down to the waterside... and there saw a lamentable fire... Everybody endeavouring to remove their goods .... into the river or into lighters that lay off; poor people staying in their houses as long as till the very fire touched them, and then running into boats, or clambering from one pair of stairs by the waterside to another... Having stayed, and in an hours time seen the fire rage every way, and nobody to my sight endeavouring to quench it ... to Whitehall and there up to the King's closet in the Chapel, where I did give them an account that dismayed them all, and the word was carried to the King. So I was called for, and did tell the King ... what I saw; and that unless His Majesty did command houses to be pulled down, nothing could stop the fire... [T]he King commanded me to go to my Mayor from him, and command him 'spare no houses'... At last met my Mayor in Canning Streete ... with a hankercher about his neck. To the King's message, he cried like a fainting woman, 'Lord, what can I do? I am spent! People will not obey me. I have been pull[ing] down houses. But fire overtakes us faster than we can do it.

Famously, Pepys wrote, on 4 September 'Sir W. Pen[n] and I did dig ... [a pit] and put our wine in it; and I my Parmazan cheese.'

Pulling down or even blowing up buildings to create firebreaks eventually proved a partially successful strategy in fighting the fire. Evelyn on 4 September noted:

[T]he blowing up of houses, as might make a [wider] gap than any yeat made by the ordinary method of pulling them downe with Engines: This some stout Seamen proposed [and] was commanded to be practised, & my concern being particularly for the Hospital of st. Bartholemeus neere Smithfield, ... made me al the more diligent to promote it... So as it pleased Almighty God by abating of the Wind, & the industrie of people, now when all was lost, infusing a new Spirit into them ... the furie of it began sensibly to abate ... so as it came no farther than the Temple West-ward, nor than the enterance of Smithfield North... It ... brake out again in the Temple: but the courage of the multitude persisting, & innumerable houses blown up with Gunpowder, such gaps & desolations were soone made ... as the back fire did not so vehemently urge upon the rest, as formerly.

Pepys also, on the 4th: 'Now begins the practice of blowing up of houses in Tower Street, ... which at first did frighten people more than any thing; but it stopped the fire when it was done.' And on the 5th: '[G]oing to the fire, I find, by the blowing up of houses ... by Sir W. Pen, there is a good stop given to it ... it having only burned the dyall of Barking Church, and part of the porch, and ... was there quenched.' Unfortunately the strategy was also one that was implemented too late to make a significant difference to the outcome (probably for fear of law-suits from 'avaritious' property owners).

The fire eventually halted in its own tracks after the wind dropped on the fourth day, although in places there were also some fresh outbreaks on the fifth day, 6 September, when Pepys wrote: 'Up about five o'clock ... to go out, ... to see how the fire is, to ... Bishop's-gate, where no fire had been near, and now there is one broke out: which did give great grounds to people, and to me too, to think that there is some kind of plot in this ... but ... we did put it out in a little time; so that all was well again.'

In the immediate aftermath, on the 7th, Pepys wrote:

Up by five o'clock; and, blessed be God! find all well; and by water to [Paul's] Wharfe. Walked thence, and saw all the towne burned, and a miserable sight of Paul's church, with all the roofs fallen, and the body of the quire fallen into St Fayth's; Paul's school also, Ludgate, and Fleet Street. My father's house, and the church, and a good part of the Temple the like... I home late to Sir W. Pen's, who did give me a bed ... but still both sleeping and waking had a fear of fire in my heart, that I took little rest. People do all the world over cry out of the simplicity of my Lord Mayor in ... this business of the fire, laying it all upon him. A proclamation is come out for markets to be kept at Leadenhall and ... several other places about the town; and Tower Hill, and all churches to be set open to receive poor people.

On the same day Evelyn wrote, elegiacally:

I wente this morning on foote ... thro the Late fleete streete, Ludgate hill, by St Paules, Cheape side, Exchange, Bishopsgate, Aldersgate, & out to Morefields, thence thro Cornehill, &c; with extraordinary difficulty, clambring over mountains of yet smoking rubbish, & frequently mistaking where I was ... in the meane time his Majestie got to the Tower by Water, to demolish the houses about [which] had they taken fire, & attaq'd the white Towre, where the Magazines of Powder lay, would undoubtedly have ... renderd ... demolition ... even ... at many miles distance: At my returne I was infinitely concerned to find that goodly Church of St Paules now a sad ruine, & that beautiful Portico (for structure comparable to any in Europe, as not long before repaird by the late King) now rent in pieces, flakes of vast Stone Split in sunder, & nothing remaining intire... It was astonishing to see what immense stones the heat had in a manner Calcin'd, so as all the ornaments, Columns, freezes, Capitels & projectures of massie Portland stone flew off, even to the very roofe, where a Sheete of Leade covering no lesse than 6 akers by measure, being totally mealted, the ruines of the Vaulted roof, falling brake into St Faithes, which being filled with ... books ... belonging to the Stationers ... carried thither for safty, they were all consumed burning for a week following... Thus lay in ashes that most venerable Church, one of the antientest Pieces of early Piety in the Christian world, beside neere 100 more: The lead, yronworke, bells, plate &c all mealted: the exquisitely wrought Mercers Chapell, the Sumptuous Exchange, the august fabrique of Christ church, all the rest of the Companies Halls, sumptuous buildings, Arches, Enteries, all in dust. The fountains dried up & ruind, whilst the very waters remained boiling; the Voragos of subterranean Cellars, Wells &

Dungeons, formerly Warehouses, still burning in stench & dark clouds of smoke like hell, so as in five or six miles traversing about, I did not see one load of timber unconsum'd, nor many stones but were calcind white as snow, so as the people who now walked about the ruines, appeard like men in some dismal desart, or rather in some greate City, lay'd waste by an impetuous & cruel Enemy.

Recriminations rapidly followed, with the Mayor Sir Thomas Bloodworth singled out for criticism over his initial complacency and subsequent indecisiveness (when first informed of the fire, he is reported to have remarked that a woman might have pissed it out, which indeed she might, if she had acted promptly – and he did not, and must soon have come to rue his rash words). The rudimentary fire brigade was also criticised for acting in an un-coordinated fashion and, in its desperation digging up roads and cutting pipes to get at the water to fill its buckets, in so doing cutting off the supply to others. This was a little unfair, given the chaotic situation they found themselves confronted with, and the tools at their disposal with which to deal with it, including primitive fire engines that looked and likely handled more like tea trolleys, and extinguishers or 'squirts' that looked like ear syringes! Eventually, the Great Fire was ascribed to an act of God, albeit one that the wit and hand of man would attempt to ensure was never repeated. At the time, though, many falsely believed it to have been deliberately set by a fanatical papist or saboteur. A Frenchman, Robert Hubert, was executed for having set it, after having confessed, probably under duress, and been convicted in a court of law – in part on the evidence of members of Farriner's family, who had their own reasons to attach the blame somewhere, anywhere. Evidence came to light shortly after his execution that Hubert had not even been in the country at the time of the fire.

The stark fact remained that the fire had largely destroyed the City that had witnessed so much history in the making. Eighty per cent of the area within the walls was more or less completely burned out, and only the extreme north and east had survived substantially intact (the walls had more or less confined the fire to the City within, although some areas without to the west had also been affected). St Paul's Cathedral was gutted, as were 85 parish churches within and immediately without the walls, alongside 45 Livery Company Halls, Baynard's Castle, the Custom House, the Guildhall, the Royal Exchange, and the Royal Wardrobe, not to mention an estimated 13,200 residences and places of business (*Figures*

28c, 29c). Damage to property and trade was on an entirely unprecedented scale, as was associated homelessness and loss of livelihood. The cost of the fire damage was estimated at around ten million pounds by John Strype in 1720. In modern terms, this equates to anywhere between one billion pounds (according to the National Archives Currency Convertor) and tens of billions (according to the Association of British Insurers). None of the cost of the fire damage was covered by insurance. The fire insurance business only came into being after, and indeed at least arguably in response to, the Great Fire (the first fire insurance company was founded by Nicholas 'If-Jesus-Christ-Had-Not-Died-For-Thee-Thou-Hadst-Been-Damned' Barbon (his actual name) in 1680. Insured properties came to be identified by plaques known as 'fire-marks', surviving examples of which may still be seen on some houses in London, notably in Spitalfields.

Around 100,000 persons were made homeless by the fire, and had to be temporarily rehoused in camps, for example in Moorfields, or in those – substantial – parts of what we might think of as Greater London that were not affected by the fire. There would appear to have been a certain amount of profiteering by landlords at this time, and a little later, as rebuilding work began, by builders' merchants, although the general mood would seem to have been one of shared hardship and public-spiritedness, somewhat akin to that of the Blitz.

Loss of life in the fire appears to have been comparatively low, although it may have been higher than reported, given that the fire had evidently been sufficiently hot as to have been able bodies to ash (hot enough to melt not only the lead on the rooves of the churches, and the iron bells within, but also glass and even pottery). The schoolboy William Taswell described encountering the body of one of the victims after the fire:

> Soon after sunrising I endeavoured to reach St Paul's. The ground was so hot as almost to scorch my shoes; and the air so intensely warm that unless I had stopped some time upon the Fleet Bridge to rest myself, I must have fainted... And now ... I perceived the metal belonging to the bells melting; the ruinous conditions of the walls; whole heaps of stone of a large circumference tumbling down with a great noise ... ready to crush me to death. [N]ear the east walls ... a human body presented itself to me, parched up, as it were, with the flames; whole as to skin, meagre as to flesh, yellow as to colour. This was an old decrepit woman who fled here for safety, imagining the flames could not have reached her ... Her clothes were burned, and evry limb reduced to a coal.

CHAPTER EIGHT

Aftermath

Would the City ever be rebuilt? Well, of course it would, not least because the prosperity of the City was essential to that of the country as a whole and more specifically powerful men with vested interests, watching anxiously from the sidelines as 'day by day the City's wealth flowed out of the gate' to other boroughs (Birch, 1887).

The Mayor initiated the process straight away, within weeks commencing a detailed survey and map of the fire-damaged area of the City to assist with the assessment of compensation claims, and to use as a template for reconstruction plans. The survey was actually commissioned by the King, Charles II, in his 'Proclamation ... to Prohibit the Rebuilding of Houses after the Great Fire of London without Conforming to the General Regulations therein premised':

> [W]e do hereby direct, that the lord mayor and court of aldermen do, with all possible expedition, cause an exact survey to be made and taken of the whole ruins occasioned by the late lamentable fire, to the end that it may appear to whom all the houses and ground did in truth belong... [W]e shall cause a plot or model to be made for the ... ruined places; which being well examined by those persons who have most concernment as well as experience, we make no question but all men will be pleased with it, and very willingly conform to those orders and rules which shall be agreed for the pursuing thereof.

Among the other stipulations in the Proclamation was that 'no man whatsoever shall presume to erect any house or building, great or small, but of brick or stone... Fleet Street, Cheapside, Cornhill, and all other eminent and notorious streets, shall be of such a breadth, as may, with God's blessing, prevent the mischief that one side may suffer if the other be on fire.' Priority was to be given to the reconstruction of churches: '[W]e do heartily pray unto Almighty God, that he will infuse it into the hearts of men, speedily to endeavour by degrees to re-edify some of those many churches, which, in this lamentable fire, have been burned down and defaced.' The survey was undertaken by one John Leake and the map drafted by Wenceslaus Hollar (1607-77), a Bohemian who had travelled widely before eventually settling in London and earning a reputation as an engraver and print-maker of some considerable skill, specialising in landscape scenes (*Figure 53*). Other maps were made in 1666 by Doornick and in 1673 by Blome, and later ones documenting the progress of the rebuilding, in 1676 by Ogilby and Morgan, and in 1682 by Morgan.

A number of revolutionary reconstruction plans for the City were submitted, by Christopher Wren, Robert Hooke and John Evelyn among others, any one of which if implemented would have given it a radically new look and feel, much more like that of the great European cities of the day such as Paris and Rome, with their broad boulevards and open piazzas. Evelyn wrote that 'In the disposure of the streets, due consideration should be had, what are the competent breadths for commerce and intercourse, cheerfulness and state' (*Figure 54*). But these plans were soon abandoned on the grounds of practicality and expediency in favour of one involving much less legal wrangling

53. The Hollar survey (1666).

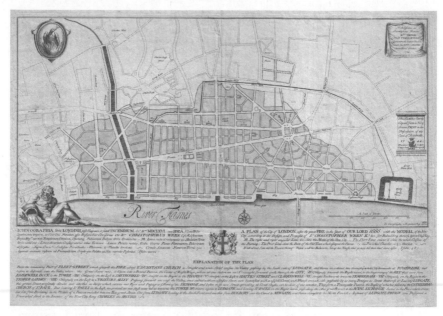

54. Wren's Plan for the Reconstruction of London (1666).

and groundwork, and a City much more like the old one. Note also that, according to the Earl of Clarendon, '[V]ery many, with more expedition than can be conceived, set up little sheds of brick and timber upon the ruins of their own houses, where they chose to inhabit rather than in more convenient places, though they knew they could not long reside in those new buildings.' So in some ways the City that might have been never came to be, and that which had been would come to be again: for the most part neither particularly beautiful nor harmonious, but rather, 'lived in' and fractious; and yet, familiar and loved.

The new City was to differ from the old one, though, in several important respects. The old narrow streets would become wider, designed simultaneously to hinder the spread of fire and unencumber the flow of traffic. In accordance with the aforementioned Royal Proclamation of 1666 and the 'Act for the Rebuilding of the City of London' of 1667 (further acts would follow in 1707, 1709 and 1774), old houses would be replaced by new ones of four categories of standard build, of fire-proof stone and brick rather than timber: those of the first category, fronting 'by-streets and lanes', of two storeys; those of the second category, fronting 'streets and lanes of note, and the Thames', of three storeys; those of the third category, fronting 'high and principal streets', of four storeys, with storey heights specified; and those of the fourth category, designed for' people of quality', also of four storeys, although with storey heights unspecified (McKellar, 1999). The old breeding-grounds for disease would be swept aside in the process, although incidentally rather than by design. As another incidental, the old organic economy would be replaced by a modern mineral economy, considerably ahead of its time, fuelled by sea-coal rather than wood.

The committee appointed by the Court and the City to oversee and implement the chosen reconstruction plan included the aforementioned Christopher Wren (1632-1723), the aforementioned Robert Hooke (1635-1703) and four others, Hugh May, Roger Pratt, Peter Mills and Edward Jerman (Wall, 1998). Wren was an architect and a member of an aristocratic family who had finally found favour in the Restoration, after years in the wilderness during the Protectorate and Commonwealth. He was also an anatomist and astronomer (one wonders whether he, like Sartre's autodidact, acquired his learning by reading an encyclopaedia, starting with the letter 'A'); a follower of the 'New Philosophy' of Francis Bacon; and an early member of the Royal Society. He was, in short, an archetypal Renaissance Man, and, most definitely, the right man, in the right place, at the right time – an unusually happy conjunction in the history of the City. Hooke was similarly an architect and surveyor. He was also a pioneer microscopist and polymath, although curmudgeonly as well as brilliant. In 1665, he published a book on his microscopical observations, described by Pepys as 'the most ingenious ... that ever I read in my life'.

Wren and his office set about their reconstruction work as speedily as practicable, so as to provide the City with the opportunity of re-establishing itself with the minimum of delay and loss. In all, they rebuilt forty-nine parish churches within and two immediately without the walls, that is, a little over half of those that had been destroyed in the Great Fire, together with St Paul's Cathedral, and also rebuilt numerous other public and private buildings, many in the – English – High Renaissance or Baroque style (*Figures 55, 31c, 32c*). Much of the rebuilding work was completed within a few short years; the cost covered by a tax on coal imposed by Act of Parliament (Baker, 2000). Samuel Pepys noted in his diary as early as 24 December 1666: ' So ... to the [rebuilt] Upper 'Change, which is almost as good as the old one; only shops are but on one side.'

Of the fifty-one churches by Wren, thirty are still standing, together with St Paul's Cathedral, and twenty-one are not. Of those lost, seventeen, far more than one might have hoped, were demolished on the orders of

55. Wren's Original Design – the so-called 'Warrant Design' – for St Paul's (1674).

our own town planners – in some cases justifiably, for safety reasons; in others, either for security reason, or to allow for site redevelopment; but some simply because they had been deemed under the incomprehensibly philistine Union of Benefices Act of 1860, to be surplus to requirements! Only four, far fewer than one might have feared, were destroyed during the Blitz, although a number were damaged to varying extents, some of which were subsequently restored and some left as empty shells (Ward, 2015). Two, St Mary Aldermanbury and St Stephen Coleman Street, were destroyed, and a number of others damaged on a single, fateful night, 29/30 December 1940, when tens of thousands of incendiary bombs were dropped on an essentially unguarded City. At least many of the original plans of these recently lost churches still survive, as do some later images, including photographs.

The most famous of Wren's many famous achievements was undoubtedly the reconstruction of St Paul's Cathedral, eventually completed after thirty-five years' work in 1710/1. The cathedral is faced in plain Portland Stone, wonderfully reflective of the City's light and mood. A staggering 66,000 tons of the stone was used to face St Paul's, having been quarried in Portland in Dorset and brought round the coast and up the Thames to London in barges. Portland Stone was also used in the construction of practically all the other churches rebuilt by Wren after the Great Fire. It was first used in London in the construction of the Banqueting House in Whitehall by Inigo Jones. St Paul's is crowned with that glorious dome, making it unique among all the cathedrals of England. The stone-work is by the Master Masons Joshua Marshall and the brothers Edward and Thomas Strong and their team, overseen by Grinling Gibbons; the wood-work by the Master Carpenter John Langland and his team, also overseen by Grinling Gibbons; and the *demi-grisaille* paintwork inside the dome by the Painter-Stainer James Thornhill and his team. Wren's simple epitaph inside the cathedral reads *Lector, si monumentum requiris, circumspice*, 'Reader, should you seek his memorial, look about you.' On the pediment above the south door is a stone bearing the image of a Phoenix rising from the ashes, together with the inscription *Resurgam*, 'I shall rise again' (a different stone bearing the same inscription had been found among the smouldering ruins of the old cathedral – a positive portent if ever there was one). And so, out of the ashes arose a new London.

Further Reading

Atkinson, 1985; Aubrey, 1696; Baker, 2000; Barker & Hyde, 1982; Beard, 1982; Birch, 1887; Campbell, 2007; Christopher, 2012; Cobb, 1942; Cooper, 2003; Cornell, 2011; de Mare, 1975; Davies, 2009; Dick, 1949; Downes, 1988; Elsden & Howe, 1923; Geraghty, 2007; Gilbert, 2002; Griffiths & Kesnerova, 1983; Hachman, 2014; Hollis, 2008; Hornak, 2016; Huelin, 1996; Hyde et al., 1992; Inwood, 2002; Jardine, 2002, 2003; Jeffery, 1996; Keene et al., 2004; Kent, 1947; McKellar, 1999; Saunders, 2012; Schofield, 2016; Smith, 1961; Stevenson, 2013; Telfer & Blackmore, 2017; Thomas, 1998; Thurley, 2013; Tindall, 2002; Tinniswood, 2001; Wall, 1998; Ward, 2015; Whinney, 1971.

Appendices

APPENDIX ONE – ROMAN LONDINIUM WALK

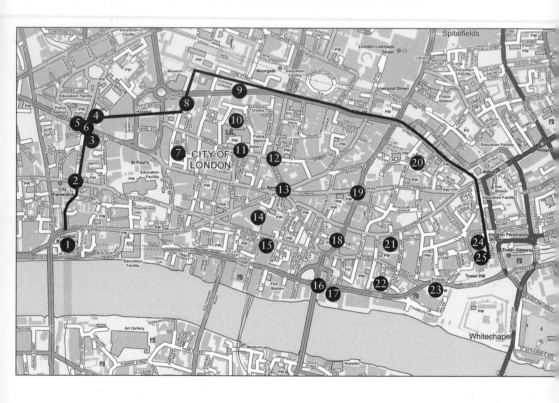

1 – Blackfriars
2 – Ludgate
3 – Central Criminal Court Building, junction of Old Bailey and Newgate Street
4 – Bank of America–Merrill Lynch Building, junction of Newgate Street and Giltspur Street
5 – Watling Street
6 – Newgate
7 – St Vedast–alias–Foster, Foster Lane
8 – Remains of Cripplegate Fort, Noble Street
9 – St Alphage Gardens, London Wall
10 – Remains of Amphitheatre, Guildhall
11 – Gresham Street
12 – Moorgate and Princes Street
13 – Poultry and Walbrook ('The Pompeii of the North')
14 – Remains of Temple of Mithras, Bloomberg Building, Walbrook
15 – Site of 'Governor's Palace', Cannon Street Station
16 – Old London Bridge (and Port of London)
17 – St Magnus the Martyr, Thames Street
18 – Ermine Street
19 – Remains of Basilica and Forum, Gracechurch Street
20 – Bury Street
21 – Fort, Plantation Place, Fenchurch Street
22 – Remains of Billingsgate Roman House, 101 Thames Street
23 – All Hallows Barking, Byward Street
24 – Site of Basilica or 'Palaeo–Christian' Church, Novotel Building, Pepys Street
25 – Cooper's Row and Tower Hill

Bold line indicates that of City wall.

Approximate distance 4.2 miles.
Start at Blackfriars tube.

1 – Blackfriars

The site of the discovery of the sunken Blackfriars I Barge, with its intact cargo of Kentish Ragstone, probably intended for use in the construction of the City wall (see Chapter Three). A little to the east is the site of the Temple of Isis, and a little further to the east, that of the Huggin Hill bath-house.

2 – Ludgate

The site of one of the seven gates in the City wall, built in the Roman period, rebuilt in the Medieval, and again in the post-Medieval, in 1586, damaged during the Great Fire, and demolished in 1760 (marked by a blue plaque). The gates were, clockwise from the west, Ludgate, Newgate, Aldersgate, Cripplegate, Moorgate, Bishopsgate and Aldgate. The wall was originally built at the turn of the second and third centuries (that is, around the time of the rival emperorships of and power-struggle between Clodius Albinus and Septimius Severus) and extended and reinforced in the late third, when a river wall was added, and in the mid fourth, when bastions were added (as defences against Saxon raids). It was originally twenty feet high, six to eight feet thick, and two miles long, and its construction involved the use of 85,000 tons of Kentish Rag, quarried near Maidstone and brought down the Medway and up the Thames to London on barges (see above). The best-preserved sections are around London Wall to the north-west and Tower Hill to the south-east (see below). A fragment is also preserved inside the church of St Martin Ludgate on Ludgate Hill.

3 – Central Criminal Court Building, junction of Old Bailey and Newgate Street

A section of City wall is preserved inside the Central Criminal Court building, popularly known as the 'Old Bailey'. It may be viewed by the public only by special arrangement.

4 – Bank of America-Merrill Lynch Building, junction of Newgate Street and Giltspur Street

Another section of City wall is preserved inside the Bank of America-Merrill Lynch building. It may be viewed by prior arrangement with BA-ML.

5 – Watling Street

The line of Watling Street is followed by Newgate Street.

6 – Newgate

The site of another of the gates in the City wall, built in the Roman period, rebuilt in the Saxon, and again in the Medieval, damaged in the Great Fire, and demolished in 1767 (marked by a blue plaque).

7 – St Vedast-alias-Foster, Foster Lane

The churchyard of St Vedast-alias-Foster contains, affixed to the wall, a surviving *ex situ* fragment of tessellated pavement discovered 18 ft below the floor of St Matthew Friday Street when it was demolished in 1886. A little to the east is the site of the Cheapside Bath-House (at Nos. 110-116).

8 – Remains of Cripplegate Fort, Noble Street

Originally built in the early second century, for a garrison of 1,500 infantry and cavalry troops, and subsequently incorporated into the City wall at the turn of the second and third. A further – substantial – portion of the fort, including the west gate, is preserved in the underground car park at the north end of the street. It may be viewed by prior arrangement with the Museum of London. A little to the west is is the site of another of the gates in the City wall, Aldersgate (marked by a blue plaque). Aldersgate was probably built in the late Roman period, rebuilt in the Medieval and again in 1617, damaged in the Great Fire and demolished in 1761. A little to the east is the site of Cripplegate (marked by a blue plaque). Cripplegate was built in the Roman period, rebuilt in the Medieval and demolished in 1760. The name became popularly understood to refer to a legend that cripples could be cured by sleeping in the gateway. In fact, it derives from the Old English *crepyl-geat*, meaning a low gate, literally for creeping through.

9 – St Alphage Gardens, London Wall
The site of a surviving section of city wall.

10 – Remains of Amphitheatre, Guildhall
Originally built in timber in the late first century, *c.* 75, rebuilt in stone in the second and renovated in the late second to third before being abandoned in the fourth, and only coming to light again during excavations in 1987. Surviving portions, some 20 ft below modern street level, may be viewed in the basement of the Guildhall Art Gallery (check opening times).

11 – Gresham Street
The site of a number of Romano-British round-houses, and of two Roman 'water-lifting machines'. A little to the north, at the junction of Moorgate and London Wall, is the site of another of the gates in the City wall, Moorgate (marked by a blue plaque). Moorgate was built in 1415 by the then- Mayor of London, Thomas Falconer and rebuilt in 1672 and demolished in 1762. There was a postern gate here in the Roman period.

12 – Moorgate and Princes Street
The area of the discovery of large numbers of so-called 'Walbrook skulls' (the streets more or less follow the line of the Walbrook, a tributary of the Thames debouching at Dowgate). It is likely that some of the skulls originated in the Roman burial ground north of the City wall in Moorfields and that they were subsequently naturally transported and deposited to the south by the waters of the Walbrook,

in the process becoming hydrodynamically sorted from their skeletons (Ranieri & Telfer, 2017). Some others, though, appear to have been deliberately placed in pits and, moreover, exhibit evidence of blunt- or sharp-force trauma, and these could be victims of gladiatorial combat, of judicial execution, or perhaps of ritual decapitation. Alternatively, they could be those of victims of the Boudiccan Revolt of 60-1, or the Carausian Revolt of 296. Or possibly of a native British uprising during the Hadrianic emperorship of 117-38, referred to by Marcus Cornelius Fronto in a letter to Marcus Aurelius, in a letter dated 162: 'under the rule of your grandfather Hadrian what a number of soldiers were killed by the ... Britons.'

13 – Poultry and Walbrook ('The Pompeii of the North')
The area of the discovery of an entire Roman waterfront, of entire streets of Roman houses, and of many, many thousands of associated artefacts, including those made of organic materials, perfectly preserved in the anaerobic sediments of the Walbrook.

14 – Remains of Temple of Mithras, Bloomberg Building, Walbrook
Originally built in the early third century, *c.* 220-40 and abandoned in the fourth when Christianity came to replace paganism throughout the Roman Empire, the remains only coming to light again during rebuilding after the Blitz. Restored portions may be viewed in the basement of the Bloomberg Building (advance booking is advisable, although not always necessary). Some of the finds from the recent archaeological excavations on and around the site may be viewed in the atrium. Other finds from the original post-war dig, including a marble bust of Mithras in his distinctive Phrygian cap, may be viewed in the Roman gallery in the Museum of London.

15 – Site of 'Governor's Palace', Cannon Street Station
Originally built during the Flavian period of the late first century, *c.* 69-96, on the then-waterfront, and in use throughout the second and third before being demolished in the late third or fourth, the remains only coming to light again during the nineteenth. Opposite, at 111 Cannon Street, is the so-called 'London Stone', which some believe to be associated in some way with the 'Governor's Palace' (it has been postulated, plausibly, that it served as a *milliarium*, or centre-stone, from which Roman roads radiated and distances were

measured). The 'London Stone' is carved out of Clipsham Stone from Rutland, which is known to have been used for construction in Roman times.

16 – 'Old London Bridge' (and Port of London)
A little to the east of the present London Bridge is the site of the Roman one, originally built in timber in *c.* 50, in stone and timber in *c.* 90 and rebuilt many, many times in the succeeding nearly two millennia.

The Roman port lay either side of the bridge. Tiles stamped *CLBR* have been found in London, suggesting at least some link between the port and the *Classis Britannica* or 'British fleet', which was the part of the Roman imperial navy responsible for supplying the province of Britannia with personnel and materiel. Foodstuffs were brought here by boat from all around the Empire, in pottery *amphorae*. Pottery, notably Samian ware, was also brought in from Gaul; brooches from Belgium; amber from the Baltic; millstones from the Rhineland; decorative marble, bronze table-ware and lamps from Italy; marble also from Greece and Turkey; glassware from Syria; and emeralds from Egypt. Slaves were also brought into London, to be sold at markets like those known to have existed on the waterfront, and then put to work. On the south side of the bridge is Southwark, which takes its name from the Old English *suth* and *weorc*, meaning defensive work or fort, in reference to the Roman defences south of the river. Borough High Street there is part of, and was once known as, Stane Street, the Roman road to the south. Interestingly, at least one woman buried in the southern cemetery in Southwark has been determined on morphometric and isotopic evidence to have been of African origin and a further two individuals to have come from the Han Empire in what is now China.

17 – St Magnus the Martyr, Thames Street
The churchyard of St Magnus contains a surviving *ex situ* fragment of timber from the Roman wharf purporting to date to 78, but in fact recently shown on tree-ring evidence to date to 62, i.e., the year after the destruction of Roman Londinium during the Boudiccan Revolt.

18 – Ermine Street
The line of Ermine Street is followed by Fish Street Hill, Gracechurch Street and Bishopsgate.

19 – Remains of Basilica and Forum, Gracechurch Street
Built in *c.* 70, and rebuilt and considerably extended in *c.* 100-30, before being substantially demolished in *c.* 300, only coming to light again during excavations at 168 Fenchurch Street in 1995-2000. A surviving pier base from the basilica may be seen in the basement of No. 90 Gracechurch Street. A little to the north is the site of another of the gates in the City wall, Bishopsgate. Bishopsgate was built in the Roman period, rebuilt in the Saxon by Erkenwald, the Bishop of London from 675-93, and again in the Medieval, and demolished in 1760. According to tradition, Erkenwald exacted a tax of one stick from all carts bringing wood into the City through the gate.

20 – Bury Street
The site of the burial of a young girl discovered during the building of 30 St Mary Axe, marked by a plaque bearing the inscription *Dis Manibus Puella Incognita Londiniensis Hic Sepulta Est* (to the spirit of an unknown girl of Roman London, who is buried here). In general, burials took place outside the City walls, for example, just outside Aldgate, Bishopsgate or Newgate, or beside the Walbrook in Moorfields, or south of the Thames in Southwark. One particular Roman woman was buried in Spitalfields, just outside Bishopsgate to the north, in a decorated lead coffin inside a plain stone sarcophagus, resting on a bed of laurel leaves, shrouded in damask silk interwoven with gold thread, and accompanied by further high-status grave goods. Isotopic evidence from her teeth indicates that she may actually have come from the imperial capital of Rome itself.

21 – Fort, Plantation Place, Fenchurch Street
Built immediately after the Boudiccan Revolt, in *c.* 63, and possibly out of use by 70. A little to the east is the site of the easternmost of the gates in the City wall, Aldgate. Aldgate was built in the Roman period, rebuilt at least twice in the Medieval and again in 1607, and demolished in 1760.

22 – Remains of Billingsgate Roman House, 101 Thames Street
Originally built in the late second to third centuries, remaining in use until the end of the fourth, before becoming abandoned in the early fifth, only coming to light again during the construction of the Coal Exchange in the nineteenth. Surviving portions, including a bath-house

with tepidarium (warm bath), caldarium (hot bath) and frigidarium (cold bath), may be viewed on guided tours organised by the Museum of London. The tours run at 11:00, 12:00 and 1:00 on Saturdays (spring, summer and autumn only).

23 – All Hallows Barking, Byward Street
The church of All Hallows Barking contains a number of Roman exhibits in its crypt, including an *in situ* portion of tessellated pavement. Also a fine dioramic reconstruction of Roman London (made before the Amphitheatre was discoved).

24 – Site of Basilica or 'Palaeo-Christian' Church, Novotel Building, Pepys Street
Built sometime in the fourth century.

25 – Cooper's Row and Tower Hill
The site of another – substantial – surviving section of City wall.

Finish at Tower Hill tube.

APPENDIX TWO – SAXON LUNDENBURG WALK

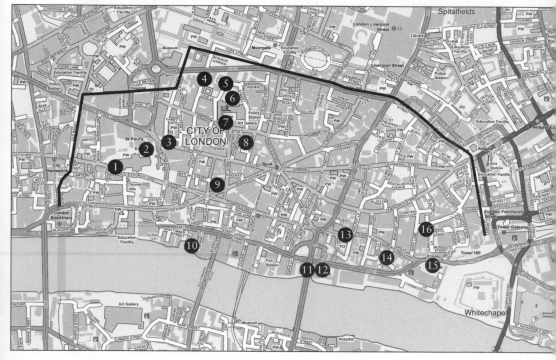

1 – St Paul's Cathedral
2 – (St) Paul's Cross
3 – Cheapside
4 – St Alban Wood Street
5 – Aldermanbury
6 – Guildhall
7 – St Lawrence Jewry, Gresham Street
8 – St Olave Jewry, Ironmonger Lane
9 – St Mary Aldermary, Watling Street
10 – Queenhithe

11 – Old London Bridge (and Port of London)
12 – St Magnus the Martyr, Thames Street
13 – Eastcheap
14 – St Dunstan–in–the–East, St Dunstan's Hill (off Great Tower Street)
15 – All Hallows Barking, Byward Street
16 – St Olave Hart Street

Bold line indicates that of City wall.

Approximate distance 2.5 miles.
Start at St Paul's tube.

1 – St Paul's Cathedral

There have been five cathedrals on the site of the present St Paul's. The first was built in 604, shortly after the first Christian mission under St Augustine landed in Kent, by the King of Kent, Ethelburg, for the Bishop of London, Mellitus, and destroyed by fire in 675. The second, 'The Church of Paulesbyri', was built between 675-85 by the Bishop Erkenwald and destroyed by the Vikings in 961. The third was built in 961, and destroyed by fire in 1087. An eleventh-century grave-slab decorated in the Viking Ringerike style and bearing a Viking Runic inscription has been found in the graveyard.

2 – (St) Paul's Cross
Built in the grounds of St Paul's Cathedral in around 1191, and demolished by order of Parliament during the Civil War, in 1643 (the statue that stands on the site today is a replica, built in 1910). Thought to have been built on the site where the Saxons held their *folkmoot*, or outdoor assembly.

3 – Cheapside
First recorded as *Westceap* in around 1100, although evidently already in existence in Saxon times, in the late ninth to tenth centuries. Takes its name from the Old English *ceap*, meaning market. A great open-air market was situated here, in what was in effect the High Street of the City, in Medieval times, where all manner of goods could be procured. At the eastern end of Cheapside, the lines of Cornhill and Leadenhall Street, also in existence in Saxon times, swing to the north and Lombard Street and Fenchurch Street to the south of the Roman Basilica and Forum.

4 – St Alban Wood Street
Originally built in the eleventh century, on the site of an eighth-century chapel believed to have been attached to the palace of the Mercian King Offa.

5 – Aldermanbury
First recorded in around 1124 as *Aldremanesburi*, from the Old English *ealdorman* (meaning, originally, shire officer eligible to take part in Parliament or *Witan*), and *burh*, meaning manor, in reference to this being the place where the Saxons held their *husting*, or indoor assembly.

6 – Guildhall
Originally built sometime before 1128, possibly on the site of an even older building, where the Saxons held their *husting*.

7 – St Lawrence Jewry, Gresham Street
Originally built in the Saxon period (wood from a coffin in the churchyard has yielded a dendrochronological date of 1046).

8 – St Olave Jewry, Ironmonger Lane

Probably originally built in the eleventh century, sometime after the martyrdom of Olave in 1030. This is only one of a number of City churches dedicated to Olave, a Norwegian who fought alongside the English against the Danish Vikings (see under 'London Bridge' below).

9 – St Mary Aldermary, Watling Street

Originally built at least as long ago as the late eleventh century, being older than the church of St Mary-le-Bow, which was completed in 1087 (hence the name). Schofield (1994) suggests that it was already established perhaps by 1020.

10 – Queenhithe

First recorded in 898 as *Aetheredes hyd*, Ethe(l)red being Alfred the Great's son-in-law. Recent archaeological excavations in Queenhithe have unearthed the skeletons of two Saxon women, one of them radio-carbon dated to 680?-810; together with re-used timbers from an arcaded 'aisled hall', likely to have been a royal palace, dendrochronologically dated to 956-79. One of the women would appear to have been executed by a blow from a bladed weapon, the other by deliberate drowning. Evidently also in the vicinity in the time of Alfred in the late ninth century were the London residences of the Archbishop of Canterbury and the Bishop of Worcester, the latter a stone building previously known as 'Hwaetmunde's Stan' (possibly a surviving part of the Roman bath-house on Huggin Hill).

11 – 'Old London Bridge' (and Port of London)

A little to the east of the present London Bridge is the site of the previous one, originally built in the Roman period, and rebuilt many, many times in the succeeding nearly two millennia. According to the Norse 'Olaf Sagas', in 1014 the Norwegian Viking Olaf, Olav or Olave Haraldsson, an ally of the English King Ethelred 'The Unready', in his fight against the Danish Vikings, destroyed the Saxon incarnation of the bridge – and the Danish Viking army assembled on it – by pulling it down with ropes tied to his long-boats. The court poet Ottar Svarte wrote, in the eleventh century, and Snorri Sturluson rewrote, in the thirteenth: 'London Bridge is broken down./Gold is won, and bright renown./Shields resounding, war-horns sounding,/ Hild is shouting in the din!/Arrows singing, mail-coats ringing –/

Odin makes our Olaf win!' Many believe this ode to be the origin of the much-loved nursery-rhyme 'London Bridge is falling down'. Olaf later converted to Christianity, and, as King Olaf II, introduced the religion to Norway in 1015. He went on to martyredom fighting heathen Danish Vikings at the Battle of Stiklestad in 1030, and to be canonised by the English Bishop of Selsey, Grimkell or Grimketel in 1031 (the local canonisation was later confirmed by Pope Alexander III in 1164). In the later Middle Ages, his tomb, in the most northerly cathedral in Christendom, in Nidaros (Trondheim), became an important pilgrimage site and the centre of a widespread 'cult of Olav'. The late Saxon port lay to either side of the bridge (the early Saxon port of Lundenwic lay a little further upstream). Goods were brought in here by boat from all around northern Europe, including the Low Countries and Scandinavia, and also, in the case of precious stones, gold, silk and other luxuries, even further afield. On the south side of the bridge is Southwark. What was later to become Southwark Cathedral was originally built there as a nunnery in 606, somewhat to the west of the southern bridge-head. The parish church of St Olave Southwark was built there, immediately to the east of the southern bridge-head, at least as long ago as 1086, being mentioned in *Domesday*.

12 – St Magnus the Martyr, Thames Street
Originally built immediately to the east of the northern bridge-head probably in the twelfth century. Magnus Erlendsson, the piously Christian Viking Earl of Orkney, was murdered by heathen Vikings in 1117 or 1118, and made a saint in 1135. Among the many treasures inside the church are a modern statue and stained-glass window depicting St Magnus in a horned Viking helmet.

13 – Eastcheap
First recorded, as *Eastceape*, in around 1100, although evidently already in existence in Saxon times. Takes its name from the Old English *ceap*, meaning market.

14 – St Dunstan-in-the-East, St Dunstan's Hill (off Great Tower Street)
Originally built at least as long ago as the twelfth century, high-quality carved stonework of this age and possibly from this site having recently been discovered in nearby Harp Lane The sometime Bishop

of London and Archbishop of Canterbury Dunstan, who famously founded Westminster Abbey in 960, died in 988 and was canonised in 1029.

15 – All Hallows Barking, Byward Street
Originally built by Ethelburga, Abbess of Barking and sister of Bishop Erkenwald in the Saxon period. A fine stone arch possibly as old as the late seventh century, *c.* 675, incorporating Roman tiles survives in the nave; and in the crypt, two stone crosses, one of 900 and the other of 1000, the former plain and simple and bearing a Saxon Runic inscription, the latter beautifully and intricately carved, and bearing a symbolic depiction of Christ over beasts, a characteristic of 'Dark Age' iconography. In one of the chapels leading off the crypt is a so-called 'Pluteus Stone' featuring two Peacocks drinking from the Fountain of Life, thought to have come from an Eastern Orthodox Church in the Byzantine region and tentatively dated to sometime in the late eleventh century (the 'East-West Schism' took place in 1054). There is an almost identical one in the iconostasis in the church of Santa Maria dell'Assunta, otherwise known as Torcello Cathedral, on the island of Torcello in the Veneto in Italy.

16 – St Olave Hart Street
Originally built in wood in the eleventh century, sometime after the canonisation of St Olave in 1031. This is one of the many London churches dedicated to Olave, the others being St Nicholas Olave, St Olave Broad Street, St Olave Jewry and St Olave Silver Street in the City, St Olave in Southwark, and St Olave in Rotherhithe.

Finish at Tower Hill tube.

APPENDIX THREE – MEDIEVAL CITY OF LONDON WALK

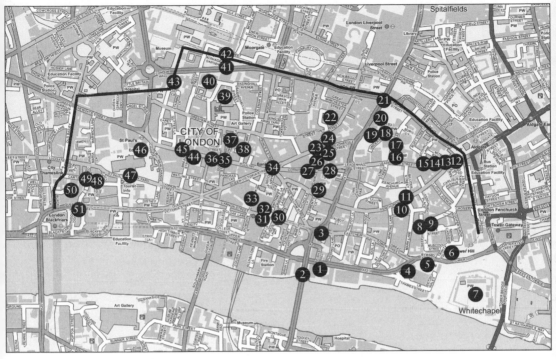

1	– St Magnus the Martyr, Thames Street	22	– Austin Friars, off Old Broad Street
2	– Old London Bridge (and Port of London)	23	– Threadneedle Street
3	– Eastcheap	24	– Site of St Anthony's Hospital, 53 Threadneedle Street
4	– Custom House, Thames Street	25	– Merchant Taylors' Hall, 30 Threadneedle Street
5	– All Hallows Barking, Byward Street		
6	– Tower Hill	26	– Site of St Benet Fink, Royal Exchange Avenue
7	– Tower of London		
8	– St Olave Hart Street	27	– Cornhill
9	– Crutched Friars	28	– St Michael Cornhill
10	– All Hallows Staining, Mark Lane	29	– Lombard Street
11	– Fenchurch Street	30	– Cannon Street
12	– Aldgate	31	– London Stone, 111 Cannon Street
13	– Leadenhall Street	32	– Catrin Glyndwr memorial, St. Swithun's Church Garden, Salter's Hall Court/Oxford Court
14	– Remains of Holy Trinity Priory, 76 Leadenhall Street		
15	– St Katharine Cree, Leadenhall Street	33	– Walbrook
16	– St Andrew Undershaft, St Mary Axe	34	– Poultry
17	– Site of church of St Mary Axe	35	– Cheapside
18	– St Helen Bishopsgate, Great St Helens	36	– Site of Cheapside Conduit, 80B Cheapside
19	– Site of Crosby Hall, Crosby Square	37	– Ironmonger Lane
20	– St Ethelburga Bishopsgate	38	– Old Jewry
21	– Bishopsgate	39	– Guildhall, Guildhall Yard

40 – Site of Aldermanbury Conduit,
Aldermanbury Square
41 – Elsing Spital
42 – St Alphage Gardens
43 – Noble Street
44 – St Mary-le-Bow, or Bow Church,
Cheapside
45 – Site of Cheapside Cross, Cheapside/
Wood Street
46 – (St) Paul's Cross, St Paul's
Churchyard

47 – St Paul's Cathedral
48 – Site of Royal Wardrobe, Wardrobe
Place, off Carter Lane
49 – Site of First Barnard's Castle,
St Andrew's Hill
50 – Remains of Blackfriars Priory,
Ireland Yard
51 – Site of Second Baynard's Castle,
Queen Victoria Street

Bold line indicates that of City wall.

Approximate distance 4 miles.
Start at the Fish Street Hill exit to Monument tube.

1 – St Magnus the Martyr, Thames Street

Probably originally built in the twelfth century. Magnus, Earl of Orkney, was martyred sometime between 1115 and 1118 and made a saint in 1135. Burned down in the Great Fire and rebuilt by Wren in 1671-87, and, despite eighteenth- to twentieth- century modifications and restorations, retains much of the 'inexplicable splendour of Ionian white and gold' alluded to by T.S. Eliot in his 1922 poem 'The Waste Land'. Henry Yevele (*c.* 1320-1400), who was the master mason to three successive Kings, Edward III, Richard II and Henry IV, *c.* 1360-1400, during which time he either built or rebuilt large parts of Westminster Abbey and the Palace of Westminster, is buried here. Among the many treasures inside the church is a modern scale-model of the bridge as it would have looked in its heyday. On the outside wall is a blue plaque marking the approach to the bridge.

2 – 'Old London Bridge' (and Port of London)

A little to the east of the present London Bridge is the site of the previous one, originally built in the Roman period, and rebuilt many, many times. The famous Medieval to post-Medieval incarnation of the bridge was originally built by Peter, chaplain of St Mary Colechurch, *c.* 1176-1209 and stood until 1831, although it had to be repaired a number of times over the centuries, and was extensively refurbished in the eighteenth. There were scores of buildings on the bridge, including a great many shops and a chapel dedicated to St Thomas Becket (it was on the pilgrimage route to Canterbury, where Archbishop Becket was the victim of the infamous 'Murder in the Cathedral' in 1170). It also had a total of nineteen arches or 'starlings', through which many of the more devil-may-care watermen would attempt to row in a dangerous practice known as 'shooting the bridge', some unfortunately losing their lives in the process. William Gregory wrote in his '*Chronicle of London*' of such an incident that took place in around 1428: 'The vii day of Novembyr the Duke of Northfolke wolde have rowed thoroughe the brygge of London, and hys barge was rente agaynste the arche of the sayde bridge, and there were drowned many men, the number of xxx personys ... of gentylmen and good yemen.' There was wisdom in the adage that 'London Bridge was made for wise men to go over, and fools to go under'! At the southern end of the bridge the heads of executed criminals were impaled on spikes. A friendly joust was held on the bridge on St George's Day, 1390 in the presence of the Richard II, between the Englishman Lord Welles and the Scotsman Sir David Lindsay. According to Hector Boece: 'At the sound of the trumpets the two champions hurled themselves at each other, and either splintered his lance without effect in dismounting his adversary. Welles had directed his spear at his opponent's head and hit him fairly on the visor, but the Scottish champion kept his seat so steadily that some of the spectators ... shouted out that Lindsay had strapped himself to his saddle. Thereupon the gallant Scot proved his honesty by vaulting to the ground and on to his horse's back again in his heavy armour. A second course followed with equal fortune, but at the third Welles was fairly overthrown. The victor at once dismounted, and in the best spirit went to assist his fallen opponent [and] never failed to call daily upon him during such time as he was confined to bed by the bruises and the severe shock of the fall.'

The Medieval port lay to either side of the bridge. A prodigious range of comestible and manufactured goods was imported there, from all over the known Old World, from the the lands bordering the English Channel, North Sea and Baltic, and further afield, from those bordering the north-east Atlantic and Mediterranean, or linked to the latter by the Silk or Spice Routes. Wool and finished woollen cloth were the most important exports, chiefly to the Low Countries, and the trade was enormously lucrative (sheepskins and other animal hides, food-stuffs, and Cornish tin were also exported). The trade with the ports on the coasts of the North Sea and Baltic came to be controlled by an alliance called the Hanseatic League, which was formally founded in 1241. The Hanseatic League had its London headquarters at the so-called Steelyard, which was essentially a semi-autonomous enclave of Germany. The Steelyard was burned down in the Great Fire of 1666, although rebuilt afterwards, only to be demolished in 1855, to make way for Cannon Street Station. On the south side of the bridge is Southwark, in the Middle Ages the site of a number of churches and religious houses, of Winchester Palace, the London residence of the Bishops of Winchester, and of a number of inns catering to pilgrims travelling to or from the shrine of St Thomas Becket in Canterbury Cathedral. Because Southwark was at this time a 'liberty', free of many of the regulations governing life in the City across the river, it became the site of a number of 'stews' or brothels. Many of the prostitutes ended up being buried, alongside the other 'Outcast Dead', in the unconsecrated burial ground known as 'Crossbones Graveyard' (on Redcross Way). Over time, Southwark became one of the poor places in which the rich City attempted to locate – and forget – some of its other 'undesirable' buildings, including prisons, and activities, including in the post-Medieval period not only prostitution but also animal-baiting and the performance of stage plays (which attracted large and unruly crowds).

A great fire in Southwark in 1212 reportedly killed thousands of people, many of them trapped on the bridge. According to a near-contemporary account: 'An exceeding great multitude of people passing the Bridge, either to extinguish or quench it, or else to gaze at and behold it, suddenly the north part, by blowing of the south wind, was also set on fire, and the people which were even now passing the Bridge, perceiving the same, would have returned, but were stopped by the fire.' The fire badly damaged the recently built bridge, leaving it only partially usable for years afterwards and necessitating a partial rebuild. It also damaged Southwark Cathedral, necessitating a partial rebuild. Some of the masonry used in the rebuilding of the cathedral was salvaged from the fire debris and shows signs of fire damage.

3 – Eastcheap

The site of the one of the principal markets in the City in the Middle Ages, where livestock would have been brought for slaughter, to be butchered and sold. The street would have been evil-smelling, and exceedingly unpleasant underfoot – whence the invention of the 'patten', the platform sole of the day (recalled in the name of the church of St Margaret Pattens).

4 – Custom House, Thames Street

Originally built at least as long ago as 1377, in Billingsgate, close to the centre of activity on the waterfront, its purpose being to collect the duties payable on exports of wool, and subsequently rebuilt following a fire, in 1559. Geoffrey Chaucer worked in the Custom House, as the 'Comptroller of the Customs and Subside of Wools, Skins and Tanned Hides', 1374-86. In the course of his work he would have met travellers from all over the country and continent, including those undertaking the pilgrimage to the shrine of Thomas Becket in Canterbury Cathedral, some of them perhaps providing inspiration for the colourful characters he wrote about in *The Canterbury Tales*, which was issued in 1387.

5 – All Hallows Barking, Byward Street

Originally built by Ethelburga, Abbess of Barking and sister of Bishop Erkenwald, in the Saxon period and considerably added to in the later Medieval and post-Medieval. The trials of certain Knights Templar took place in the church in 1311. Among the many surviving Medieval features here are an undercroft chapel and an altar table of stone salvaged by the Knights Templar from the thirteenth-century Crusaders' castle at At(h)lit below Mount Carmel in the Holy Land; numerous monuments, including brasses to William Tong (d. 1389) and John Bacon (d. 1437), and a canopied tomb to John Croke (d. 1477); a fine Flemish painted panelled altar-piece, known as the Tate Panel, dating to at least the fifteenth century; and numerous sculptures, including a carved wooden one of St James of Compostela, dating to the fifteenth century.

6 – Tower Hill

The site of public executions in the Middle Ages. Among those executed here were Robert Hales, who was the Lord High Treasurer and Simon Sudbury, the Archbishop of Canterbury, both during the Peasants' Revolt of 1381. Somewhat to the east, in East Smithfield, is the recently excavated 'plague pit' in which many victims of the Black Death of 1348-49 were buried Grainger & Phillpotts, 2011).

7 – Tower of London

Originally built under William I, William II and Henry I in the late eleventh to earliest twelfth century (the keep), added to by Henry III in the late thirteenth (the inner curtain wall), Edward I in the late thirteenth to early fourteenth (outer curtain wall), and a succession of later kings and queens, many of whom used it as a royal residence, through to the seventeenth. The chapel of St Peter ad Vincula within is arguably of even older, Saxon origin. The Tower features in the earliest known painting of London, by an unknown artist, dating to the late fifteenth century, and commissioned to illustrate a book of poems written by Charles, Duc d'Orleans, who was imprisoned here for twenty-five years after his capture at the Battle of Agincourt in 1415. Hundreds were imprisoned here over the centuries; and scores were tortured and/or executed in a variety of horrible ways. The remarkable menagerie established here in the thirteenth century was eventually closed down in the nineteenth by the then Constable of the Tower, the Duke of Wellington, who did not want it interfering with military matters any longer. The animals were rehomed in Regent's Park, in what was to become the zoo there.

8 – St Olave Hart Street, corner of Hart Street and Seething Lane
Originally built in wood in the eleventh century, sometime after the canonisation of St Olave in 1031. Subsequently rebuilt in stone in the late twelfth to early thirteenth century, and again around 1450, and extended in the sixteenth to seventeenth. Undamaged in the Great Fire, but damaged by bombing on the last night of the continuous Blitz, 10/11 May, 1941, and rebuilt again in the post-war period (1951-4). The thirteenth-century crypt, some thirteenth- and fifteenth- century walls and the fifteenth-century tower survive. In the late fourteenth century, one Robert Knollys, a soldier, and his wife Constance, who lived nearby, on Seething Lane, were made to pay a token fine to the Mayor, William Walworth, in the form of an annual floral tribute, for undertaking some building work without having previously sought what at the time passed for planning permission. Quaintly, the practice continues to this day, as the 'Knollys' Rose Ceremony', with the Master of the Company of Watermen and Lightermen of the River Thames, accompanied by a guard of honour formed by the Doggett's Badge winners, picking a single red rose from Seething Lane Garden and presenting it to the Mayor at the Mansion House, every June (on the occasion of the Feast of St John the Baptist).

9 – Crutched Friars

Named after the Augustinian Friars of the Holy Cross, also known as the *fratres cruciferi* or, in Middle English, *crouched freres*, established here under Ralph Hosiar and William Sabernes in the late thirteenth century.

10 – All Hallows Staining, Mark Lane

Originally built around 1177 and rebuilt in the fourteenth or fifteenth century (sources differ). Undamaged in the Great Fire, most of the church fell down in 1671, due to undermining of the foundations by – mostly plague – burials, and it had to be rebuilt in 1674-5 before being substantially demolished in 1870, when the parish was merged with St Olave Hart Street. The fourteenth- or fifteenth- century tower still stands, thanks to the initiative of the Clothworkers' Company, who were also responsible for restoring it in 1873. The foundations are original, twelfth-century. The crypt is also twelfth-century, although it has been transported from its original location in the chapel of St James-in-the-Wall.

11 – Fenchurch Street

First recorded as *Fancherchestrate* in 1283, although evidently already in existence in Saxon times. Takes its name from the nearby church of St Gabriel, now no longer standing, and the nearby 'fen' or marshy ground of the Langborne or Langbourn. Rather wonderfully, the surrounding ward was once known as 'Langbourn and Fennie About'.

12 – Aldgate

The site of one of the seven gates in the City wall, originally built in the Roman period, and subsequently rebuilt at least twice in the Medieval, and again in 1607 before being eventually demolished in 1760 (marked by a blue plaque). Geoffrey Chaucer is known to have lived in the gate-house 1374-86, and would have worked from there to his then place of work in the Custom House in Billingsgate (see above). Somewhat to the north, on Aldgate High Street, stands the Hoop and Grapes public house, originally built as a private house in 1290.

13 – Leadenhall Street

First recorded in 1605, although evidently already in existence in Saxon to Medieval times. Takes its name from the lead-roofed manor house of the Neville family that stood here in the thirteenth and fourteenth centuries (Milne, 1992). The building was converted into a market by Hugh Neville in 1309, acquired by Dick Whittington after the death of Alice Neville in 1394, and given by him to the City in 1411. It was rebuilt as a market and 'garner' (grain-store) by John Croxton in 1440-55, at the instigation of the sometime Mayor, Simon Eyre, before being damaged in the Great Fire and eventually demolished in stages 1793-1812. The present Leadenhall Market, at the junction of Leadenhall Street and Gracechurch Street, was built by Horace Jones in 1880-81.

14 – Remains of Holy Trinity Priory, 76 Leadenhall Street
Holy Trinity Priory was originally founded by the secular priests known as the Canons of Augustine in around 1108, on the site of an even older, eleventh-century parish church; added to 1197-1221 and rebuilt in the years up to 1350, only to be voluntarily dissolved in 1532 (Schofield & Lea, 2005). After the Dissolution, the site came to be owned initially by Sir Thomas Audley, subsequently by the Duke of Norfolk (whence, nearby 'Duke's Place'), and finally by the City. There is some surviving stonework from the priory, including a fine probably fifteenth-century arch from 'Chapel 2', inside No. 76 Leadenhall Street.

15 – St Katharine Cree, Leadenhall Street
Originally built in around 1280-1303, and rebuilt between 1500-4, in the Late Gothic style, and again between 1628 and1631, this time in the Renaissance style. Undamaged by the Great Fire, although later requiring restoration in 1878-79, and again, after being damaged in the Blitz. The tower dates to 1500-1504, the porch to 1628-31, and the gateway to the churchyard on Mitre Street by William Avenon to 1631. The interior contains some Late Gothic elements, such as the east window, in the form of an elaborately stylised Catherine wheel, and the intricately ribbed ceiling; and some Renaissance ones, such as the Corinthian columns in the nave.

16 – St Andrew Undershaft, St Mary Axe
Originally built in the twelfth century, rebuilt in the fourteenth and again, in the Perpendicular Gothic style, around 1520-32. Undamaged both in the Great Fire and in the Blitz, although the seventeenth-century stained-glass windows were destroyed by an IRA bomb in 1992.

17 – Site of Church of St Mary Axe

Built around 1197, and suppressed as idolatrous in 1561. According to one contemporary account, the church was the home of an unusual superstitious relic, namely 'one of the two [axes] that the eleven thousand Virgins [accompanying St Ursula on her ill-fated pan-European pilgrimage] were beheaded with [by a Hunnish chief, possibly Attila]' (Wheatley & Cunningham, 1891). Its site is marked by a blue plaque.

18 – St Helen Bishopsgate, Great St Helens

The original parish church dates back to the eleventh century, possibly around 1010, the later Benedictine nunnery, built immediately alongside to the left, to around 1210, and later rebuilds, additions and embellishments to the fourteenth through early seventeenth. The nunnery was suppressed in 1538, whereupon the nunnery church was incorporated into the parish church, and the remaining nunnery buildings and land were given to Thomas Cromwell's adopted son Richard Wyllyams, who sold them to the Leathersellers' Company. Undamaged by the Great Fire, although nonetheless requiring to be restored in 1893, only to be damaged by IRA bombs in 1992 and 1993 and restored again in 1993-5. The church is dubbed 'The Westminster Abbey of the City' because of the beauty of its interior and the richness of its memorials. The alabaster effigies of Sir John de Oteswich and his wife, salvaged from the church of St Martin Outwich, are from the late fourteenth or early fifteenth century. Numerous other monuments date from the fifteenth to seventeenth centuries, including that of the wealthy grocer and sometime Sheriff Sir John Crosby (d. 1476), who lived nearby, in Crosby Hall. Crosby had been knighted in 1471 for his role in the City's defence during the so-called 'Bastard Fauconberg's assault' (one of the actions of the Wars of the Roses) and is represented in armour. The arcade separating the former nuns' quire from the nave dates to 1475. The exterior is substantially thirteenth-century, although both west front doors are later replacements. The construction of the church made use of much Roman dressed stone and tile, most likely sourced either from a Roman building that was once on the site or from the City wall that once stood a short distance away. Helen was the mother of the first Christian Roman Emperor, Constantine.

19 – Site of Crosby Hall, Crosby Square

Originally built by Sir John Crosby (see above) 1466-75, and described by John Stow in his *Survay of London* of 1598 as 'very large and beautiful'. Survived the Great Fire. Relocated stone-by-stone to Cheyne Walk in Chelsea in 1909, where it may still be seen to this day. There are some wonderfully evocative old black-and-white photographs of the Hall in its original location in 1907 in Philip Davies' 'haunting and heartbreaking' book *Lost London* (English Heritage, 2009).

20 – St Ethelburga Bishopsgate

Originally built in around 1250, possibly on the site of an even older Saxon church, extended in 1390 and again in the fifteenth and sixteenth centuries. Undamaged in the Great Fire, although nonetheless restored in 1861-2, and again, by Ninian Comper, in 1912, and described by Nairn in 1966 as 'one of the sweetest things in the City'. Severely damaged by an IRA bomb on 24 April, 1993 and substantially rebuilt and reopened in 2002 as a Centre for Peace and Reconciliation, focussing on the role of faith in conflict resolution. The west front was rebuilt using stone from the Medieval church, the doorway along the lines of the fourteenth-century one, and the three-light window along the lines of the fifteenth-century one. 'The Tent' and 'Peace Garden' at the back were built at the same time, to encourage inter-faith dialogue. Ethelburga was the sister of the seventh-century Saxon Bishop Erkenwald. She was also the Abbess of Barking and founder of the church of All Hallows Barking.

21 – Bishopsgate

The site of another of the gates in the City wall, originally built in the Roman period, and subsequently rebuilt in the Saxon by Erkenwald, the Bishop of London from 675-93, and again in the Medieval, before being eventually demolished in 1760. To the north and east is Spitalfields, named after the priory of St Mary Spital; to the north and west, the priory of St Mary of Bethlehem, otherwise known as 'Bedlam'.

22 – Austin Friars, off Old Broad Street

Named after the Austin Friars Priory originally built around 1253 by Humphrey de Bohun, Constable of England, the priory church incorporating the existing parish church of St Peter-le-Poer as a private chapel, and extended in 1354. The priory was attacked during the Peasants' Revolt of 1381, when 13 Flemings were dragged from its sanctuary and beheaded. Many of the barons killed at the Battle of

Barnet in the Wars of the Roses in 1471 were buried here. Most of the buildings on the site were destroyed during the Great Fire. The salvaged altar table from the priory church may be seen in the present Dutch Church.

23 – Threadneedle Street
First recorded as *Three needle Street*, in 1598, and as Thred-needle-street in 1616, although evidently already in existence in Medieval times. Thought to take its present name from the arms of either the Needlemakers or the Merchant Taylors, whose Halls were here in Medieval times.

24 – Site of St Anthony's Hospital, 53 Threadneedle Street
Originally founded in 1242, on the site of a former synagogue, as the Hospital of St Antoine de Viennois, a hospital specifically for the treatment of sufferers of 'St Anthony's Fire', or ergotism, a disease caused by eating cereals contaminated by an alkaloid-secreting fungus. Expanded in 1429 to incorporate a hospice; in 1440, a school, where Thomas More (1478-1535) studied; and, in 1550, a chapel where Protestant Huguenots fleeing religious persecution in Catholic France worshipped. All burned down in the Great Fire. The site is marked by a blue plaque.

25 – Merchant Taylors' Hall, 30 Threadneedle Street
Originally built in around 1392. Damaged, but not destroyed, in the Great Fire, and rebuilt afterwards, only to be substantially destroyed by bombing during the Blitz and rebuilt again in the post-war period. Parts of the fifteenth-century Great Kitchen survive (alongside the crypt of the chapel). In the Middle Ages, Merchant Taylors made not only clothes but also protective quilted and padded waistcoats (the 'stab-proof vests' of the day) and linings for suits of armour. They were granted their Royal Charter by Edward III in 1326.

26 – Site of St Benet Fink, Royal Exchange Avenue
Originally built at least as long ago as 1216, burned down in the Great Fire, and rebuilt by Wren in 1670-5, only to be demolished, to make way for the rebuilding of the Royal Exchange in 1841, when the parish was merged with St Peter-le-Poer. The site is marked by a blue plaque.

27 – Cornhill

First recorded as *Cornehull* in around 1100, although evidently already in existence in Saxon times. Takes its name either from the hill on which corn was grown, or 'of a corn market time out of mind there holden' (Stow). The Cornhill 'Tun' was built here in the thirteenth century to incarcerate 'street walkers and loose women'. It was later replaced with stocks and a pillory.

28 – St Michael Cornhill

Originally built in the Saxon period and burned down in the Great Fire. Subsequently rebuilt by Wren's office 1669-72 and by Hawksmoor 1715-24 in the Gothic style, and modified by Sir George Gilbert Scott 1857-60 in the Victorian Gothic style (probably incorporating parts of the Medieval Gothic building that were still standing after the Great Fire). Repaired after having been damaged by an IRA bomb in 1993.

29 – Lombard Street

First recorded as *Langburnestrate* in 1285 and as *Lumbardstret* in 1318, although evidently already in existence in Saxon times. Takes its present name from the Lombards from northern Italy, who took over banking and money-lending after the Jews who had formerly fulfilled those roles were expelled from the City following the 'Edict of Expulsion' issued by Edward I in 1290. Took its previous name from the Langborne or Langbourn.

30 – Cannon Street

First recorded as *Candelewrithstret* in 1183, although evidently already in existence in Saxon times. Took its original name from the Middle English *candelwricht*, meaning candle-wright or chandler, in reference to such work in the Middle Ages. The smell associated with the rendering of the animal fat to make the tallow for the candles caused so many complaints from the neighbouring populace that the manufactories eventually had to be moved into the surrounding countryside.

31 – London Stone, 111 Cannon Street

The so-called 'London Stone' now stands at 111 Cannon Street, although unfortunately in an easily overlooked position at street level, and behind a somewhat unprepossessing steel grille. From 1798 it had been incorporated into the south wall of the church of St Swithin London Stone and was preserved when the church was demolished in

1957, according to a stipulation in the conditions for the redevelopment of the site. Previously it stood in the middle of the street, as indicated on the map of 1520, and was apparently used as a place from which to make important public pronouncements throughout the Middle Ages, being evidently richly endowed with symbolic significance. During the failed rebellion of 1450 that ended with the 'Harvest of the Heads' of the leaders, one of the same, Jack Cade, alias Mortimer, struck the stone with his sword, and declared himself to be 'Lord of this City', an act immortalised thus by Shakespeare in *Henry VI, Part II*, Act IV, Scene VI: 'Now is Mortimer Lord of this City. And here, sitting upon London-stone, I charge and command that, of the city's cost, the pissing-conduit run nothing but claret wine this first year of our reign.' The first (Lord) Mayor of London, appointed in 1189, was Henry FitzAilwyn de Londonestone, who evidently hailed from hereabouts.

32 – Catrin Glyndwr memorial, St. Swithun's Church Garden, Salter's Hall Court/Oxford Court

The Welsh freedom fighter Owain Glyndwr's daughter Catrin and two of her daughters were buried in the church of St Swithin London Stone here after dying in captivity in the Tower of London in 1413, the year in which Henry IV died. The circumstances were suspicious, as Catrin's daughter, by Edmund Mortimer, who was descended from Edward III, had a claim to the English throne. Some suspect that they were done to death so as to prevent them from making any such claim.

A modern Gelligaer bluestone sculpture by Nic Stradlyn-John and Richard Renshaw, inscribed with a Welsh *englyn* by Menna Elfyn, marks the spot. Freely (by me) rendered into English, the englyn reads: 'In the Tower, now her home,/' before 'Her heart-song turns to longing:/ The exile's silent lament'.

33 – Walbrook

First recorded as *Walbrokstrate* in 1274. Named after the Walbrook, a tributary of the Thames which rose in the area around Moorfields to the north of the City wall, flowed south through the City, and debouched at Dowgate (it is now covered over).

34 – Poultry

First recorded as *Poletria* in 1301, although evidently in existence in Saxon times. Poultry Compter was built here in the fourteenth century.

35 – Cheapside
First recorded, as *Westceap* in around 1100, although evidently already in existence in Saxon times. Takes its name from the Old English *ceap*, meaning market. A great open-air market was situated here, in what was in effect the High Street of the City in Medieval times, where all manner of goods could be procured.

36 – Site of Cheapside Conduit, 80B Cheapside
Part of the Medieval and later water supply system. The site is marked by two plaques.

37 – Ironmonger Lane
'Ismongerelane' is recorded in the twelfth century. Thomas Becket is said to have been born on the corner of Cheapside and Ironmonger Lane.

38 – Old Jewry
Named after the Jewish community established here in the twelfth century, and expelled in the thirteenth. The site of a number of synagogues, including the Great Synagogue (marked by a blue plaque). The remains of Jewish ritual baths or mikva'ot have been found here.

39 – Guildhall, Guildhall Yard
Originally built sometime before 1128, possibly on the site of an even older building, where the Saxons held their *husting*, or indoor assembly. Subsequently substantially rebuilt 1298-1356 and rebuilt again by the Master Mason John Croxton between 1411 and 1430. Damaged in the Great Fire and repaired in the aftermath, only to be badly damaged by bombing on the night of 29/30 December 1940, and repaired again after that. The lower levels of the walls (up to the level of the clerestorey) still survive from the Medieval period, as do some of the original windows, made from slivers of horn, and the crypts. The porch is a later, eighteenth-century addition by George Dance, in a bizarre style described as Hindoo Gothic. The Medieval frontage had featured statues of the civic virtues of Temperance, Fortitude, Justice and Prudence (or Discipline). Inside, the famous statues of the mythical giants Gog and Magog replace two sets of earlier ones, the first destroyed in the Great Fire, and the second in the Blitz. Nearby, also in Guildhall Yard, is the site of Bakewell or Blackwell Hall, the home of the Bakewell family and also the centre of the important wool

trade in Medieval times. The hall was burned down in the Great Fire, rebuilt in the 1670s and demolished in 1820.

40 – Site of Aldermanbury Conduit, Aldermanbury Square

Another part of the originally Medieval water supply system. The site is marked by a blue plaque.

41 – Elsing Spital

Also known as the Hospital of St Mary within Cripplegate. Founded in 1331 by William de Elsing as a hospital for the blind, it became an Augustinian priory in 1340. After the Dissolution, the hospital chapel became the new parish church of St Alphage (the old one, a little to the north and abutting the City wall, was demolished). The fourteenth-century tower survives.

42 – St Alphage Gardens

The site of a substantial surviving section of Roman, Medieval and post-Medieval City wall. The Medieval portion dates in part to the mid-thirteenth century, to the reign of Henry III (stonework), and in part to the fifteenth, around 1477, to the reign of Edward IV (brickwork).

43 – Noble Street

The site of another surviving section of City wall. The Medieval portion dates to the mid-thirteenth century and includes a number of stone bastions. To the north is the Medieval church of St Giles Cripplegate and to the west is West Smithfield.

44 – St Mary-le-Bow, or Bow Church, Cheapside

Originally built in around 1077-87 by the Norman King William I's Archbishop of Canterbury, Lanfranc, possibly on the site of an older Saxon church; subsequently rebuilt following damage by a tornado in 1091, following a fire in 1196, following a partial collapse in 1271, following the Great Fire of 1666, and following damage sustained on the last night of the continuous Blitz of the Second World War, 10/11 May 1941. The tornado virtually levelled the church and drove four 26-ft rafters vertically into the ground. From accounts of the damage, meteorologists estimate that it would have rated T8 on the T scale, which runs from T1 to T10, with winds in excess of 200 mph. It also damaged 600 other buildings, including

London Bridge, but caused only two fatalities. Only the crypt of the eleventh-century church survives. The famous bells, used to sound the nine o'clock 'curfew' in the Medieval era, were destroyed during the Blitz (only those born within earshot of the bells could truly call themselves 'Cockneys'). Here ended the Rebellion of William Longbeard (William Fitz Osbert) in 1196, when, according to a contemporary account, Longbeard 'flying into the church of St Mary of the Arches, demanded the protection of our Lord, St Mary, and her church ... His expostulations, however, were not listened to ... and the archbishop ... ordered that he should be dragged from the church to take a trial, because he had created a sedition... When this was told to William, he took refuge in the tower of the church, for he knew that the mayors ... sought to take away his life. In their obstinacy they applied fire, and sacrilegiously burned down a great part of the church. Thus William was forced to leave.' This early champion of the poor was 'drawn asunder by horses' and then hanged.

45 – Site of Cheapside Cross, Cheapside/Wood Street
The Cheapside Cross was built by Edward I in 1290 to mark one of the twelve locations where his late wife Eleanor of Castile's body was rested overnight on its journey from Nottinghamshire, where she died, to Westminster, where she was buried. It was subsequently demolished by what Evelyn called 'furious and zealous' Parliamentarians in 1643 during the Civil War.

46 – (St) Paul's Cross, St Paul's Churchyard
Built in the grounds of St Paul's Cathedral in around 1191, damaged in 1382, possibly by the earthquake of that year, repaired in 1387, rebuilt as a sort of open-air pulpit by Bishop Kempe in 1448/9, and demolished by order of Parliament during the Civil War, in 1643 (the statue that stands on the site today is a replica, built in 1910).

47 – St Paul's Cathedral
The fourth St Paul's Cathedral, Old St Paul's, was built in the Norman, or Romanesque, style in the years after 1087 by the Bishop, Maurice and his successors; partially rebuilt and extended in the Gothic style 1221-1240, and in the 'New Work' of 1269-1332; renovated in the Renaissance style by Inigo Jones in 1633-1641, and again by Wren, after the Civil War, during which it had been occupied by Parliamentary

troops and horses, in 1660. It was burned down in the Great Fire. There are models of Old St Paul's in the modern Cathedral and also in the Museum of London. It was clearly an impressive building, measuring some 600 ft in length, and, according to some estimates, over 500 ft in height, inclusive of the spire (which was destroyed by lightning in 1444, rebuilt in 1462, and destroyed by lightning again in 1561). John Denham wrote in 1624: 'That sacred pile, so vast, so high/That whether 'tis a part of earth or sky/Uncertain seems, and may be thought a proud/Aspiring mountain or descending cloud.' The Chapter House was built by the Master Mason William Ramsay in 1332 in the Perpendicular Gothic style, with only the octagonal outline of foundations surviving, in the churchyard on the south side of the cathedral (Sankey, in Cotton *et al.*, 2014).

48 – Site of Royal Wardrobe, Wardrobe Place, off Carter Lane
Built as an office for managing Royal assets and provisions, and a storehouse for clothes worn on ceremonial occasions and such like, in the reign of Edward III in the late fourteenth century, around 1361, and burned down in the Great Fire. The site is marked by a Corporation blue plaque.

49 – Site of First Barnard's Castle, St Andrew's Hill
Originally built by Ralph Baynard, one of William I's noblemen, in the late eleventh century, and demolished in the early thirteenth, after the baronial conspiracy against King John in 1212, in which the Constable, Robert FitzWalter, was implicated. Essentially nothing of the castle remains above ground today, other than, arguably, part of the outline of the moat, traced by the curved northern end of St Andrew's Hill.

50 – Remains of Blackfriars Priory, Ireland Yard
Built on the site of the first Baynard's Castle in 1278 and dissolved in the reign of Henry VIII in 1538 (a copy of the Dissolution document can be seen in the church of St Andrew-by-the-Wardrobe). Most of the buildings on the former site were burned down in the Great Fire, although part of the wall of the Provincial Prior's house can still be seen in in Ireland Yard. According to a contemporary account, a large number of needy poor people were crushed to death in a rush to get alms food and money at the gates of the priory in 1322.

51 – Site of Second Baynard's Castle, Queen Victoria Street
Built in a river-front location in the early fourteenth century, around
1338, rebuilt around 1428, and possibly again in the late fifteenth.
It was used by a succession of Kings and Queens in the late fifteenth
to sixteenth centuries, before being essentially completely destroyed
in the Great Fire. It was the London headquarters of the House of
York during the Wars of the Roses, and Edward IV was hailed King
here in 1461 (moreover, Richard III is believed to have asserted his
claim to the throne here, in 1483). A Corporation blue plaque on
the Embankment marks the site of the castle, parts of which were
uncovered during building works in 1972.

Finish at Blackfriars tube.

APPENDIX FOUR – TUDOR AND STUART CITY OF LONDON WALK

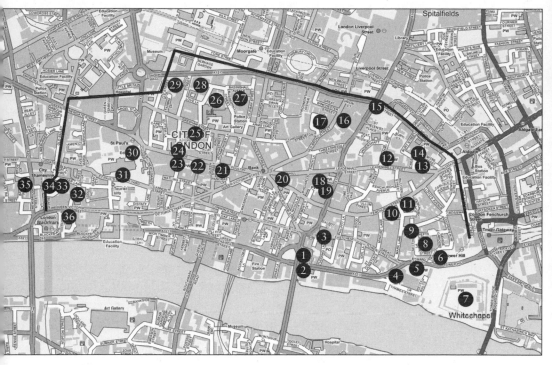

1 – Monument, Monument Street
2 – Old London Bridge (and Port of London)
3 – Eastcheap
4 – Custom House, Thames Street
5 – All Hallows Barking, Byward Street
6 – Tower Hill
7 – Tower of London
8 – Site of Navy Office, Seething Lane
9 – St Olave Hart Street
10 – All Hallows Staining, Mark Lane
11 – Site of East India House, Fenchurch Street
11 – St Andrew Undershaft, St Mary Axe
13 – St Katharine Cree, Leadenhall Street
14 – Site of First Synagogue after Resettlement, Creechurch Lane
15 – Bishopsgate
16 – Site of Gresham College, Old Broad Street
17 – Austin Friars, off Old Broad Street
18 – Site of 'Pasqua Rosee's Head', St Michael's Alley, off Cornhill
19 – Site of 'Bell Inn', Bell Inn Yard, off Gracechurch Street
20 – Royal Exchange

21 – Site of Cheapside Conduit, 80B Cheapside
22 – St Mary–le–Bow, or Bow Church, Cheapside
23 – Bread Street, off Cheapside
24 – Site of Cheapside Cross, Cheapside/ Wood Street
25 – Milk Street
26 – Guildhall, Guildhall Yard
27 – Masons Avenue, off Basinghall Street
28 – Aldermanbury Square
29 – Site of St Olave Silver Street
30 – St Paul's Cross
31 – St Paul's Cathedral
32 – Site of 'Shakespeare's House', Ireland Yard, off St Andrew's Hill
33 – Site of Blackfriars Theatre, Playhouse Yard
34 – Apothecaries' Hall, Blackfriars Lane
35 – Site of Bridewell Palace, New Bridge Street
36 – Site of Second Baynard's Castle, Queen Victoria Street

Bold line indicates that of City wall.

Approximate distance 4.4 miles.
Start at the Fish Street Hill exit to Monument tube.

1 – Monument, Monument Street

Built between 1671-7 as a monument to the Great Fire by Sir Christopher Wren, whose original plan had been to crown the edifice with a symbolic and dramatic Phoenix rising. The monument stands 202 ft high, the vertical distance from the base to the top being the same as the horizontal distance from the base to the seat of the fire in Pudding Lane. Archaeological excavations at nearby Monument House uncovered a layer of debris from the Great Fire, including charred imported Dutch and Spanish tiles – and a waffle iron!

2 – 'Old London Bridge' (and Port of London)

A little to the east of the present London Bridge is the site of the previous one. The famous Medieval to post-Medieval incarnation of the bridge was originally built by Peter, chaplain of St Mary Colechurch, in *c.* 1176-1209, and stood until 1831, although having to be repaired a number of times over the centuries, and extensively refurbished in the eighteenth. There is a fine scale-model of it as it would have looked in the church of St Magnus the Martyr on Thames Street. There were scores of buildings on it then, including a great many shops, a chapel dedicated to St Thomas Becket; and from the late sixteenth century until the mid-eighteenth, a palatial residence known as Nonsuch House. Nonsuch House was built between 1577 and 1579 and eventually demolished in 1757 to allow for the widening of the road. The construction of the house was remarkable for the amount of pre-fabrication involved, with sections manufactured in Holland and shipped across the North Sea packed flat for assembly on site; and also for the quality of the craftsmanship employed, it being claimed that all the sections fitted together with wooden pegs and without a single nail. The completed House, with its gaudy paintwork, intricately carved carapace and ornate cupolas, was one of the wonders of its age. Fortunately, it stood just long enough, albeit apparently in a state of some disrepair, to be immortalised in a Canaletto drawing of c. 1750, now in the British Museum in London. Unfortunately, we know very little of its nearly two-hundred year history – not even who its occupants were!

The bridge had a total of nineteen arches or 'starlings', through which many of the more devil-may-care watermen would attempt to row in a dangerous practice known as 'shooting the bridge', some unfortunately losing their lives in the process. Only the northern end of the bridge was affected by the Great Fire of 1666, the southward progress of which across the river was halted at a gap in the buildings that formed a natural firebreak – ironically, the result of another fire in 1633. The post-Medieval port lay chiefly on the downstream side of the bridge, at least in part because the drawbridge that had allowed large vessels to pass upstream had become unusable by the end of the fifteenth century. A prodigious range of comestible and manufactured goods was imported in, from not only the Old World but also the New. The trade with the ports on the coasts of the North Sea and Baltic continued to be controlled by the Hanseatic League, headquartered at the Steelyard. However, the former privileges extended to the League were revoked by Edward VI in 1551, and some foreign merchants belonging to the League and based in London were deported – albeit only temporarily – in 1598. The Steelyard was burned down in the Great Fire, although rebuilt afterwards, only to be demolished in 1855 to make way for Cannon Street Station. The trade with ports further afield came to be controlled by the merchant-adventurers of the Muscovy Company, formed in 1555; the Levant Company, formed in 1581; the (Honourable) East India Company, formed in 1600; the Virginia Company (of London), formed in 1606; and the Royal African Company, formed in 1660. The so-called Cheapside Hoard, believed to have been buried in or shortly after 1640, that is, on the eve of the Civil War, includes not only various types of jewel and jewelry from continental Europe, and Sinai, Iran, Afghanistan, India and Sri Lanka in Asia, but also heliodors (a type of beryl) from Brazil and emeralds from Colombia. On the south side of the bridge is Southwark, which was in the post-Medieval period the site of a number of animal-baiting arenas and playhouses. Famously, there were also some fifty inns and other drinking establishments on and around Borough High Street at the time of the Great Fire, including the White Hart, which was written about by Shakespeare. They all survived that fire, although many were burned down in the Great Fire of Southwark in 1676. The George was rebuilt after that second Great Fire as a galleried inn, and still stands.

3 – Eastcheap

The site of the Boar's Head, where, in Shakespeare, Falstaff frolicked with Mistress Quickly (marked by the figure of a boar's head on the nineteenth-century building at No. 33).

4 – Custom House, Thames Street

Originally built at least as long ago as 1377, in Billingsgate, close to the centre of activity on the waterfront, its purpose being to collect the duties payable on exports of wool, and subsequently rebuilt, following a fire, in 1559. Burned down in the Great Fire in 1666 and rebuilt yet again by Christopher Wren in 1668-71.

5 – All Hallows Barking, Byward Street

Originally built by Ethelburga, Abbess of Barking and sister of Bishop Erkenwald, in the Saxon period, and considerably added to in the later Medieval and post-Medieval. Undamaged in the Great Fire, although nonetheless partially rebuilt in the late nineteenth century. Gutted in the Blitz and rebuilt again by Lord Mottistone, in a 'happy blend' of Ancient and Neo-Perpendicular styles in the post-war period. Among the many surviving post-Medieval features of the church are a carved ivory figure of Christ salvaged from the flagship of the Spanish Armada in 1588, and the seventeenth-century tower, from which Samuel Pepys watched the Great Fire (noting in his diary entry for Wednesday 5 September, 'I up to the top of Barkinge steeple, and there saw the saddest sight of desolation I ever saw'). Also of note are the pulpit, originally from St Swithin London Stone, dating to 1678; and the exquisitely intricately carved lime-wood font-cover by Grinling Gibbons, dating to 1682. The headless bodies of Bishop John Fisher and Sir Thomas More, beheaded on nearby Tower Hill in 1535, and that of Archbishop William Laud, beheaded in 1645, were once temporarily buried here before being moved to their final resting places (Fisher's and More's in the chapel of St Peter ad Vincula in the Tower of London). In 1698, the annual 'Beating of the Bounds' ceremony at Rogatontide ended in a boundary dispute with the Warders of the Tower of London, during which, as one historical account put it: '[T]he warders used their halberds to some purpose, and several parishioners were seriously injured.' To this day, every third year, the event is re-enacted during a 'Boundary Dispute Ceremony'.

6 – Tower Hill

The site of public executions in the post-Medieval period. Among those executed here were John Fisher, Thomas More, Thomas Cromwell, Thomas Wyatt the Younger, Robert Devereux, and in the Stuart period Thomas Wentworth, William Laud, Harry Vane and, in 1683, Algernon Sidney. Somewhat to the east, in East Smithfield, is the site of the Royal Naval Victualling Yard.

7 – Tower of London

Originally built under William I, William II and Henry I In 1602, Frederic Gershow, the secretary to Philipp Julius, the Duke of Stettin-Pomerania, wrote in his diary with startling vagueness: '[H]is princely Grace, having obtained permission, visited the Tower of London, an old but strong castle built by Julius Caesar, where they keep the prisoners. At first we were led into a long hall, full of harness, maybe for a hundred thousand men, as one might say; but this armour was not properly arranged, nor kept clean.' Though the start of the Tudor period has in fact seen the Tower fall out of favour as a royal residence, becoming an armoury and prison. The Tower was a target for Charles I during the English Civil War, he wanting and needing its cache of money and munitions.

8 – Site of Navy Office, Seething Lane

Originally built in 1659 on the site of a mansion owned by Elizabeth I's spymaster Francis Walsingham. Undamaged in the Great Fire, but destroyed in another fire in 1673, subsequently rebuilt in 1674-5 and eventually demolished in 1788 (when the Navy Board moved to Somerset House). The site then came to be occupied by warehouses owned by the East India Company in the late eighteenth century and by the Port of London Authority Building in the early twentieth. Recent archaeological work undertaken during the course of the conversion of that building into a hotel uncovered a seventeenth-century ground surface with a pit in it. Is it too fanciful to imagine that the pit might have been the very one in which Pepys, who lived and worked nearby, buried his parmesan cheese and wine for safe keeping in 1666?

9 – St Olave Hart Street

Originally built in wood in the eleventh century, sometime after the canonisation of St Olave in 1031. Subsequently rebuilt in stone in the late twelfth to early thirteenth century, and again in the mid-fifteenth, around 1450, and extended in the sixteenth to seventeenth. Undamaged in the Great Fire, but damaged in the Blitz and rebuilt again in the post-war period, between 1951-4. The thirteenth-century crypt, some thirteenth- and fifteenth- century walls, the fifteenth-century tower, the gateway, dating to 1658, and the vestry, dating to 1662, survive. A number of sixteenth- and seventeenth- century memorials also survive, including ones to the Florentine merchant – and rumoured informant to Elizabeth's spymaster Walsingham – Piero Capponi, who died of the plague in 1582, the diarist Samuel Pepys, who died in 1703, and Pepys's long-suffering wife Elizabeth, who pre-deceased him in 1669 (and whose expression suggests she is 'admonishing her wayward husband'). The gateway to the churchyard is especially memorable for its adornment of skulls and cross-bones, from a design by Hendrik de Keyser.

10 – All Hallows Staining, Mark Lane
Originally built around 1177 and rebuilt in the fourteenth or fifteenth century (sources differ). Undamaged in the Great Fire, most of the church fell down in 1671, due to undermining of the foundations by mostly plague burials, making it one of the last buildings to be destroyed by the fire. It had to be rebuilt in 1674-5, before being substantially demolished in 1870, when the parish was merged with St Olave Hart Street. The fourteenth- or fifteenth- century tower still stands, thanks to the initiative of the Clothworkers' Company, who were also responsible for restoring it in 1873.

11 – Site of East India House, Fenchurch Street
Originally built in 1648, on the site of the residence of the one-time Mayor, William Craven (d. 1618). Survived the Great Fire, together with its content of spices and other immensely valuable merchandise, thanks to the action of an Alderman, who handed out sums of money to anyone who helped hold back the encroaching blaze. Nonetheless rebuilt in 1726, and again in 1799-1800. Sold after the Government took control of the Company's possessions in India in 1858, Britannia thus 'Receiving the Riches of the East', as depicted on an overmantel bas-relief in the Directors' Court Room. It was demolished in 1861, when many of the furnishings were moved to the India Office. The site is now occupied by the Lloyd's of London Building.

12 – St Andrew Undershaft, St Mary Axe

Originally built in the twelfth century, and rebuilt in the fourteenth, and again in the Perpendicular Gothic style in around 1520-32. Undamaged both in the Great Fire and in the Blitz, although the seventeenth-century stained-glass windows were destroyed by an IRA bomb in 1992. Among the many memorials inside the church is one to the Merchant Taylor and amateur antiquarian John Stow (d. 1605), the author of *A Survey of London*. Stow appears with a quill-pen in his hand. Every third year, on or around the anniversary of his death on 5 April, as part of a special service in his memory he is ceremonially presented with a new quill. The church gains its peculiar name from a huge maypole that was put up on feast days, purportedly taller than the spire.The revelries were curtailed after 1517 wan the London apprentices went on a rampage and the pole was removed.

13 – St Katharine Cree, Leadenhall Street

Originally built around 1280-1303, rebuilt between 1500-1504 in the Late Gothic style, and again 1628-31, this time in the Renaissance style. Undamaged by the Great Fire, although later requiring restoration in 1878-79, and again, after being damaged in the Blitz. The tower dates to 1500-1504, the porch to 1628-31 and the gateway to the churchyard, on Mitre Street, by William Avenon, to 1631 (nearby St Helen Bishopsgate also has a Renaissance porch, dating to 1633). The interior contains some Late Gothic elements, such as the east window and the intricately ribbed ceiling; and some Renaissance ones, such as the Corinthian columns in the nave. It also contains monuments to Sir Nicholas Throkmorton (d. 1570) and Sir John Gayer (d. 1649), a marble font of around 1631, and a Father Smith organ of 1686, once played by Handel and Purcell (as well as some memorial plaques and a reredos salvaged from St James Duke's Place). The church is the home of the 'Lion Sermons', given each year on or around 16 October in remembrance of the Merchant Adventurer of the Levant Company and former Mayor Sir John Gayer being spared by a lion in Syria on that day 1643. It has associations from that same Civil War period with the Royalist cause, and even contains a wooden statue of Charles I, depicted as a martyr and saint. Archbishop William Laud, who reconsecrated the church in 1631, was executed in 1645 for his support of Charles, his High Church views, and his persecution of Puritans.

14 – Site of First Synagogue after Resettlement, Creechurch Lane

Creechurch Lane is the site of the first synagogue after the resettlement of the Jews in 1656 (marked by a blue plaque). The synagogue was built in 1657 and enlarged in 1673 (having survived the Great Fire of 1666). It was demolished in 1701 and replaced by an even larger synagogue on an adjacent site just off Bevis Marks, which still stands.

15 – Bishopsgate

The site of one of the gates in the City wall, originally built in the Roman period, and subsequently rebuilt in the Saxon by Erkenwald, the Bishop of London from 675-93, and again in the Medieval, before being eventually demolished in 1760. To the north is Shoreditch, the site of 'The Theatre', built in 1576, on the site of the dissolved Holywell Priory, and of 'The Curtain', built in 1577; to the northwest, 'Bedlam'.

16 – Site of Gresham College, Old Broad Street

Originally founded in 1597 through the benefaction of the financier Thomas Gresham, on the site of his house and grounds, situated between Bishopsgate and Old Broad Street. Subsequently relocated to Gresham Street, in 1842 and then to Barnard's Inn in 1991. Rather wonderfully, free public lectures are still given here, and in the Museum of London, on the topics of Divinity, Music, Astronomy, Law, Rhetoric, Physic, Geometry and Commerce. The Royal Society's first meetings were held at Gresham College between 1660 and 1665. They were then temporarily suspended during the Great Plague of 1665 and temporarily moved to Arundel House after the Great Fire of 1666, when the business of Gresham's Exchange (the Royal Exchange), which had been burned down, was moved to Gresham College, which had survived.

17 – Austin Friars, off Old Broad Street

Named after the Austin Friars Priory built here in the thirteenth century. Erasmus of Rotterdam, the Dutch priest, theologian and philosopher, the so-called 'Prince of the Humanists', lodged here in 1513, complained about the quality of the wine on offer and left without settling his bill! Miles Coverdale worked on his English translation of the Bible here in 1529 and Thomas Cromwell, the lawyer, banker, soldier and sometime statesman, Vicar-General and Vice-Gerent in Spirituals to Henry VIII, lived here from the 1520s until his execution in 1540 (the past site of his house being presently occupied by the Draper's Hall on Throgmorton Street). After the Dissolution of the Monasteries in 1538 much of the priory precinct came into the possession of Sir William Paulet, the First Marquess of Winchester, who built himself a substantial town-house here (whence Great Winchester Street). In 1550, under Edward VI, part of the priory church was converted into a Dutch Church ('notwithstanding that they do not conform with the rites and ceremonies used in our Kingdom'), and the remaining part reverted to being the parish church of St Peter-le-Poer. Most of the buildings in the former precinct were destroyed during the Great Fire. Paulet's town-house and the Dutch Church survived, although the former was subsequently demolished in 1830, and the latter destroyed in a fire in 1863, rebuilt, destroyed again during the Blitz, and rebuilt again. The church of St Peter-le-Poer also survived the fire, although ash from the fire settled on an open prayer book in the interior and obscured the text. However, it subsequently fell into disrepair and had to be repaired in 1716 and rebuilt in 1788-92, and was eventually demolished in 1907-08.

18 – Site of 'Pasqua Rosee's Head', St Michael's Alley, off Cornhill
The first coffee-house in the City, established in 1652, destroyed in the Great Fire, and rebuilt as the 'Jamaica' in the 1670s (the site is marked by a blue plaque on the present 'Jamaica Wine-House'). The eponymous Pasqua Rosee was employed as a man-servant by one Daniel Edwards, a London merchant, member of the Levant Company and trader in Turkish goods, and he appears to have run the coffee-shop as a sideline. It is thought that Rosee and Edwards met in Smyrna in Anatolia.

19 – Site of 'Bell Inn', Bell Inn Yard, off Gracechurch Street
Built in the fourteenth century, and burned down in the Great Fire in the seventeenth. Early plays were performed in the purpose-adapted inn from at least as long ago as 1576, that is, before any purpose-built playhouses existed.

20 – Royal Exchange (best viewed from Bank Junction)
Originally built by the City financier and philanthropist Sir Thomas Gresham between 1566 and1569, being modelled on the Bourse in Antwerp, and officially opened by Queen Elizabeth I in 1570 or 1571. Subsequently burned down in the Great Fire, one Thomas Vincent writing: 'The Royal Exchange itself, the glory of the merchants [was]

invaded with much violence. And when once the fire was entered, how quickly did it run round the galleries, filling them with flames [and] giving forth flaming volleys... By and by, down fell all the [statues of] Kings [in the alcoves] upon their faces, and the greatest part of the ... building after them, with such a noise as was dreadful and astonishing.' Rebuilt in 1669, only to be burned down again in 1838 and rebuilt yet again in 1842-44. A centre of commerce until 1939, it is currently a shopping centre. The grasshopper insignia is that of Gresham and is also to be seen on the former Gresham's Bank building on nearby Lombard Street.

21 – Site of Cheapside Conduit, 80B Cheapside
Part of the Medieval and later water supply system. The site is marked by two plaques.

22 – St Mary-le-Bow, or Bow Church, Cheapside
Originally built in around 1077-87 by the Norman King William I's Archbishop of Canterbury, Lanfranc, possibly on the site of an older Saxon church; and subsequently rebuilt following damage by a tornado in 1091, following a fire in 1196, and following a partial collapse in 1271. St Mary-le-Bow was considered second only to St Pauls in all of London. Burned down in the Great Fire and rebuilt again by Wren 1670-83. Gutted by bombing on the last night of the continuous Blitz of the Second World War, 10/11 May, 1941, and rebuilt yet again in the post-war period, between 1956-64. The churchyard contains a statue to Captain John Smith, parishioner, Citizen and Cordwainer, 'first among the leaders of the settlement at Jamestown in Virginia [in 1607] from which began the overseas expansion of the English-speaking peoples'. Smith later returned to London and died there in 1631, He is buried in the church of St Sepulchre Newgate Street.

23 – Bread Street, off Cheapside
'So called of bread in old time there sold' (Stow). The site of the Mermaid Tavern, where Shakespeare, Ben Jonson and Christopher Marlowe were wont to gather, Francis Beaumont memorably writing of their encounters: 'What things have we seen/Done at the Mermaid! Heard words that have been/So nimble, and so full of subtle flame/As if that every one from whence they came/Had meant to put his whole wit in a jest,/And had resolv'd to live a fool the rest/Of his dull life.'

Also the site of the birthplace of John Milton, at the sign of the 'Spread Eagle', in 1608 (marked by a blue plaque) and of the Bread Street Compter, opened in the fifteenth century, and closed in the sixteenth.

24 – Site of Cheapside Cross, Cheapside/Wood Street
Demolished by Parliamentarians in 1643 during the Civil War. The so-called Cheapside Hoard was buried nearby in or shortly after 1640 on the eve of the war, and discovered in 1912, the greatest single collection of Elizabethan and Stuart jewellery ever found. A purpose-built gallery for the hoard's exhibition is planned for 2021 in Smithfield.

25 – Milk Street
The site of the birthplace of Thomas More (marked by a blue plaque).

26 – Guildhall, Guildhall Yard
Built in the Medieval period to rival Westminster Hall. The site of a number of important trials in the post-Medieval, including those of Anne Askew in 1546, Nicholas Throckmorton, Lady Jane Grey and Archbishop Thomas Cranmer in 1554, and Father Henry Garnet in 1606.

27 – Masons Avenue, off Basinghall Street
Immediately to the east of the Guildhall, off Basinghall Street, is Masons Avenue, a row of houses built in 1928 in the 'Mock Tudor'or 'Tudor Revival' style, which gives some sense of how parts of pre-Great Fire London might have looked. The architectural historian Nikolaus Pevsner evidently rather disapproved of the standard of the twentieth-century craftsmanship, and the 'flimsy applied half-timbering'.

28 – Aldermanbury Square
The site of a bust of Shakespeare that also commemorates his fellow-actors John Heminge and Henry Condell, parishioners at the church of St Mary Aldermanbury, who, on his death, gathered together all his unpublished manuscripts and published them as the *First Folio* in 1623. The inscription on the bust reads in part: 'They alone collected his dramatic writings regardless of pecuniary loss and without the hope of any profit gave them to the world. They thus merited the gratitude of mankind.' The church of St Mary Aldermanbury was originally built at least as long ago as 1181 and extended in 1438. It was subsequently rebuilt by Wren in 1671-5, after having burned

down in the Great Fire, only to be substantially destroyed by bombing on the night of 29/30 December, 1940. Only the foundations remain at the site, which has been a city garden since 1966 (there is also an informative plaque). Much of the building material salvaged from the church survive, in the remarkable reconstruction, true to Wren's design, on the campus of Westminster College in Fulton, Missouri (where Churchill gave his famous 'Iron Curtain' speech).

29 – Site of St Olave Silver Street
Originally built around 1181, subsequently burned down in the Great Fire and never rebuilt, the parish being merged with that of St Alban Wood Street. The former churchyard survives as a city garden. Parish records show that in 1665-6 the corpses of 119 people hanged at Tyburn were handed over to the nearby Barber-Surgeons' Hall for the purposes of dissection. Silver Street itself was essentially obliterated during the Blitz and even its name – and indeed its line – disappeared in post-war redevelopment. Shakespeare once lodged here with a family of Huguenots (Nicholl, 2007). To the north is the church of St Giles Cripplegate, where Oliver Cromwell was married in 1620, and where John Milton was buried in 1674 (also buried here are Martin Frobisher, seeker after the North-West Passage and Scourge of the Armada, who died in another naval action against the Spanish in 1594; and John Speed, historian and map-maker extraordinary, who died in 1629).

30 – (St) Paul's Cross
Built in the around 1191 and demolished by order of Parliament during the Civil War, in 1643 (the statue that stands on the site today is a replica, built in 1910). One Dr Beal or Bell gave an inflammatory speech here on May Day, 1517, inciting the crowd 'to cherish and defend themselves, and to hurt and grieve aliens for the common weal', which they duly did, with great gusto, in the infamous so-called 'Evil May Day' riots (at the time there was considerable popular resentment towards foreigners in general and foreign merchants in particular, on account of their perceived preferential treatment by City authorities). The riots were eventually broken up only after thousands of troops were called in and hundreds of rioters taken prisoner. The ring-leaders were then more or less immediately hanged, drawn and quartered, and their remains gibbeted. The remainder, though, despite also facing the death penalty for the treason of 'breaking the peace of Christendom',

were eventually pardoned by Henry VIII, probably largely thanks to pleas for mercy made by his Queen, Catherine of Aragon, and by Thomas Wolsey. At this, the prisoners 'took the halters from their necks and danced and sang'. In the aftermath of the riots, the annual May Day celebrations that had taken place for hundreds of years were discontinued and the May Pole that gave Undershaft its name was taken away. According to a contemporary account, in the 'The Chronicle of the Grey Friars': 'Thys yere was yell [evil] May Day, that yong men and prentes of London rose in the nyght, and wolde have had James Mottas an owte-landych mane [foreigner] slayne ... but he hyde hym in hys gotters in hys howse; and from thence they wente un to sent Martyns, and there spoyled the ... shoppes; and thane rose the mayer and shreffes and wolde have cessyd them, but they cowed not. ... And iiij or v days after ... at the last there were dyvers of them hongyd within the citte on gallos... And within shorte space the kynge satte in Westmyster halle, and there was commandyd the ... rest of them ... to come with halters abowte their neckes ... to ask pardone, and soo a generall pardone was gevyne unto theme alle that came that tyme.' In 1549 a rabble-rousing Protestant preacher incited the congregation to sack the Cathedral, seen as a symbol of Catholicism, which they did with great zeal, rampaging through the interior, destroying the high altar and wall-hangings, and desecrating the tombs.

In 1612 John Chamberlain wrote: 'This last Sunday Moll Cut-purse, a notorious baggage (that used to go into man's apparel and challenged the field of diverse gallants) was brought to [Paul's Cross], where she wept bitterly and seemed very penitent, but it is since doubted she was maudlin drunk. Being discovered to have tippled off three quarts of sack before she came to her penance.' Moll Cut-purse, whose real name was Mary Frith, was the model for Thomas Dekker and Thomas Middleton's 'The Roaring Girle', written in 1611. On 5 November 1622 the then Dean of the Cathedral, the priest and metaphysical poet John Donne, delivered his famous 'Gunpowder Plot Sermon' here, reassuring the congregation as to the ongoing commitment to the Protestant cause of the King, who was himself widely suspected of harbouring Catholic sympathies.

31 – St Paul's Cathedral

The fourth, 'Old St Paul's', was built in the Norman, or Romanesque, style in the years after 1087 by Bishop Maurice and his successors; partially rebuilt and extended in the Gothic style in 1221-1240, and in the 'New Work' of 1269-1332; renovated in the Renaissance style by Inigo Jones 1633-1641, again by Wren after the Civil War in 1660; and burned down in the Great Fire. There are models of Old St Paul's in the modern Cathedral and also in the Museum of London. The fifth, present cathedral was built in the Baroque style by Wren between 1675-1710/1 (*Figures 31c, 32c*). There are a great many important memorials in the interior of the cathedral. The one in the south quire aisle to the metaphysical poet John Donne (1572-1631) survived the Great Fire, although if you look carefully, you can still see scorch-marks around its base. The ones in the crypt to, among others, Nicholas Bacon (d. 1579), and Thomas Heneage (d. 1594), also survived the fire, although again not without a certain amount of charring. The cathedral famously survived the Blitz essentially intact: some would say due to divine intervention; others, to the heroism of the St Paul's Watch, who extinguished around 30 fires caused by incendiary bombs on the night of 29/30 December 1940 alone.

32 – Site of Shakespeare's House, Ireland Yard, off St Andrew's HIll

What had been the gate-house of the dissolved Blackfriars Priory, adjacent to the later Blackfriars Theatre, was purchased by Shakespeare in 1613 (according to the Deed of Conveyance in the London Metropolitan Archives, which incidentally bears one of the few surviving examples of his signature, it cost him £140, at a time when the annual salary for a teacher was £20). The site is marked by a blue plaque. What may once have been part of the cellar is preserved in what is now the public house known as the 'Cockpit'.

33 – Site of Blackfriars Theatres, Playhouse Yard

Built on the site of the Great Hall of the Blackfriars Priory by Richard Farrant in 1576; rebuilt by James Burbage on the site of the Parliament Hall 1596-1600; closed down by the Puritans in 1642 and demolished in 1655. In the Parliament Hall in 1529 a real-life drama was enacted when the Legatine Court, under the Papal Legate, Cardinal Lorenzo Campeggio, and King Henry VIII's representative, Cardinal Thomas Wolsey, met to discuss the proposed annulment of Henry's marriage to Catherine of Aragon. The rebuilt theatre, the 'Second Blackfriars', was – like the first – indoors, and was used by theatre companies throughout the year. Open-air playhouses such as the Globe on Bankside in Southwark were unusable in bad weather.

The 'Second Blackfriars' was also an 'all-seater', seating 6-700 in some – although not much – comfort, and charging a minimum of 6*d* a head. In contrast, the Globe seated or stood more (2-3000), but charged less (a minimum of only 1*d*). In time, the theatre became extremely popular with the fashionable set, and equally profitable. From 1600 to 1608, it housed performances by a troupe of boy-actors under Henry Evans and Nathaniel Giles, some of the boys evidently forcibly taken from their homes and families and pressed into service through 'impressment warrants' authorised by the Crown. From 1609, it housed performances by Shakespeare's 'King's Men', who also owned it. The recently completed Wanamaker Playhouse inside the reconstruction of the Globe on Bankside is similar in design to the 'Second Blackfriars' (*Figure 35*).

34 – Apothecaries' Hall, Blackfriars Lane
Originally built in 1633, on part of the site of the former Blackfriars Priory, which was dissolved in 1538. Substantially burned down in the Great Fire, and rebuilt by Thomas Lock in 1668. The walls of the original building survive.

35 – Site of Bridewell Palace, New Bridge Street
Originally built by Henry VIII in 1520, granted by Edward VI in 1553 to the City of London to house a hospital, hostel, work-house and prison, and burned down in the Great Fire in 1666. Subsequently rebuilt in 1667, and demolished between 1864 and 1871. The new building on the old site bears a commemorative plaque.

36 – Site of Second Baynard's Castle, Queen Victoria Street
Built in a river-front location around 1338, rebuilt around 1428 and possibly again in the late fifteenth century. It was used by a succession of Kings and Queens in the late fifteenth to sixteenth centuries, before being essentially completely destroyed in the Great Fire in the seventeenth. It was the London headquarters of the House of York during the Wars of the Roses, and Edward IV was hailed King here, in 1461 (moreover, Richard III is believed to have asserted his claim to the throne here in 1483). Both Lady Jane Grey and, nine days later, Mary, were proclaimed Queen here in 1553. A Corporation blue plaque on the Embankment marks the site of the castle, parts of which were uncovered during building works in 1972.

Bibliography and References

LAMAS = London and Middlesex Archaeological Society; MoLA(S) = Museum of London Archaeology (Service); PCA = Pre-Construct Archaeology.

Ackroyd, P., 1998. *The Life of Thomas More*. Chatto.

Ackroyd, P., 2000. *London – The Biography*. Chatto & Windus.

Ackroyd, P., 2004. *Chaucer*. Chatto & Windus.

Ackroyd, P., 2005. *Shakespeare*. Chatto & Windus.

Ackroyd, P., 2011. *The History of England. Volume I – Foundation* ... . MacMillan.

Ackroyd, P., 2012. *The History of England. Volume II – Tudors* ... . MacMillan.

Ackroyd, P., 2014. *The History of England. Volume III – Civil War* ... . MacMillan.

Adams, A. & Forbes, S., 2015. *The Syon Abbey Herbal – AD1517*. AMCD.

Adams, J.C., 1961. *The Globe Playhouse* ... . Constable & Company Ltd.

Albert, E. & Tucker, K., 2014. *In Search of Alfred the Great*. Amberley.

Aldhouse-Green, M., 2018. *Sacred Britannia – The Gods and Rituals of Roman Britain*. Thames & Hudson.

Alford, S., 2017. *London's Triumph – Merchant Adventurers and the Tudor City*. Allen Kane.

Allderidge, P., 1997. *Bethlem Hospital 1247-1997*. Phillimore.

Ambler, S., Baker, P., Ball, S. *et al.*, 2015. *The Story of Parliament* ... . The History of Parliament Trust.

Ames-Lewis, F. (ed.), 1999. *Sir Thomas Gresham and Gresham College – Studies in the Intellectual History of London in the Sixteenth and Seventeenth Centuries*. Ashgate.

Andrews, J., Briggs, A., Porter, R. *et al.*, 1997. *The History of Bethlem*. Routledge.

Anonymous, 1632. *The Lawes Resolutions of Women's Rights*.

Anonymous, 1827. *A Chronicle of London from 1089 to 1483; Written in the Fifteenth Century and For the First Time Printed from MSS in the British Museum*. Longman, Rees, Orme, Brown, and Green.

Anonymous, 1932. *Chartulary of the Hospital of St Thomas the Martyr, Southwark (1213 to 1525)*. Privately printed.

Anonymous, 1938. *Scenes from the Life of St Thomas's Hospital from 1106 to the Present Time*. Surrey Fine Arts Press.

Anonymous, 1996. *Southwark*. Southwark Heritage Association.

Anonymous, undated. *Greensted Church Guidebook*.

Anonymous, undated. *A Guide to St Pancras Old Church* ... .

Anonymous, undated. *The Parish Church of St Martin, Ruislip*. Beric Tempest.

Appleford, A., 2015. *Learnig to Die in London 1380-1540*. University of Pennsylvania Press.

Arber, E., 1890. *A List ... of ... London Publishers ... between 1553 and 1640*. [Guildhall Library].

Archer, J.E., Goldring, E. & Knight, S. (eds.), 2011. *The Intellectual and Cultural World of the Early Modern Inns of Court*. Manchester University Press.

Archer, I.W., 2004. *The Haberdashers' Company* ... . Phillimore.

Archer, I.W., 2017. *The History of the Haberdashers' Company*. Phillimore.

Arnold, C., 2010. *City of Sin*. Simon & Schuster.

Arnold, C., 2015. *Globe – Life in Shakespeare's London*. Simon & Schuster.

Aston, M., 2000. *Monasteries in the Landscape*. Tempus.

Atkinson, D. & Oswald, A., 1969. London Clay Tobacco Pipes. *Journal of the Archaeological Association, Third Series*, 32: 172-227.

Atkinson, F., 1985. *St Paul's and the City*. Michael Joseph/Park Lane.

Aubrey, J., 1669-96. '*Brief Lives', Chiefly of Contemporaries* ... .

Auer, J. & Maarleveld, T.J. (Eds.), 2014. *The Gresham Ship Project – A 16th-Century Merchantman Wrecked in the Princes Channel, Thames Estuary. Volume I – Excavation and Hull Studies*. British Archaeological Reports.

Ayre, J. & Wroe-Brown, R., 2015. The Post-Roman Foreshore and the origins of the Late Anglo-Saxon Waterfront and Dock of Aethelred's Hithe. *Archaeological Journal*, 172(1): 123-94.

Baddeley, J.J., 1952. *The Guildhall of the City of London. Eighth Edition*. Spottiswoode-Ballantyne.

Baker, H.B., 1904. *History of the London Stage and its Famous Players (1576-1903)*. Benjamin Blom.

Baker, T., 1970. *Medieval London*. Cassell.

Baker, T.M.M., 2000. *London – Rebuilding the City after the Great Fire*. Phillimore.

Barber, B. & Bowsher, D., 2000. *The Eastern Cemetery of Roman London*. MoLA (Monograph 4).

Barber, B., Chew, S., Dyson, T. & White, B., 2004. *The Cistercian Abbey of St Mary Stratford Langthorne, Essex*. MoLA (Monograph 18).

Barber, B. & Thomas, C., 2002. *The London Charterhouse*. MoLA (Monograph 10).

Barber, B., Thomas, C. & Watson, B., 2013. *Religion in Medieval London*. MoLA.

Barber, P., 2012. *London – A History in Maps*. The London Topographical Society/The British Library.

Barclay, B. & Lindley, D., 2017. *Shakespeare, Music and Performance*. Cambridge University Press.

Bard, R., 2013. *London's Lost Battlefields*. Fonthill.

Barker, F. & Jackson, P., 2008. *Pleasures of London*. London Topographical Society (Publication No. 167).

Barker, F. & Hyde, R., 1982. *London as it Might Have Been*. John Murray.

Barnett, L.D., 1940. *Bevis Marks Records ... . Part I – The Early History of the Congregation from the Beginning until 1800*. Oxford University Press.

Barnett, R. & Jay, M., 2008. *Medical London*. Wellcome Trust.

Barron, C.M., 1974. *The Mediaeval Guildhall of London*. Corporation of London.

Barron, C.M., 2004. *London in the Later Middle Ages ...* . Oxford University Press.

Barton, N. & Myers, S., 2016. *The Lost Rivers of London. Revised and Extended Edition*. Historical Publications.

Barty-King, H., 1994. *The Salters' Company 1394-1994*. James & James.

Bastable, J., 2011. *Inside Pepys' London*. F & W Media.

Bateman, N., 2000. *Gladiators at the Guildhall*. MoLA.

Bateman, N., 2011. *Roman London's Amphitheatre*. MoLA.

Bateman, N., Cowan, C. & Wroe-Brown, R., 2008. *London's Roman Amphitheatre, Guildhall Yard, City of London*. MoLA (Monograph 35).

Beadle, R. (ed.), 1994. *The Cambridge Companion to Medieval English Theatre*. Cambridge University Press.

Beard, G., 1982. *The Work of Christopher Wren*. John Bartholomew & Son.

Bebbington, G., 1972. *London Street Names*. Batsford.

Bedford, J., 1966. *London's Burning*. Abelard Schuman.

Belcher, V., Bond, R., Gray, M. & Wittrick, A., 2004. *Sutton House*. English Heritage/National Trust.

Bell, W.G., 1912. *Fleet Street in Seven Centuries ...* . Sir Isaac Pitman & Sons Ltd.

Bell, W.G., 1951a. *The Great Fire of London in 1666. Revised Edition*. The Bodley Head.

Bell, W.G., 1951b. *The Great Plague in London. Revised Edition*. The Bodley Head.

Bell, W.G., Cottrill, F. & Spon, C., 1937. *London Wall through Eighteen Centuries ...* . Balding and nMansell.

Benham, W., 1902. *Old St Paul's*. Seeley and Co. Ltd.

Bennett, J.G., 2009. *E1 – A Journey through Whitechapel and Spitalfields*. Five Leaves.

Bergeron, D.M., 2017. *Shakespeare's London 1613*. Manchester University Press.

Berry, G., 1978. *Taverns and Tokens of Pepys' London*. Seaby Publications Limited.

Berry, H. (ed.), 1979. *The First Public Playhouse – The Theatre in Shoreditch 1576-1598*. McGill-Queen's University Press.

Berry, H., 1989. The First Public Playhouses, especially the Red Lion. *Shakespeare Quarterly*, **40**(2): 133-48.

Berry, H., 1986. *The Boar's Head Playhouse*. Folger Books.

Besant, W., 1894. *London*. Chatto & Windus.

Besant, W., 1903. *London in the Time of the Stuarts*. Adam & Charles Black.

Besant, W., 1904. *London in the Time of the Tudors*. Adam & Charles Black.

Besant, W., 1925. *Westminster*. Chatto & Windus.

Betjeman, J., 1993. *City of London Churches*. Pitkin.

Bicheno, H., 2012. *Elizabeth's Sea Dogs*. Conway.

Biggs, C.R.D., 1912. *All Hallows Barking ...* . Waterlow and Sons Ltd.

Birch, W. de G., 1887. *The Historical Charters and Constitutional Documents of the City of London*. Whiting & Co.

Birchenough, A., Dwyer, E., Elsden, N. & Lewis, H., 2009. *Tracks through Time – Archaeology and History from the London Overground East London Line*. MoLA/Transport for London.

Bird, J., Hassall, M. & Sheldon, H. (eds.), 1996. *Interpreting Roman London ...* . Oxbow (Monograph 58).

Bird, R., 1949. *The Turbulent London of Richard II*. Longmans, Green and Co.

Bishop, B., Cotton, J. & Humphrey, R., 2017. 'Mesolithic Activity and early Neolithic Earthworks at 41-42 Kew Bridge Road, Hounslow'. *Transactions, London and Middlesex Archaeological Society*, 68: 1-40.

Bisschop, W.R., 1968. *The Rise of the London Money Market 1640-1826*. Frank Cass & Co. Ltd.

Bisson, D.R., 1993. *The Merchant Adventurers of England – The Company and the Crown 1474-1564*. University of Delaware Press.

Black, G., 2003. *Jewish London*. Tymsder.

Black, J., 2009. *London – A History*. Carnegie.

Blair, I. & Sankey, D., 2007. *A Roman Drainage Culvert, Great Fire Destruction Debris and Other Evidence from Hillside Sites North-East of London Bridge*. MoLA (Archaeology Studies Series 17).

Bland, D.S., 1984. *Three Revels from the Inns of Court*. Avebury Publishing Company.

Blatherwick, S. & Bluer, R., 2009. *Great Houses, Moats and Mills on the South Bank of the Thames*. MoLA (Monograph 47).

Boffey, J., 2012. *Manuscript and Print in London c. 1475-1530*. British Library.

Bolton, J.L., 1998. *The Alien Communities in London in the Fifteenth Century – The Subsidy Rolls of 1440 & 1483-4*. Richard III & Yorkist History Trust in association with Paul Watkins, Stamford.

Borman, T., 2015. *The Story of the Tower of London*. Merrell.

Boswell, E., 1932. *The Restoration Court Stage (1660-1702) ...* . George Allen & Unwin Ltd.

Boulter, C.B., 1935. *History of St Andrew Undershaft ...* . Eden Fisher & Co. Ltd.

Boulton, W.B., 1901. *The Amusements of Old London*. John C. Nimmo.

Boulton, J., 1987. *Neighbourhood and Society – a London Suburb in the Seventeenth Century*. Cambridge University Press.

Bowsher, D., Dyson, T., Holder, N. & Howell, I., 2007. *The London Guildhall*. MoLA (Monograph 36).

Bowsher, J., 2012. *Shakespeare's London Theatreland*. MoLA.

Bowsher, J. & Miller, P., 2009. *The Rose and the Globe*. MoLA (Monograph 48).

Boyd, P., 1928. *Index to London Lay Subsidy 1412*. [MS in Guildhall Library].

Boyd, P.D.A. 1981. 'The Micropalaeontology and Palynology of Medieval Estuarine Sediments from the Fleet and Thames in London'. Pp. 274-92 in Neale, J.W. & Brasier, M.D. (eds.): *Microfossils from Recent and Fossil Shelf Seas*. Ellis Horwood.

Bradley, S. & Pevsner, N., 1997. *London 1 – The City of London*. Penguin (The Buildings of England).

Bradley, S. & Pevsner, N., 1998. *London – The City Churches*. Penguin.

Bradley, S. & Pevsner, N., 2003. *London 6 – Westminster*. Yale University Press (The Buildings of England).

Bramley, Z., 2015. *The Shakespeare Trail … *. Amberley.

Brandon, D. & Brooke, A., 2006. *London – The Executioner's City*. Sutton.

Brandon, D. & Brooke, A., 2011. *Bankside*. Amberley.

Breay, C. & Story, J. (eds.), 2018. *Anglo-Saxon Kingdoms – Art, Word, War*. British Library.

Brechin, D., 1968. *The Conqueror's London*. MacDonald (Discovering London 2).

Brenner, R., 1993. *Merchants and Revolution – Commercial Change, Political Conflict and London's Overseas Traders, 1530-1653*. Cambridge University Press.

Brereton, G., 1978. *Froissart Chronicles. Revised Edition*. Penguin Books.

Brett-James, N.G., 1935. *The Growth of Stuart London*. George Allen & Unwin Ltd.

Brickley, M., Miles, A. & Stainer, H., 1999. *The Cross Bones Burial Ground, Redcross Way, Southwark, London … *. MoLA (Monograph 3).

Brigden, S., 1989. *London and the Reformation*. Oxford University Press.

Brigham, T. & Woodger, A., 2001. *Roman and Medieval Townhouses on the London Waterfront*. MoLA (Monograph 9).

Brooke, A., 2010. *Fleet Street*. Amberley.

Brooke, A. & Brandon, D., 2004. *Tyburn*. Sutton.

Brooke, A. & Brandon, D., 2010. *Olde London Punishments*. The History Press.

Brooke, C., 2003. *The Age of the Cloister*. Revised Edition (of *The Rise and Fall of the Medieval Monastery*). Sutton Publishing (reprinted in 2006 by the Folio Society).

Brooke, C.N.L., 1975. *London 800-1216 – The Shaping of a City*. Secker & Warburg.

Brooke-Hunt, V., 1902. *The Story of Westminster Abbey*. James Nisbet & Co.

Brotton, J., 2016. *This Orient Isle – Elizabethan England and the Islamic World*. Allen Lane.

Brown, B., 1921. *Law Sports and Gray's Inn (1594)*. Privately printed.

Brown, C., 2009. *Whitehall*. Simon & Schuster.

Brown, P., 2012. *Shakespeare's Local*. MacMillan.

Brown, R.L., 1996. *A History of the Fleet Prison, London*. The Edwin Mellen Press.

Bruce, J., 1868. *Diary of John Manningham of the Middle Temple, … 1602-1603*. The Camden Society.

Bucholz, R.O. & Ward, J.P., 2012. *London – A Social and Cultural History, 1550-1750.* Cambridge University Press.

Bull, R., Davis, S., Lewis, H. & Phillpotts, C., 2011. *Holywell Priory and the Development of Shoreditch to c1600.* MoLA (Monograph 53).

Bumpus, T.F., 1927. *Ancient London Churches.* T. Werner Laurie Ltd.

Burch, M. & Treveil, P., 2011. *The Development of Early Medieval and Later Poultry.* MoLA (Monograph 38).

Burford, E.J., 1973. *The Orrible Synne – A Look at London Lechery from Roman to Cromwellian Times.* Calder & Bryars.

Burford, E.J., 1977. *In the Clink.* W.H. Allen.

Burford, E.J., 1990. *London – The Synfulle Citie.* Robert Hale.

Burford, E.J., 1993. *The Bishop's Brothels* [previously published as *Bawds and Lodgings – A History of the London Bankside Brothels*]. Robert Hale.

Burford, E.J. & Wotton, J., 1995. *Private Vices, Public Virtues – Bawdry in London from Elizabethan Times to the Regency.* Robert Hale.

Butler, J., 2005. *Saxons, Knights and Lawyers in the Inner Temple.* PCA (Monograph 4).

Butler, J., 2006. *Reclaiming the Marsh – Archaeological Excavations at Moor House, City of London.* PCA (Monograph 6).

Butler, L. & Given-Wilson, C., 1979. *Medieval Monasteries of Great Britain.* Michael Joseph.

Byrne, M. & Bush, G.R. (eds.), 2007. *St Mary-le-Bow – A History.* Wharncliffe.

Callaway, E., 2011. The Black Death Decoded – The Genome of a 660-Year-Old Bacterium is Revealing Secrets from One of Europe's Darkest Chapters. *Nature,* 478: 444-6.

Campbell, J.W.P., 2007. *Building St Paul's.* Thames & Hudson.

Campbell, K.E., Tomalak, A. & Manning, P., 2013. *A Brief History and Account of St Katharine Cree Church. Revised and Updated Edition.* The Guild Church Council of St Katharine Cree.

Capper, E., Desmond, E., Finch, S. *et al.*, 2009. *St Helen's Church ... .* Jarrold..

Carlin, M., 1996. *Medieval Southwark.* Hambledon.

Carlin, M. & Rosenthal, J.T. (eds.), 2017. *Medieval London – Collected Papers of Caroline M. Barron.* Medieval Institute Publications, Western Michigan Unversity.

Carpenter, E. (ed.), 1966. *A House of Kings – The Official History of Westminster Abbey.* John Baker.

Carruthers, B. (ed.), 2013. *The Anglo-Saxon Chronicle.* Pen & Sword.

Carson, C. & Karim-Cooper, F. (eds.), 2008. *Shakespeare's Globe.* Cambridge.

Cartwright, J.J., 1875. *The Memoirs of Sir John Reresby ... .* Longmans, Green & Co.

Carus-Wilson, E.M., 1967. *Medieval Merchant Venturers ... . Second Edition.* Methuen & Co. Ltd.

Casson, L., Drummond-Murray, J. & Francis, A., 2014. *Romano-British Round Houses to Medieval Parish – Excavations at 10 Gresham Street, City of London ... .* MoLA (Monograph 67).

Cavert, W.M., 2016. *The Smoke of London – Energy and Environment in the Early Modern City.* Cambridge University Press.

Chambers, E.K., 1906. *Notes on the History of the Revels Office under the Tudors*. A.H. Bullen.

Chambers, P., 2009. *Bedlam – London's Hospital for the Mad*. Ian Allan.

Chambers, R.W. & Daunt, M. (eds.), 1931. *A Book of London English 1384-1425*. Clarendon Press.

Champion, J.A.I., 1995. *London's Dreaded Visitation – The Social Geography of the Great Plague in 1665*. Centre for Metropolitan History.

Chartres, R. & Vermont, D., 1998. *A Brief History of Gresham College 1597-1997*. Gresham College.

Chaudhuri, K.N., 1965. The English East India Company … . Frank Cass & Co. Ltd.

Chaudhuri, K.N., 1978. *The Trading World of Asia and the English East India Company 1660-1760*. Cambridge University Press.

Christ's Hospital, 1953. *Christ's Hospital – Four Hundred Years Old*. Christ's Hospital.

Christiansen, C.P., 1987. *Memorials of the Book Trade in Medieval London …* . D.S. Brewer.

Christiansen, C.P., 1990. *A Directory of London Stationers and Book Artisans 1300-1500*. Bibliographic Society of America.

Christiansson, C.P., 2005. *The Riverside Gardens of Thomas More's London*. Yale University Press.

Christopher, J., 2012. *Wren's City of London Churches*. Amberley.

Chute, M., 1949. *Shakespeare of London*. E.P. Dutton.

Clark, D., 2007. *Barnet – 1471 … *. Pen and Sword.

Clark, J., 1989. *Saxon and Norman London*. Her Majesty's Stationery Office/ Museum of London.

Clark, J., 2018. The Walbrook Skulls Revisited. *London Archaeologist*, **15**(4): 99-109.

Clayton, A., 2003. *London's Coffee Houses … *. Historical Publications.

Clements, D., 2010. *The Geology of London*. Geologists' Association.

Clout, H. (ed.), 2004. *The Times History of London. Fourth Edition*. Times Books.

Coates, R., 1998. A New Explanation of the Name of London. *Transactions of the Philological Society*. **96**(2): 203–29.

Cobb, G., 1942. *The Old Churches of London*. Batsford.

Cohen, N. & Stevens, N., 2011. Medieval Fishing on the Isle of Dogs. *London Archaeologist*, **13**(2): 55.

Cohen, N. & Wragg, E., 2017. 'The River's Tale' – Archaeology on the Thames Foreshore in Greater London. MoLA.

Connell, B., Jones, A.G., Redfern, R. & Walker, D., 2012. *A Bioarchaeological Study of Medieval Burials on the Site of St Mary Spital*. MoLA (Monograph 60).

Connell, C., 1982. *They Gave Us Shakespeare – John Heminge & Henry Condell*. Oriel Press.

Cook, A.J., 1981. *The Privileged Playgoers of Shakespeare's London, 1576-1642*. Princeton University Press.

Cook, G., 1955. *Old St Paul's Cathedral – A Lost Story of Mediaeval London*. Phoenix House.

Cook, G., 1999. *St Clement Danes*. Pitkin.

Cooper, M., 2003. *'A More Beautiful City' – Robert Hooke and the Rebuilding of London after the Great Fire.* Sutton.

Corfield, P.J. & Harte, W.B. (eds.), 1990. *London and the English Economy, 1500-1700.* The Hambledon Press.

Cooper, T. (ed.), 2014. *Elizabeth I and Her People.* National Portrait Gallery.

Cornell, H. (ed.), 2011. *St Paul's Cathedral.* Scala.

Cornford, M.E., 1910. *Paul's Cross – A History.* S.P.C.K.

Cotton, J., Hall, J., Keily, J. *et al.*, 2014. *Hidden Histories and Records of Antiquity.* London and Middlesex Archaeological Society (Special Paper 17).

Cowie, R., 2013. The Gardens and Inner Gatehouse of the Abbey of St Mary Stratford Langthorne and Post-Dissolution Settlement. *Transactions, London and Middlesex Archaeological Society,* **64**: 163-200.

Cowie, R., 2018. Saxon London – Milestones and Challenges. *London Archaeologist,* **15**(5): 123-30.

Cowie, R. & Blackmore, L., 2008. *Early and Middle Saxon Rural Settlement in the London Region.* MoLA (Monograph 41).

Cowie, R. & Blackmore, L., 2012. *Lundenwic ... .* MoLA (Monograph 63).

Cox, J. & Chessun, C., 2002. *St Dunstan and All Saints, Stepney.* Jarrold.

Craven, W.F., 1957. *The Virginia Company of London.* Clearfield.

Craven, W.F., 1964. *Dissolution of the Virginia Company – The Failure of a Colonial Experiment.* Peter Smith, Gloucester, Mass.

Crawford, A., 1977. *A History of the Vintners' Company.* Constable.

Crawforth, H., Dustagheer, S. & Young, J., 2014. *Shakespeare in London.* Bloomsbury.

Crew, A., 1933a. *London Prisons of Today and Yesterday ... .* Ivor Nicholason and Watson Limited.

Crew, A., 1933b. *The Old Bailey – History, Constitutions, Functions, Notable Trials.* Ivor Nicholson & Watson Lrd.

Crowfoot, E., Pritchard, F. & Staniland, K., 2001. *Textiles and Clothing 1150-1450. New Edition.* Boydell/Museum of London.

Cruickshank, D., 2016. *Spitalfields ... .* Random House.

Cunningham, K., 1992. *St Etheldreda's Ely Place.* Jarrold.

Dale, T.C., 1931. *The Inhabitants of London in 1638.* Society of Genealogists.

Davey, J. (ed.), 2018. *Tudor & Stuart Seafarers – The Emergence of a Maritime Nation, 1485-1707.* Adlard Coles/National Maritime Museum Greenwich.

Davey, P., 1981. *Pipes and Kilns in the London Region.* British Archaeological Reports (No. 97).

Davies, F.G., 1999. *The Royal African Company.* Routledge.

Davies, G.S., 1921. *Charterhouse in London – Monastery, Mansion, Hospital, School.* John Murray.

Davies, J.D., 2008. *Pepys's Navy – Ships, Men & Warfare, 1649-1689.* Seaforth.

Davies, K.G., 1957. *The Royal African Company.* Longmans, Green and Co.

Davies, P., 2009. *Lost London 1870-1945.* Transatlantic/English Heritage.

Davies, P., 2012. *London – Hidden Interiors.* Atlantic/English Heritage.

Davies, R.G. & Denton, J.H. (eds.), 1981. *The English Parliament in the Middle Ages.* Manchester University Press.

Day, B., 1996. *This Wooden 'O' – Shakespeare's Globe Reborn.* Oberon/The Shakespeare Globe Trust.

Day, M., 2011. *Shakespeare's London*. Batsford.

De la Bedoyere, G. (ed.), 1995. *The Diary of John Evelyn*. The Boydell Press.

De la Bedoyere, G (ed.), 2006. *The Letters of Samuel Pepys*. The Boydell Press.

Da la Bedoyere, G., 2013. *Roman Britain*. Revised Edition. Thames & Hudson.

De la Ruffiniere du Prey, P., 2000. *Hawksmoor's London Churches*. The University of Chicago Press.

De Mare, E., 1975. *Wren's London*. The Folio Society.

Defoe, D., 1722. *A Journal of the Plague Year ...* . E. Nutt.

Deiter, K., 2008. *The Tower of London in English Renaissance Drama –* Icon of Opposition. Routledge.

Dekker, T., 1603. *The Wonderfull Yeare 1603*. Thomas Creede.

Dennis, G., 2004. *Red Lion Theatre, Whitechapel ...* . Crossrail (Documentary Research Report 1E0418-C1E00-00004).

Derwent, G., 1968. *Roman London*. MacDonald (Discovering London 1).

Derwent, K., 1968. *Medieval London*. MacDonald (Discovering London 3).

Dick, O.D., 1949. *Aubrey's Brief Lives*. Secker & Warburg.

Dickinson, H.W., 1954. *Water Supply of Greater London*. The Newcomen Society/Courier Press.

Dietz, B. (ed.), 1972. *The Port and Trade of Early Elizabethan London ...* . London Record Society.

Ditchfield, P.H., 1926. *The Story of the City Companies*. Burleigh Press.

Divers, D., Mayo, C., Cohen, N. & Jarrett, C., 2008. *A New Millennium at Southwark Cathedral – Investigations into the First Two Thousand Years*. PCA (Monograph 8).

Dobbs, B., 1972. *Drury Lane – Three Centuries of the Theatre Royal, 1663-1971*. Cassell.

Dockray, K., 2002. *William Shakespeare, the Wars of the Roses and the Historians*. Tempus.

Doolittle, I., 1994. *The Mercers' Company 1579-1959*. W.S. Hervey & Son.

Doolittle, I., 2010. *The City of London and its Livery Companies*. Guildhall Library Publications.

Douglas-Smith, A.E., 1965. *The City of London School*. Second Edition. Blackwell.

Downes, K., 1970. *Hawksmoor*. Thames & Hudson.

Downes, K., 1988. *The Architecture of Wren*. Third Edition. Redhedge.

Draper, F.W.M., 1962. *Four Centuries of Merchant Taylors' School*. Oxford University Press.

Dudley, M., 1999. *Saint Bartholomew the Great*. The Priory Church of St Bartholomew the Great and Jarrold Publishing.

Duff, E.G., 1906. *Westminster and London Printers 1476-1535*. Cambridge University Press.

Dunning, G.C., 1945. Two Fires in Roman London. *Antiquaries Journal*, **25**: 48-77.

Dunwoodie, L., 2004. *Pre-Boudican and Later Activity on the Site of the Forum*. MoLA (Archaeology Studies Series 13).

Dunwoodie, L., Harward, C. & Pitt, K., 2016. *An Early Roman Fort and Urban Development of Londinium's Eastern Hill ...* . MoLA (Monograph 65).

Dustagheer, S., 2017. *Shakespeare's Two Playhouses – Repertory and Theatre Space at the Globe and the Blackfriars, 1599-1613*. Cambridge University Press.

Dutton, R., 2018. *Shakespeare's Theatre.* Wiley Blackwell.

Dyson, T., Samuel, M., Steele, A. & Wright, S.M., 2011. *The Cluniac Priory and Abbey of St Saviour, Bermondsey, Surrey.* MoLA (Monograph 50).

Egan, G., 2010. *The Medieval Household. New Edition.* Boydell/Museum of London.

Egan, G. & Pritchard, F., 2002. *Dress Accessories 1150-1450. New Edition.* Boydell/Museum of London.

Ekwall, E., 1951. *Two Early London Subsidy Rolls.* C.W.K. Gleerup, Lund.

Ekwall, E., 1956. *Studies on the Population of Medieval London.* Almqvist & Wiksell, Stockholm.

Elborough, T. & Rennison, N. (eds.), 2013. *A London Year.* Frances Lincoln.

Elliott, S., 2018. *Ragstone to Riches – Imperial Estates, Metalla and the Roman Military in the South East of Britain during the Occupation.* BAR.

Elsden, J.V. & Howe, J.A., 1923. *The Stones of London ... .* Colliery Guardian Company Limited.

Elsden, N.J., 2002. *Excavations at 25 Cannon Street, City of London – From the Middle Bronze Age to the Great Fire.* MoLA (Archaeology Studies Series 5).

Epstein, M., 1908. *The English Levant Company.* George Routledge & Son Limited.

Etherington-Smith, M. (ed.), 2009. *Somerset House.* Cultureshock Media (for The Somerset House Trust).

Evans, J., 2013. *Merchant-Adventurers – The Voyage of Discovery that Transformed Tudor England.* Weidenfeld & Nicolson.

Fairfield, S., 1983. *The Streets of London – A Dictionary of their Names and their Origins.* MacMillan.

Field, J., 1980. *Place names of Greater London.* Batsford.

Fincham, H.W., 1933. *The Order of the Hospital of St John of Jerusalem.* The Grand Priory in the British Realm of the Veritable Order of the Hospital of St John of Jerusalem.

Firstbrook, P., 2014. *A Man Most Driven – Captain John Smith, Pocahontas and the Founding of America.* Oneworld.

Fitzstephen, T., 1183. *Vita Sancti Thomae [et] Descriptio Nobilissimi Civitatis Londoniae.*

Flanders, D., 1974. *The Great Livery Companies of the City of London ... .* Charles Skilton.

Flintham, D., 2017. *Civil War London – A Military History of London under Charles I and Oliver Cromwell.* Helion & Company.

Foley, M., 2018. *City of London.* Amberley.

Forshaw, A., 2015 *Smithfield.* Robert Hale.

Forsyth, H., 2013. *The Cheapside Hoard.* Museum of London/Philip Wilson Publishers.

Forsyth, H., 2016. *Butcher, Baker, Candlestick Maker – Surviving the Great Fire of London.* Museum of London/I.B. Tauris.

Foster, W., 1924. *The East India House ... .* John Lane, The Bodley Head Limited.

Fowler, L. & Taylor, R., 2013. *At the Limits of Lundenwic ... .* MoLA (Archaeology Studies Series 27).

Fox, A., 1968. *A Brief Description of the Worshipful Company of Skinners.* Revised Edition. Privately printed.

Foxell, S., 2007. *Mapping London*. Black Dog.

Frame, P., 2015. *Liberty's Apostle – Richard Price, His Life and Times*. University of Wales Press.

Francia, S. & Stobart, A. (eds), 2014. *Critical Approaches to the History of Western Herbal Medicine* ... . Bloomsbury Academic Press..

Francis, A., 2017. *The Deptford Royal Dockyard and Manor of Sayes Court, London* ... . MoLA (Monograph 71).

Franciscus, A., 1497. *Itinerarium Britanniae*.

Fraser, A., 1973. *Cromwell* ... . Weidenfeld & Nicolson.

Fraser, A., 1996. *The Gunpowder Plot*. Weidenfeld & Nicolson.

Freeth, S., 2016. *A Guide to the Merchant Taylors Company of the City of London*. Leachprint.

Fuller, J.O., 1981. *Sir Francis Bacon* ... . East-West Publications.

Gadd, I.P. & Wallis, P. (eds.), 2002. *Guilds, Society and Economy in London 1450-1800*. Institute of Historical Research.

Gair, R., 1982. *The Children of Paul's – The Story of a Theatre Company 1553-1608*. Cambridge University Press.

Gardiner, D., 1930. *The Story of Lambeth Palace – A Historical Survey*. Constable & Co. Ltd.

Geraghty, A., 2007. *The Architectural Drawings of Sir Christopher Wren*. Lund Humphries.

Gerhold, D., 2016. *London Plotted – Plans of London Buildings c. 1450-1720*. London Topographical Society (Publication No. 178).

German, L. & Rees, J., 2012. *A People's History of London*. Verso.

Gilbert, A., 2002. *The New Jerusalem – Rebuilding London* ... . Bantam Press.

Girling, B., 2010. *The City of London*. The History Press.

Girtin, T., 1958. *The Golden Ram – A Narrative History of the Clothworkers' Company 1528-1958*. Hunt, Barnard & Co. Ltd.

Glover, E., 1991. *A History of the Ironmongers' Company*. Biddles Ltd.

Gordon, C. & Dewhirst, W., 1985. *The Ward of Cripplegate in the City of London*. Cripplegate Ward Club.

Gordon, E.O., 1932. *Prehistoric London – Its Mounds and Circles*. The Covenant Publishing Co., Ltd.

Goss, C.W.F., 1930. *Sir Paul Pindar and his Bishopsgate Mansion*. Cambridge.

Graeme, B., 1929. *The Story of St James's Palace* ... . Hutchison & Co. Ltd.

Grainger, I, Hawkins, D., Cowal, L. & Mikulski, R., 2008. *The Black Death Cemetery, East Smithfield, London*. MoLA (Monograph 43).

Grainger, I. & Phillpotts, C., 2010. *The Royal Navy Victualling Yard, East Smithfield, London*. MoLA (Monograph 45).

Grainger, I. & Phillpotts, C., 2011. *The Cistercian Abbey of St Mary Graces, East Smithfield, London*. MoLA (Monograph 44).

Graves, C., 1947. *The Story of St Thomas's 1106-1947*. Faber and Faber Ltd.

Graves, C., 1963. *Palace Extraordinary – The Story of St James's*. Cassell.

Graves, T.S., 1913. *The Court and the London Theatres during the Reign of Elizabeth* I. Russell & Russell.

Green, M., 2013. *The Lost World Of The London Coffee-House*. Idler Books.

Green, M., 2015. *London – A Travel Guide Through Time*. Michael Joseph.

Greg, W.W., 1956. *Some Aspects and Problems of London Publishing between 1550 and 1650.* Clarendon Press (Oxford).

Grew, F. & de Neergaard, M., 2001. *Shoes and Pattens. New Edition.* Boydell/Museum of London.

Grey, E., Calder, P.R. & Manning, P., 2014. *Our Own Church – Aspects & Images of St Olave Hart Street, All Hallows Staining and St Catherine Coleman.* St Olave Hart Street PCC.

Grey, E.C.W., 1905. *St Giles of the Lepers.* Longmans, Green & Co.

Griffin, A. & Hill, M., undated. *St Bartholomew's Hospital.* A.G. Bishop & Sons Ltd.

Griffith, E., 2013. *A Jacobean Company and its Playhouse – the Queen's Servants at the Red Bull Theatre (c. 1605-1619).* Cambridge University Press.

Griffith-Jones, R. & Park, D. (eds.), 2010. *The Temple Church in London ...* . The Boydell Press.

Griffiths, A. & Kesnerova, G., 1983. *Wenceslas Hollar.* British Museum/ Museum of London.

Griffiths, D., 2006. *Fleet Street – Five Hundred Years of the Press.* British Library.

Griffiths, P., 2008. *Lost Londons – Change, Crime and Control in the Capital City, 1550-1660.* Cambridge University Press.

Griffiths, P. & Jenner, M.S.R. (eds.), 2000. *Londinopolis – Essays on the Cultural and Social History of Early Modern London.* Manchester University Press.

Grimes, W.F., 1968. *The Excavation of Roman and Medieval London.* Routledge and Kegan Paul.

Groom, S., Souden, D., Spooner, J. & Dixon-Smith, S., 2011. *Discover the Banqueting House.* Historic Royal Palaces.

Grovier, K., 2008. *The Gaol – The Story of Newgate, London's Most Notorious Prison.* John Murray.

Grueninger, N., 2017. *Discovering Tudor London.* The History Press.

Grummett, A., 2015. *All Hallows by the Tower.* Scala.

Gurr, A., 2004. *Playgoing in Shakespeare's London ... . Third Edition.* Cambridge University Press.

Gurr, A. & Karim-Cooper, F. (eds.), 2014. *Moving Shakespeare Indoors – Performance and Repertoire in the Jacobean Playhouse.* Cambridge University Press.

Gurr, E., 2009. *The Rose Theatre.* Elizabeth Gurr (for The Rose Theatre Trust).

Hachman, G., 2014. *Stones to Build London – Portland's Legacy.* Folly Books.

Hahn, D., 2003. *The Tower Menagerie.* Simon & Schuster.

Hakluyt, R. (ed.), 1600. *The Principal Navigations, Voyages, Traffiques and Discoveries of the English Nation ... . Second Edition.* Printed by George Bishop and Ralph Newberie, deputies to Christopher Barker, printer to the Queen's Most Excellent Majestie (Vol. 1 1598; Vol. 2 1599; Vol. 3 – 'Including the English Valiant Attempts in Searching Almost all the Corners of the Vaste and New World of America, Whereunto is Added the Last Most Renowned English Navigation Round About the Whole Globe of the Earth' – 1600).

Hall, J. & Merrifield, R., 1986. *Roman London.* Her Majesty's Stationery Office/Museum of London.

Halliday, S., 2006. *Newgate – London's Prototype of Hell*. Sutton.

Hamilton, W.D. (ed.), 1875. *A Chronicle of England During the Reign of the Tudors, from AD1485 to 1559, by Charles Wriothesley ...* . The Camden Society.

Hammer, P.E.J., 2008. Shakespeare's *Richard II*, the Play of 7 February 1601, and the Essex Rising. *Shakespeare Quarterly*, 59(1): 1-35.

Hampden, J. (ed.), 1970. *The Tudor Venturers ...* . Folio Society.

Hanawalt, B.A., 1993. *Growing Up in Medieval London*. Oxford University Press.

Hanawalt, B.A., 2017. *Ceremony and Civility – Civic Culture in Late Medieval London*. Oxford University Press.

Handover, P.M., 1960. Printing in London from 1476 to Modern Times. Geo. Allen & Unwin.

Hanson, N., 2001. *The Dreadful Judgement – The True Story of the Great Fire of London*. Doubleday.

Hanson, N., 2003. *The Confident Hope of a Miracle – The True History of the Spanish Armada*. Doubleday.

Harkness, D.E.., 2007. *The Jewel House – Elizabethan London and the Scientific Revolution*. Yale University Press.

Harris, E., 2009. *Walking London Wall*. The History Press.

Harrison, B.A., 2004. *The Tower of London Prisoner Book – A Complete Chronology of the Persons known to have been detained at Their Majesties' Pleasurre, 1100-1941*. Royal Armouries.

Hartle, R., 2017. *The New Churchyard – From Moorfields Marsh to Bethlem Burial Ground, Brokers Row and Liverpool Street*. MoLA (Crossrail Archaeology Publication Series, No. 10).

Harvey, J.H., 1944. *Henry Yevele*. B.T. Batsford.

Harvey, J., 1947. *Gothic England – A Survey of National Culture, 1300-1550*. B.T. Batsford.

Harvey, W. & Harvey, J.H., 1936. *Master Hugh Herland, Chief Carpenter to King Richard II ...* .

Harward, C., Holder, N. & Jeffries, N., 2015. *The Spitalfields Suburb 1539-c 1880*. MoLA (Monograph 61).

Harward, C., Holder, N., McKenzie, M., Pitt, K., Thomas, C., Aitken, R., and Bowsher, D., in preparation, *The Medieval Priory and Hospital of St Mary Spital and the Bishopsgate Suburb...* . MoLA (Monograph 59).

Hatfield, E., 2015. *London's Lord Mayors ...* . Amberley.

Hausner, S.L., 2016. *The Spirits of Crtossbones Graveyard*. Indiana University Press.

Hawkins, D. & Phillpotts, C., 2005. The Priory of St Leonard Stratford-at-Bow and Parish Church of St Mary Bromley-by-Bow. *London Archaeologist*, Autumn 2005: 38-46.

Hayward, M., 2004. *The 1542 Inventory of Whitehall ...* . The Society of Antiquaries of London/Illuminata Publishers.

Hazelwood, N., 2004. *The Queen's Slave Trader – John Hawkyns, Elizabeth I, and the Trafficking of Human Souls*. William Morrow.

Heard, K. & Goodburn, D., 2003. *Investigating the Maritime History of Rotherhithe*. MoLA (Archaeology Studies Series 11).

Hearsey, J.E.N., 1965. *London and its Great Fire.* John Murray.

Heath, B., 1869. *Some Account of the Worshipful Company of Grocers in the City of London.* Privately printed.

Herber, M., 1999. *Legal London* ... . Biddles Ltd.

Herbert, W., 1884. *The History of the Twelve Great Livery Companies in London.* Augustus M. Kelley, New York.

Heyman, P., Simons, L. & Cochez, C., 2014. Were the English Sweating Sickness and the Picardy Sweat Caused by Hantaviruses? *Viruses*, **6**(1): 151-71.

Hibbert, C., 1969. *London – The Biography of a City.* Longmans.

Hill, J. & Rowsome, P., 2011. *Roman London and the Walbrook Stream Crossing.* MoLA (Monograph 37).

Hill, J. & Woodger, A., 1999. *Excavations at 72-78 Cheapside/83-93 Queen Street, City of London.* MoLA (Archaeology Studies Series 2).

Hill, R., 2000. *Middle Temple Hall – An Architectural Appreciation.* The Middle Temple.

Hill, T., 2010. *Pageantry and Power – A Cultural History of the Early Modern Lord Mayor's Show, 1585-1639.* Manchester University Press.

Hinde, T., 1995. *Carpenter's Children – The Story of the City of London School.* James & James.

Hingley, R., 2018. *Londinium – A Biography* ... . Bloomsbury.

Hinkle, W.G., 2006. *A History of Bridewell Prison 1553-1700.* The Edwin Mellen Press.

Historic Royal Palaces, 2010. *Tower of London Souvenir Guidebook.* Historic Royal Palaces.

Hodges, C.W., 1968. *The Globe Restored – A Study of the Elizabethan Theatre. Second Edition.* Oxford University Press.

Holder, N., 2017. *The Friaries of Medieval London* ... . Boydell & Brewer.

Holder, N., Samuel, M. & Betts, I., 2013. The Church and Cloister of Austin Friars. *Transactions, London and Middlesex Archaeological Society*, **64**: 143-62.

Holland, P., 1993. *St Margaret's Westminster* ... . Aidan Ellis.

Hollis, L., 2008. *The Men Who Made Modern London.* Weidenfeld & Nicolson.

Hollis, L., 2011. *The Stones of London – A History in Twelve Buildings.* Weidenfeld & Nicolson.

Hollyer, B. (ed.), 2001. *Walter George Bell – The Great Plague.* The Folio Society.

Hollyer, B. (ed.), 2003. *Walter George Bell – The Great Fire of London in 1666.* The Folio Society.

Holmes, M., 1969. *Elizabethan London.* Cassell.

Holmes-Walker, A., 2005. *Sixes & Sevens – A Short History of the Skinners' Company.* Information Press.

Home, G., 1931. *'Old London Bridge'.* John Lane at the Bodley Head.

Home, G., 1948. *Roman London A.D.43-457.* Eyre and Spottiswoode.

Home, G., 1994. *Medieval London. Revised Edition.* Bracken Books.

Hooper, W.F., 1935. *The History of Newgate and the Old Bailey* ... . Underwood Press Ltd.

Hope, A., 1990. *Londoners' Larder – English Cuisine from Chaucer to the Present*. Mainstream Publishing.

Hope, W.St.J., 1925. *The History of the London Charterhouse from its Foundation until the Suppression of the Monastery*. Society for Promoting Christian Knowledge.

Hopkinson, H.L., 1931. *The History of the Merchant Taylors' Hall*. Cambridge University Press.

Hornak, A., 2016. *After the Fire – London Churches in the Age of Wren, Hooke, Hawksmoor and Gibbs*. Pimpernel.

Horsman, V., Milne, C., Milne, G. *et al.*, 1988. *Aspects of Saxo-Norman London*. London and Middlesex Archaeological Society (Special Papers, Nos. 11 & 12).

Hostettler, E., 2000. *The Isle of Dogs, 1066-1918*. Island History Trust.

Hotson, L., 1928. *The Commonwealth and Restoration Stage*. Harvard Universty Press.

Hotson, L., 1959. *Shakespeare's Wooden O*. Rupert Hart-Davis.

Houses of Parliament, 2012. *The Palace of Westminster Official Guide*. Houses of Parliament.

Howard, J.E., 2007. *Theater of a City – The Places of London Comedy 1598-1642*. University of Pennsylvania Press.

Howell, J., 1657. *Londinopolis – An Historical Discourse or Perlustration of the City of London ... .*

Howgego, J., 1978. *Printed Maps of London circa 1553-1850*. Dawson.

Howse, G., 2012. *A History of London's Prisons*. Wharncliffe Books.

Huelin, G., 1996. *Vanished Churches of the City of London*. Guildhall Library Publications.

Hunting, P., 1981. *Royal Westminster*. Penshurst.

Hurst, G., 1946. *A Short History of Lincoln's Inn*. Constable.

Hutton, A.W., 1908. *A Short History and Description of Bow Church, Cheapside*. Elliot Stock.

Hyde, E. (1st Earl of Clarendon), 1702-4. *The History of the Rebellion and Civil Wars in England*.

Hyde, R., 1999. *London in Paintings*. Guildhall Art Gallery.

Hyde, R., Fisher, J. & Cline, R., 1992. *The A to Z of Restoration London*. London Topographical Society (Publication No. 145).

Impey, E. (ed.), 2008. *The White Tower*. Yale University Press/Historic Royal Palaces.

Impey, E. & Parnell, G., 2011. *The Tower of London. Second Revised Edition*. Merrell/Historic Royal Palaces.

Inwood, S., 1998. *A History of London*. MacMillan.

Inwood, S., 2002. *The Man Who Knew Too Much – The Strange and Inventive Life of Robert Hooke 1653-1703*. MacMillan.

Inwood, S., 2008. *Historic London*. MacMillan.

Jackson, P., 2002. *London Bridge. Revised Edition*. Historical Publications.

Jardine, L., 2002. *On a Grander Scale – The Outstanding Career of Sir Christopher Wren*. HarperCollins.

Jardine, L., 2003. *The Curious Life of Robert Hooke – The Man who Measured London*. HarperCollins.

Jeffery, P., 1996. *The City Churches of Sir Christopher Wren*. Continuum.

Jenkinson, W., 1917. *London Churches before the Great Fire*. Society for Promoting Christian Knowledge.

Jenkinson, W., 1921. *The Royal & Bishops' Palaces in Old London*. Society for Promoting Christian Knowledge.

Jenkyns, R., 2011. *Westminster Abbey. Revised and Updated Edition*. Profile.

Jewett, C., 2017. *The History of Newgate Prison*. Pen & Sword.

Johnson, A.H., 1914-22. *The History of the Worshipful Company of Drapers of London*. Clarendon Press.

Johnson, L., 2017. *Shakespeare's Lost Playhouse – Eleven Years at Newington Butts*. Routledge.

Johnson, M., 2013. *Crypts of London*. The History Press.

Jones, D., 2009. *Summer of Blood – The 'Peasants' Revolt' of 1381*. Harper.

Jones, D., 2014a. *Magna Carta*. Head of Zeus.

Jones, D., 2014b. *The Hollow Crown – The Wars of the Roses and the Rise of the Tudors*. Faber and Faber.

Jones, F., 2014. *The Battle of Barnet. Revised Edition*. Barnet Museum and Local History Society.

Jones, N., 2011. *Tower*. Hutchison.

Jones, P.E. & Smith, R., 1951. *A Guide to the Records in the Corporation of London Records Office and the Guildhall Library Muniments Room*. English Universities Press Ltd.

Jones, R.W., 2012. *The Lost City of London*. Amberley.

Jones, R.W., 2015. *The Lost City of London. Second Edition*. Amberley.

Jones, T. & Ereira, A., 2004. *Medieval Lives*. BBC.

Jordan, D., 2017. *The King's City …* . Little, Brown.

Jordan, D. & Walsh, M., 2012. *The King's Revenge*. Little, Brown.

Jordan, W.K., 1960. *The Charities of London 1480-1660 …* . George Allen & Unwin Ltd.

Jowett, C., 2017. *The History of Newgate Prison*. Pen and Sword.

Judges, A.V., 1930. *The Elizabethan Underworld*. George Routledge & Son.

Kahl, W.F., 1960. *The Development of London Livery Companies …* . Harvard Graduate School of Business Administration.

Karim-Cooper, F. & Stern, T., 2013. *Shakespeare's Theatres and their Effects on Performance*. Bloomsbury.

Kaufmann, M., 2017. *Black Tudors …* . One World.

Keay, A., 2001. *The Elizabethan Tower of London – The Haiward and Gascoyne Plan of 1597*. London Topographical Society (Publication No. 158).

Keay, J., 2010. *The Honourable Company – A History of the English East India Company*. HarperCollins.

Keene, D. & Archer, I.W. (eds.), 2014. *The Singularities of London, 1578 …* . London Topographical Society (Publication No. 175).

Keene, D., Burns, A. & Saint, A., 2004. *St Paul's – The Cathedral Church of London, 604-2004*. Yale University Press.

Keevill, G., 2004. *The Tower of London Moat*. Historic Royal Palaces.

Kelly, J., 2017. *Tunnel – The Archaeology of Crossrail*. Crossrail.

Kensey, M.F., 2013. *London's New River in Maps, Volume 1, Part 2 – c. 1600 to 1850 (Robert Mylne's Survey, Enfield Flash to New River Head)*. M.F. Kensey.

Kent, W., 1947. *The Lost Treasures of London*. Phoenix House.

Kent, W., 1949. *London for the Literary Pilgrim*. Rockliff.

Kent, W., 1970. *An Encyclopaedia of London*. J.M. Dent & Sons.

Kenyon, N. (ed.), 2011. *The City of London*. Thames & Hudson.

Kerling, N.J.M., 1973. *Cartulary of St Bartholomew's Hospital, Founded 1123*. St Batrholomew's Hospital.

Keynes, S. & Lapidge, M., 1983. *Alfred the Great – Asser's Life of King Alfred and other Contemporary Sources*. Penguin Classics.

Khan, S.A., 1973. *The East India Trade in the XVIIth Century*. D. Appleton-Century Company Incorporated.

Killock, D., Shepherd, J., Gerrard, J. *et al.*, 2015. *Temple and Suburbs – Excavations at Tabard Square, Southwark*. PCA (Monograph 18).

Kingsford, C.L., 1915. *The Grey Friars of London*. Aberdeen University Press.

Knight, C. (ed.), 1841. *London*. Charles Knight & Co.

Knight, H., 2002. *Aspects of Medieval and Later Southwark*. MoLA (Monograph 13).

Knighton, C.S. (ed.), 2004. *Pepys's Later Diaries*. Sutton Publishing.

Knowles, D. & Grimes, W.E., 1954. *Charterhouse – The Medieval Foundation in the Light of Recent Discoveries*. Longman's, Green & Co.

La Gallienne, R. (ed.), 2001. *The Diary of Samuel Pepys*. The Modern Library.

Lang, J., 1975. *Pride without Prejudice – The Story of London's Guilds & Livery Companies*. Perpetua.

Lang, J., 1984. *The Billesdon Award*. Westerham Press.

Lang, R.G. (ed.), 1993. *Two Tudor Subsidy Assessment Rolls for the City of London – 1541 and 1582*. London Record Society.

Lanson, P., 1993. *The East India Company – A History*. Longman.

Larman, A., 2016. *Restoration – The Year of the Great Fire*. Head of Zeus.

Lavigne, F., Degeai, J.-P., Komorowski, J.C., *et al.*, 2013. Source of the Great 1257 Mystery Eruption Unveiled, Samalas Volcano, Rinjani Volcanic Complex, Indonesia. *Proceedings of the National Academy of Sciences of the U.S.A., Earth, Atmospheric and Planetary Sciences*, 110(42): 16742-7.

Laurence, A., 1994. *Women in England 1500-1760*. Weidenfeld & Nicolson.

Leary, J., Branch, N. & Rayner, L., 2011. Prehistoric Southwark – Neolithic, Bronze Age and Iron Age Activity on Horselydown Eyot. *London Archaeologist*, 13(2): 31-5.

Leary, J., Brown, G., Rackham, J. *et al.*, 2004. *Tatberht's Lundenwic*. PCA (Monograph 2).

Leasor, J., 1962. *The Plague and the Fire*. George Allen & Unwin Ltd.

Lethaby, W.R., 1902. *London before the Conquest*. MacMillan and Co.

Lewer, D. & Dark, R., 1997. *The Temple Church in London*. Historical Publications.

Lewis, J.E. (ed.), 2008. *London – The Autobiography*. Constable & Robinson.

Leyser, H., 1995. *Medieval Women – A Social History of Women in England from 450-1500*. Weidenfeld & Nicolson.

Lincoln, M. (ed.), 2015. *Samuel Pepys – Plague, Fire, Rebellion*. Thames & Hudson.

Lindeboom, J., 1950. *Austin Friars – History of the Dutch Reformed Church in London 1550-1950*. Martinus Nijhoff, The Hague.

Lindley, K., 1997. *Popular Politics and Religion in Civil War London*. Scolar Press.

Lipscombe, S., 2012. *A Visitor's Companion to Tudor England*. Ebury.

Littlehales, H., 1898. *Some Notes on the Road from London to Canterbury in the Middle Ages*. The Chaucer Society.

Lobel, M.D. (ed.), 1989. *The British Atlas of Historic Towns, Vol. III – The City of London from Prehistoric Times to c. 1520*. Oxford.

Lockyer, R. (ed.), 1967. *The History of the Great Rebellion (Edward Hyde: Earl of Clarendon)*. Oxford University Press for the Folio Society.

Longman, W., 1873. *A History of Three Cathedrals Dedicated to St Paul …*. Longmans, Green & Co.

Lubbock, P.J.A. (ed.), 1981. *The Halls of the Livery Companies of the City of London*. The Company of Chartered Surveyors.

Lyon, J., 2007. *Within These Walls – Roman and Medieval Defences North of Newgate at the Merrill Lynch Financial Centre, City of London*. MoLA (Monograph 33).

MacDonald, M., 1981. *Mystical Bedlam*. Cambridge University Press.

Mackinder, A., 2013. *The Hope Playhouse, Animal Baiting and later Industrial Activity on Bankside …*. MoLA (Studies Series, No. 25).

Macy, G., 2007. *The Hidden History of Women's Ordination – Female Clergy in the Medieval West*. Oxford University Press.

Major, F., 2000. *St Giles' Church, Cripplegate*. St Giles' Church, Cripplegate, PCC.

Malcolm, G. & Bowsher, D., 2003. *Middle Saxon London*. MoLA (Monograph 15).

Malcolm, J.P., 1827. *Londinium Redivivum*, or *An Antient History and Modern Description of London …*. Rivington.

Mancall, P.C. & Shammas, C. (eds.), 2015. *Governing the Sea in the Early Modern Era …*. Huntington Library.

Manley, L. (ed.), 1986. *London in the Time of Shakespeare – An Anthology*. Crook Helm.

Marriott, J., 2011. *Beyond the Tower – A History of East London*. Yale University Press.

Marsden, P., 1975. The Excavation of a Roman Palace Site in London, 1961-1972. *Transactions of the London and Middlesex Archaeological Society*, **26**: 1-102.

Marsden, P., 1980. *Roman London*. Thames and Hudson.

Marsden, P., 1987. *The Roman Forum Site in London*. HMSO/Museum of London.

Marsden, P., 1994. *Ships of the Port of London – First to Eleventh Centuries AD*. English Heritage.

Marsden, P., 1996. *Ships of the Port of London – Twelfth to Seventeenth Centuries AD*. English Heritage.

Marsden, P., 2018. The Purpose of the Cripplegate Roman Fort. *London Archaeologist*, 15(5): 137-44.

Marshall, P., 2002. *Beliefs and the Dead in Reformation England*. Oxford University Press.

Martin, P.H., 2016. *Elizabethan Espionage – Plotters and Spies in the Struggle between Catholicism and the Crown*. McFarland Inc.

Mason, A.E.W., 1920. *The Royal Exchange*. The Royal Exchange.

Matthews, P., 2008. *London's Bridges*. Shire.

McDonnell, K.G.T., 1978. *Medieval London Suburbs*. Phillimore.

McDonnell, M.F.J., 1909. *A History of St Paul's School*. Chapman & Hall, Ltd.

McIlwain, J., 1994. *Prisoners in the Tower*. Pitkin.

McInnes, E.M., 1963. *St Thomas's Hospital*. George Allen & Unwin Lrd.

McKellar, E., 1999. *The Birth of Modern London – The Development and Design of the City, 1660-1720*. Manchester University Press.

McKenzie, M. & Thomas, C., in preparation. *The Northern Cemetery of Roman London*. MoLA (Monograph 58).

Meadows, C.A., 1957. *Trade Signs and their Origins*. Routledge & Kegan Paul.

Meara, D., 2004. *St Bride's Church, Fleet Street, City of London*. Jarrold.

Medvei, V.C. & Thornton, J.L. (eds.), 1974. *The Royal Hospital of Saint Bartholomew 1123-1973*. W.S. Cowell.

Megarry, R., 1972. *Inns Ancient and Modern ... .* Selden Society.

Melling, J.K., 2003. *Discovering London's Guilds and Liveries. Sixth Edition.* Shire.

Mendle, M. (ed.), 2001. *The Putney Debates of 1647*. Cambridge University Press.

Merrifield, R., 1969. *Roman London*. Cassell.

Merrifield, R., 1983. *London – City of the Romans*. Guild.

Merriman, N., 1990. *Prehistoric London*. Her Majesty's Stationery Office/ Museum of London.

Merritt, J.F. (ed.), 2001. *Imagining Early Modern London – Perceptions & Portrayals of the City from Stow to Strype 1598-1720*. Cambridge University Press.

Metcalf, P., 1977. *The Halls of the Fishmongers' Company ... .* Phillimore.

Miles, A. & White, W., 2008. *Burial at the Site of the Parish Church of St Benet Sherehog before and after the Great Fire*. MoLA (Monograph 39).

Millen, R., 2007. *St Dunstan-in-the-West – The Church and its History*. Barnard & Westwood.

Mills, A.D., 2001. *A Dictionary of London Place Names*. Oxford University Press.

Millward, J.S., 1961. *Portraits & Documents – The Seventeenth Century, 1603-1714*. Hutchinson Educational.

Millward, J.S., 1968. *Portraits & Documents – The Sixteenth Century, 1485-1603. Second Edition.* Hutchinson Educational.

Milne, G., 1985. *The Port of Roman London*. Batsford.

Milne, G., 1986. *The Great Fire of London*. Historical Publications.

Milne, G. (ed.), 1992. *From Roman Basilica to Medieval Market – Archaeology in Action in the City of London*. HMSO.

Milne, G., 1995. *Roman London*. English Heritage.

Milne, G., 2003. *The Port of Medieval London*. Tempus.

Milne, G., 2014. *St Bride's Church London*. English Heritage.

Milne, G. & Cohen, N., 2002. *Excavations at Medieval Cripplegate, London*. English Heritage.

Milne, G. & Sully, D. (eds.), 2014. *The Gresham Ship Project – A 16th-Century Merchantman Wrecked in the Princes Channel, Thames Estuary. Volume II – Contents and Context*. British Archaeological Reports.

Milton, G., 2000. *Big Chief Elizabeth – How England's Adventurers Gambled and Won the New World*. Hodder & Stoughton.

Mishra, R., 2018. *A Business of State – Commerce, Politics and the Birth of the East India Company*. Harvard University Press (Harvard Historical Series, No. 188).

Mitchell, R.J. & Leys, M.D.R., 1958. *A History of London Life*. Pelican.

Moore, N., 1918. *The History of St Bartholomew's Hospital*. C. Arthur Pearson Limited.

Moorhouse, G., 2005. *Great Harry's Navy – How Henry VIII Gave England Sea Power*. Weidenfeld & Nicolson.

Moote, A.L. & Moote, D.C., 2004. *The Great Plague – The Story of London's Most Deadly Year*. Johns Hopkins University Press.

Morris, D., 2011. *Whitechapel 1600-1800*. The East London History Society.

Morris, D. & Cozens, K., 2009. *Wapping 1600 1800*. The East London History Society.

Morris, D. & Cozens, K., 2014. *London's Sailortown 1600-1800*. The East London History Society.

Morris, J., 1982. *Londinium – London in the Roman Empire*. Book Club Associates/Weidenfeld & Nicolson.

Mortimer, I., 2008. *The Time Traveller's Guide to Medieval England*. The Bodley Head.

Mortimer, I., 2012. *The Time Traveller's Guide to Elizabethan England*. The Bodley Head.

Mortimer, I., 2017. *The Time Traveller's Guide to Restoration Britain*. Pegasus.

Mostafavi, M. & Binet, H., 2015. *Nicholas Hawksmoor London Churches*. Lars Muller.

Mount, T., 2014. *Everyday Life in Medieval London*. Amberley.

Mount, T., 2015. *Medieval Medicine ... .* Amberley.

Munro, L., 2005. *Children of the Queen's Revels – A Jacobean Theatre Repertory*. Cambridge Universty Press.

Myers, A.R., 2009. *Chaucer's London. Revised Edition*. Amberley.

Nairn, I., 1966. *Nairn's London*. Penguin.

Neill, E.D., 1869. *History of the Virginia Company of London*. Bart Frankin, New York.

Nicholl, C., 1995. *The Creature in the Map – A Journey to El Dorado*. Jonathan Cape.

Nicholl, C., 2005. *Shakespeare and his Contemporaries*. National Portrait Gallery.

Nicholl, C., 2007. *The Lodger – Shakespeare on Silver Street*. Allen Lane.

Nichols, J.G. (ed.), 1848. *The Diary of John Machyn, Citizen and Merchant-Taylor of London, from AD1550 to AD1563.* The Camden Society.

Nichols, J.G. (ed.), 1852. *Chronicle of the Grey Friars of London.*

Nicoll, A. (ed.), 1964. *Shakespeare in his own Age.* Cambridge University Press.

Norman, P., 1905. *London Vanished and Vanishing.* Black.

Nurse, B., 2017. *London Prints and Drawings before 1800.* The London Topographical Society.

O'Donoghue, E.G., 1914. *The Story of Bethlehem Hospital from its Foundation in 1247.* T. Fisher Unwin.

O'Havery, R. (ed.), 2011. *History of the Middle Temple.* Hart Publishing.

Olusoga, D., 2016. *Black and British ... .* Pan MacMillan.

Ormond, R., 1979. *National Portrait Gallery ... .* Studio Vista.

Orridge, D.B., 1867. *Some Account of the Citizens of London and their Rulers from 1060 to 1867.* William Tegg.

Osborn, J.M. (ed.), 1960. *The Quenes Maiesties Passage through the Citie of London and Westminster the Day before her Coronacion.* Yale University Press.

Page, W.S., 1912. *The Russia Company from 1553 to 1660.* Willliam Brown & Co. Limited.

Palfreyman, D., 2010. *London's Livery Companies.* Oracle.

Palfreyman, D., 2011. *London's Inns of Court.* Oracle.

Palme, P., 1956. *Triumph of Peace – A Study of the Whitehall Banqueting House.* Almqvist & Wiksell, Stockholm.

Panton, K., 2001. *Historical Dictionary of London.* Scarecrow Press.

Panton, K., 2005. *London – A Historical Companion. Revised Edition.* Tempus.

Parnell, G., 1999. *The Royal Menagerie at the Tower of London.* Royal Armouries.

Parnell, G., 2009. *The Tower of London. Revised Edition.* The History Press.

Parrott, D., 2014. *St Lawrence Jewry ... .* Pitkin.

Parsons, F.G., 1927. *The Earlier Inhabitants of London.* Cecil Palmer.

Parsons, F.G., 1932-36. *The History of St Thomas's Hospital ... .* Methuen & Co. Ltd.

Parsons, M., 2005. *Fleet Street and the Strand.* Tempus.

Partridge, R.B., 1998. *'O Horrable Murder' – The Trial, Execution and Burial of King Charles I.* The Rubicon Press.

Payne, H., 2011. The First Olympic Village – Finished 3000 Years ahead of Schedule (Bronze Age Settlement at the Olympic Aquatics Centre). *London Archaeologist,* **12**(12): 315-20.

Pearce, E.H., 1908. *Annals of Christ's Hospital. Second Edition.* Hugh Rees Ltd.

Pearce, J.E., Vince, A.G. & Jenner, M.A., 1985. *Medieval Pottery – London-Type Ware.* LAMAS (Special Paper, No. 6).

Pearl, V., 1961. *London and the Outbreak of the Puritan Revolution – City Government and National Politics, 1625-43.* Oxford University Press.

Pearson, A., 2006. *The Work of Giants – Stone and Quarrying in Roman Britain.* Tempus.

Pearson, D. (ed.), 2011. *London: 1000 Years – Treasures from the Collections of the City of London*. Scala.

Perring, D., 1991. *Roman London*. Routledge.

Perring, D., 2017. London's Hadrianic War? *Britannia*, **48**: 1-40.

Pettigrew, W.A., 2013. *Freedom's Debt – The Royal African Company and the Politics of the Atlantic Slave Trade, 1672-1752*. University of North Carolina Press.

Pfizenmaier, S., 2016. *Charterhouse Square – Black Death Cemetery and Carthusian Monastery, Meat Market and Suburb*. MoLA (Crossrail Archaeology Publication Series, No. 7).

Philp, B., 1996. *The Roman Villa Site at Orpington, Kent*. Kent Archaeological Rescue Unit.

Picard, L., 1997. *Restoration London*. Weidenfeld & Nicolson.

Picard, L., 2003. *Elizabeth's London*. Weidenfeld & Nicolson.

Pierce, P., 2001. *'Old London Bridge'*. Headline.

Pimm, G., 2017. *The Dark Side of Samuel Pepys*. Pen & Sword.

Pitt, K., Blackmore, L., Dyson, T. & Tyson, R., 2013. *Medieval to early Post-Medieval Tenements and Middle Eastern Imports – Excavations at Plantation Place, City of London, 1997-2005*. MoLA (Monograph, No. 66).

Polk, W.R., 2006. *The Birth of America – From Columbus to the Revolution*. HarperCollins.

Pooley, E., 1945. *The Guilds of the City of London*. Collins.

Porter, R., 2000. *London – A Social History. Revised Edition*. Penguin.

Porter, S. (ed.), 1996. *London in the Civil War*. MacMillan.

Porter, S., 2008. *The Plagues of London. Revised Edition*. Tempus.

Porter, S., 2009. *The Great Fire of London. Revised Edition*. The History Press.

Porter, S., 2010. *Charterhouse*. Amberley.

Porter, S., 2011a. *Pepys's London*. Amberley.

Porter, S., 2011b. *Shakespeare's London. Revised Edition*. Amberley.

Porter, S., 2012. *The Tower of London*. Amberley.

Porter, S., 2016. *Everyday Life in Tudor London*. Amberley.

Porter, S., 2018. *Black Death – A New History of the Bubonic Plagues of London*. Amberley.

Porter, S. & Marsh, S., 2010. *The Battle for London*. Amberley.

Power, E., 1975. *Medieval Women*. Cambridge University Press.

Prest, E.R., 1972. *The Inns of Court under Elizabeth I and the Early Stuarts 1590-1640*. Longman.

Prockter, A., Taylor, R. & Fisher, J., 1979. *The A to Z of Elizabethan London*. London Topographical Society (Publication No. 122).

Pulley, J., 2006. *Streets of the City*. Capital History.

Ranieri, S. & Telfer, A., 2017. *Outside Roman London – Roadside Burials by the Walbrook Stream*. MoLA (Crossrail Archaeology Publication Series, No. 9).

Rappaport, S., 1989. *Worlds within Worlds – Structures of Life in Sixteenth-Century London*. Cambridge University Press.

Rawley, J.A., 2003. *London, Metropolis of the Slave Trade*. University of Missouri Press.

Reddaway, T.F., 1973. *The Early History of the Goldsmith's Company ...* . Edward Arnold.

Redfern, R. & Bonney, H., 2016. Headhunting and Amphitheatre Combat in Roman London, England – New Evidence from the Walbrook Valley. *Journal of Archaeological Science*, **43**: 214-26.

Redfern, R.C., Grocke, D.R., Millard, A.R. *et al.,* 2016. Going South of the River – A Multidisciplinary Analysis of Ancestry, Mobility and Diet in a Population from Roman Southwark, London. *Journal of Archaeological Science*, **74**: 11-22.

Reed, R.R., Jr., 1952. *Bedlam on the Jacobean Stage*. Harvard University Press.

Rees, G.L., 1978. *The History of the London Commodity Markets*. Commodity Analysis Limited.

Rees, J.A., 1923. *The Worshipful Company of Grocers – An Historical Retrospective, 1345-1923*. Chapman and Dodd.

Reid, C.L., 1967. *Commerce and Conquest – The Story of the Honourable East India Company*. C. & J. Temple Limited.

Reid, D. & Bowen, H. (eds.), 2015. *Lord Mayor's Show – 800 Years, 1215-2015*. Third Millennium.

Rendle, W., 1878. *Old Southwark and its People*. W. Drewett.

Rendle, W. & Norman, P., 1888. *The Inns of Old Southwark ...* . Longmans, Green and Co.

Renn, D., 2014. Pause and Cause – The 'Building Break' in the White Tower of London. *Transactions, London and Middlesex Archaeological Society*, **65**: 221-30.

Richardson, J., 1988. *Islington Past*. Historical Publications.

Richardson, J., 1995. *London and its People – A Social History from Medieval Times to the Present Day*. Barrie & Jenkins.

Richardson, J., 2000. *The Annals of London ...* . Cassell.

Richardson, T., 2016. *The Tower Armoury in the Fourteenth Century*. Royal Armouries.

Riches, C. (ed.), 2011. *The Times Atlas of London*. Times Books.

Rideal, R., 2016. *1666 – Plague, War and Hellfire*. John Murray.

Ridgeway, V., Leary, K. & Sudds, B., 2013. *Roman Burials in Southwark – Excavations at 52-56 Lant Street and 56 Southwark Bridge Road, London SE1*. PCA (Monograph, No.17).

Riley, H.T. (transl.), 1861. *Liber Albus – The White Book of the City of London ...* . Richard Griffin and Company.

Riley, H.T., 1863. *Chronicles of the Mayors and Sheriffs of London A.D.1188 to A.D.1274... .* Turner and Co.

Robertson, A.G., 1968. *Tudor London*. MacDonald (Discovering London 4).

Robertson, D.W., Jr., 1968. *Chaucer's London*. John Wiley & Sons, Inc.

Robins, N., 2012. *The Corporation that Changed the World – How the East India Company Shaped the Modern Multinational. Second Edition*. Pluto.

Rodwell, W. & Mortimer, R. (eds.), 2010. *Westminster Abbey Chapter House – The History, Art and Architecture of 'A Chapter House Beyond Compare'*. Society of Antiquaries of London.

Rogers, M., 1921. *Down Thames Street*. Robert Scott.

Roose-Evans, J., 1977. *London Theatre from the Globe to the National*. Phaidon.

Rosewell, R., 2012. *The Medieval Monastery*. Shire.

Ross, C. (ed.), 2016. *Revealing the Charterhouse ...* . The Charterhouse/D. Giles.

Ross, C. & Clark, J., 2008. *London – The Illustrated History*. Allen Lane/ Museum of London.

Ross, S., 1965. *The Plague and Fire of London*. Faber and Faber.

Rounding, V., 2017. *The Burning Time – The Story of the Smithfield Martyrs*. MacMillan.

Rowles, R., 2018. *The Civil War in London ...* . Pen & Sword.

Rowse, A.L., 1972. *The Tower of London in the History of the Nation*. Weidenfeld & Nicolson.

Rowsome, P., 2000. *Heart of the City – Roman, Medieval and Modern London Revealed by Archaeology of No. 1 Poultry*. MoLA.

Rowston, G., 2010. *Southwark Cathedral – The Authorized Guide. Amended Edition*. Robert James Publications.

Roxburgh, R., 1963. *The Origin of Lincoln's Inn*. Cambridge University Press.

Rudden, B., 1985. *The New River ...* . Clarendon Press.

Rule, F., 2017. *The Oldest House in London*. The History Press.

Rumbelow, D., 1982. *The Triple Tree – Newgate, Tyburn and the Old Bailey*. Harrap.

Rutter, C.C., 1984. *Documents of the Rose Playhouse*. Manchester University Press.

Ryrie, A., 2017. *The Age of Reformation ...* . Routledge.

Saint, A. & Darley, G.,1994. *The Chronicles of London*. Weidenfeld & Nicolson.

Salgado, G., 1977. *The Elizabethan Underworld*. J.M. Dent & Sons.

Salkeld, D., 2018. *Shakespeare & London*. Oxford University Press.

Sandling, T., 2016. *London in Fragments – A Mudlark's Treasures*. Frances Lincoln.

Sankey, D., 2015. *Stepney Gree – Moated Manor House to City Farm*. MoLA.

Saunders, A. (ed.), 1997. *The Royal Exchange*. London Topographical Society (Publication No. 152).

Saunders, A., 2001. *St Paul's*. Collins & Brown.

Saunders, A., 2012. *St Paul's Cathedral*. Scala.

Saunders, H.St.G., 1951. *Westminster Hall*. Michael Joseph.

Sayle, R.T.B., 1945. *A Brief History of the Worshipful Company of Merchant Taylors ...* . The Eastern Press Limited.

Schofield, P., 1984. *The Building of London from the Conquest to the Great Fire*. Colonnade/British Museum.

Schofield, J. (ed.), 1987. *The London Surveys of Ralph Treswell*. London Topographical Society (Publication No. 135).

Schofield, J., 1994. Saxon and Medieval Parish Churches in the City of London – A Review. *Transactions, London and Middlesex Archaeological Society*, 45: 23-246.

Schofield, J., 1995. *Medieval London Houses*. Yale University Press.

Schofield, J., 2011a. *London 1100-1600*. Equinox.

Schofield, J., 2011b. *St Paul's Cathedral before Wren*. English Heritage.

Schofield, J., 2016. *St Paul's Cathedral – Archaeology & History*. Oxbow.

Schofield, J., Blackmore, L. & Pearce, J., 2018. *London's Waterfront 1100-1666 – Excavations in Thames Street, London, 1974-84*. Archaeopress.

Schofield, J. & Lea, R., 2005. *Holy Trinity Priory, Aldgate, City of London*. MoLA (Monograph 24).

Schofield, J. & Pearce, J., 2009. Thomas Soane's Buildings near Billingsgate, London, 1640-66. *Post-Medieval Archaeology*, 43: 282-341.

Schuler, C.J., 2011. *Mapping the City from Antiquity to the Twentieth Century*. Editions Places des Victoires.

Seeley, D., Phillpotts, C. & Samuel, M., 2006. *Winchester Palace*. MoLA (Monograph 31).

Sergeaunt, J., 1898. *Annals of Westminster School*. Methuen & Co.

Seward, D., 2000. *The Monks of War – The Military Orders*. The Folio Society.

Shami, J., 1996. *John Donne's 1622 Gunpowder Plot Sermon … .* Duquesne University Press, Pittsburgh, Pennsylvania.

Shapiro, J., 2005. *1599 – A Year in the Life of William Shakespeare*. Faber and Faber.

Shapiro, J., 2015. *1606 – William Shakespeare and the Year of Lear*. Faber and Faber.

Sharland, E., 1997. *From Shakespeare to Coward, from the Globe to the Phoenix Theatre … .* Barbican Press.

Sharpe, R.R., 1899-1912. *Calendar of Letter-Books preserved among the Archives of the Corporation of the City of London at the Guildhall*. John Edward Francis.

Shelley, H.C., 1909. *Inns and Taverns of Old London*.

Shenton, C., 2012. *The Day Parliament Burned Down*. Oxford University Press.

Shepherd, C.W., 1971. *A Thousand Years of London Bridge*. John Baker.

Shepherd, J., 1998. *The Temple of Mithras, London*. English Heritage.

Shepherd, R., 2012. *Westminster*. Bloomsbury.

Sheppard, E., 1902. *The Old Royal Palace of Whitehall*. Longmans, Green and Co.

Shrimplin, V., 2017. *Sir Thomas Gresham and his Vision for Gresham College*. Pitkin.

Sibun, L. & Ponce, P., 2018. *Life and Death – Archaeological Excavations at the Queens Chapel Savoy, London*. SpoilHeap Monograph (No. 17).

Sidell, J., Wilkinson, K., Scaife, R. & Cameron, N., 2000. *The Holocene Evolution of the London Thames*. MoLA (Monograph 5).

Simpson, J.W., 1928. *Some Account of the Old Hall of Lincoln's Inn*. The Dolphin Press.

Sinclair, G., 2009. *Historic Maps and Views of London*. Black Dog & Leventhal.

Sinclair, W., 1909. *Memorials of St Paul's Cathedral*. Chapman & Hall.

Sisson, C.J., 1972. The Boar's Head Theatre – *Theatre – An Inn-Yard Theatre of the Elizabethan Age*. Routledge & Routledge.

Sloane, B., 2011. *The Black Death in London*. The History Press.

Sloane, B., 2012. *The Augustinian Nunnery of St Mary Clerkenwell, London*. MoLA (Monograph 57).

Sloane, B. & Malcolm, G., 2004. *Excavations at the Priory of the Order of the Hospital of St John of Jerusalem, Clerkenwell, London*. MoLA (Monograph 20).

Smith, B., 1961. *Sea-Coal for London – History of the Coal Factors in the London Market*. Longmans.

Smith, S., 2014. 'Pleasing Strains' – The Dramaturgical Role of Music in 'The Winter's Tale'. Pp. 372-83 in Holland, P. (ed.): *Shakespeare Survey 67 – Shakespeare's Collaborative Works*. Cambridge University Press.

Smith, S., 2017. *Musical Response in the Early Modern Playhouse, 1603-1625*. Cambridge University Press.

Smither, P., 2017. Weighing up the Economy of Roman London. *Transactions, London and Middlesex Archaeological Society*, **68**: 41-58.

Somerville, R., 1960. *The Savoy: Manor: Hospital: Chapel*. R. & R. Clark Ltd.

Souden, D., 2008. *The Royal Palaces of London*. Merrell/Historic Royal Palaces.

Spencer, B., 2010. *Pilgrim Souvenirs and Secular Badges. New Edition*. Boydell/Museum of London.

Spencer, C., 2014. *Killers of the King*. Bloomsbury.

Stanley, A.P., 1868. *Historical Memorials of Westminster Abbey*. John Murray.

Stanhope, N., 1887. *Monastic London* … . Remington & Co.

Statham, E.P. (ed.), 1920. *A Jacobean Letter-Writer – The Life and Times of John Chamberlaine*. Kegan Paul, Trench, Trubner & Co.

Steckley, G.F. (ed.), 1984. *The Letters of John Paige, London Merchant, 1648-1658*. London Record Society.

Stedall, R., 2016. *Men of Substance – The London Livery Companies' Reluctant Part in the Plantation of Ulster*. Austin Macauley.

Stevenson, C., 2013. *The City and the King – Architecture and Politics in Restoration London*. Yale University Press.

Stone, L., 2002. *Causes of the English Revolution, 1529-1642*. Third Edition. Routledge.

Stone, P., 2017. *The History of the Port of London* … . Pen & Sword.

Stow, J., 1598. *A Survay of London Written in the Year 1598*.

Streitberger, W.R., 2016. *The Masters of the Revels and Elizabeth I's Court Theatre*. Oxford Unversity Press.

Strohm, P., 2014. *Chaucer's Tale – 1386 and the Road to Canterbury*. Viking.

Strype, J., 1720. *A Survey of the Cities of London and Westminster*.

Stubbs, J., 2006. *Donne – The Reformed Soul*. Viking.

Sullivan, D., 1994. *The Westminster Corridor – The Anglo-Saxon Story of Westminster Abbey and its Lands in Middlesex*. Historical Publications.

Sullivan, D., 2006. *The Westminster Circle – The People who Lived and Worked in the Early Town of Westminster, 1066-1307*. Historical Publications.

Summerson, J., 2000. *Inigo Jones. Revised Edition*. Yale University Press.

Sutcliffe, A., 2006. *London – An Architectural History*. Yale University Press.

Sutton, A.F., 2005. *The Mercery of London – Trade, Goods and People, 1130-1578*. Ashgate.

Sutton, A.F., 2016. *Wives and Widows of Medieval London*. Shaun Tyas.

Sutton, J., 1981. *Lords of the East – The East India Company and its Ships*. Conway Maritime Press Ltd.

Taggart, C., 2012. *The Book of London Place Names*. Ebury.

Tames, R., 1995. *City of London Past*. Historical Publications.

Tames, R., 1999. *Clerkenwell and Finsbury Past*. Historical Publications.

Tames, R., 2002. *A Traveller's History of London. Fourth Edition*. Cassell/Windrush.

Tames, R., 2004. *East End Past*. Historical Publications.

Tames, R., 2006a. *The City of London Book*. Historical Publications.

Tames, R., 2006b. *London – A Literary and Cultural History*. Signal.

Tames, R., 2006c. *Theatrical London*. Historical Publications.

Tames, R., 2008. *The London We Have Lost*. Historical Publications.

Tames, R., 2009. *Shakespeare's London on Five Groats a Day*. Thames & Hudson.

Tames, R., 2012. *Parliament and its Buildings*. Shire.

Tatlock, J.S.P., 1906. The Duration of the Canterbury Pilgrimage. *Publications of the Modern Language Associaton*, **21**(2): 478-85.

Tatton-Brown, T., 2000. *Lambeth Palace – A History of the Archbishops of Canterbury and their Houses*. Society for Promoting Christian Knowledge.

Tatton-Brown, T. & Mortimer, R. (eds.), 2003. *Westminster Abbey – The Lady Chapel of Henry VII*. Boydell.

Taylor, A.J., 1999. *The Jewel Tower*. English Heritage.

Taylor, B. (ed.), 2002. *Foreign-Language Printing in London 1500-1900*. British Library.

Taylor, J., 2018. Prehistoric Landscape at Harold Wood ... . *London Archaeologist*, **15**(6): 164-73.

Taylor, W.F., 1912. *The Charterhouse of London – Monastery, Palace and Thomas Sutton's Foundation*. J.M. Dent & Sons Ltd.

Telfer, A. & Blackmore, L., 2017. 'In the Path of the Flames: Evidence for Daily Life before and after the Great Fire, from Excavations at 11-23 New Fetter Lane, 25 New Street Square, 11 Bartlett Court, 1 and 8-9 East Harding Street, London EC4'. *Transactions, London and Middlesex Archaeological Society*, **68**: 151-90.

Telford, L., 2016. *Tudor Victims of the Reformation*. Pen & Sword.

Telford, L., 2018. *Women in Medieval England*. Amberley.

Temple, P., 2010. *The Charterhouse*. English Heritage.

The Clothworkers' Company, 2005. *The History of the Clothworkers' Company*. The Clothworkers' Company.

Thomas, C., 2002. *The Archaeology of Medieval London*. Sutton.

Thomas, C., 2003. *London's Archaeological Secrets*. Yale University Press/ MoLA.

Thomas, C., 2004. *Life and Death in London's East End – 2000 Years at Spitalfields*. MoLA.

Thomas, C., Cowie, R. & Sidell, J., 2006. *The Royal Palace, Abbey and Town of Westminster on Thorney Island*. MoLA (Monograph 22).

Thomas, C., Sloane, B. & Phillpotts, C., 1997. *Excavations at the Priory and Hospital of St Mary Spital, London*. MoLA (Monograph 1).

Thomas, D., 2016. *A Visitor's Guide to Shakespeare's London*. Pen & Sword.

Thomas, J., 1998. *Discover Dorset Stone Quarrying*. The Dovecot Press.

Thomson, P., 1983. *Shakespeare's Theatre*. Routledge & Kegan Paul.

Thompson, W., 1894. *The History and Antiquities of the Collegiate Church of St Saviour (St Marie Overie), Southwark*. Ash & Co.

Thrupp, S.L., 1948. *The Merchat Class of Medieval London 1300-1500*. University of Chicago Press.

Thurley, S., 1998. *The Lost Palace of Whitehall*. Historic Royal Palaces.

Thurley, S., 1999. *Whitehall Palace*. Yale University Press/Historic Royal Palaces.

Thurley, S., 2009. *Somerset House*. London Topographical Society (Publication No. 168).

Thurley, S., 2013. *The Building of England*. William Collins.

Thurley, S., 2017. *Houses of Power ... .* Bantam Press.

Timbs, J., 1865. *The Romance of London*. Frederick Warne & Co.

Tindall, G., 2002. *The Man Who Drew London – Wenceslas Hollar in Reality and Imagination*. Chatto & Windus.

Tinniswood, A., 2001. *His Invention So Fertile – A Life of Christopher Wren*. Jonathan Cape.

Tinniswood, A., 2003. *By Permission of Heaven – The Story of the Great Fire of London*. Jonathan Cape.

Tomalin, C., 2002. *Samuel Pepys*. Viking.

Tomlin, R.S.O., 2016. *Roman London's First Voices ... .* MoLA (Monograph 72).

Tomory, L., 2017. *The History of London's Water Industry 1580-1820*. Johns Hopkins University Press.

Toynbee, J.M.C., 1986. *The Roman Art Treasures from the Temple of Mithras*. LAMAS (Special Paper, No. 7).

Tosh, W., 2018. *Playing Indoors – Staging Early Modern Theatre in the Wanamaker Playhouse*. Bloomsbury.

Trowles, T., 2016. *Treasures of Westminster Abbey. Revised Edition*. Scala.

Tucker, T., 2010. *The Visitor's Guide to the City of London Churches*. Horizon.

Tudor-Craig, P., 2004. *'Old St Paul's' – The Society of Antiquaries' Diptych, 1616*. London Topographical Society/The Society of Antiquaries of London.

Unwin, G., 1963. *The Gilds and Companies of London*. Frank Cass & Company Ltd.

Vince, A., 1990. *Saxon London ... .* Seaby.

Vince, J., 1973. *Fire-Marks*. Shire.

Wadmore, J.F., 1902. *Some Account of the Worshipful Company of Skinners of London ... .* Blades, East & Blades.

Walford, E., 1872. *Old and New London ... .*

Wall, C., 1988. *The Literary and Cultural Spaces of Reestoration London.* Cambridge University Press.

Wallace, C.W., 1908. *The Children of the Chapel at Blackfriars 1597-1603.* University of Nebraska.

Wallace, L., 2014. *The Origin of Roman London.* Cambridge University Press.

Walsh, D., 2018. *The Cult of Mithras in Late Antiquity – Development, Decline and Demise, ca. AD270-410.* Brill.

Walvin, J., 2011. *The Slave Trade.* Thames & Hudson.

Ward, L., 2015. *The London County Council Bomb Damage Maps 1939-1945.* Thames & Hudson.

Ward, R., 2003. *London's New River.* Historical Publications.

Warner, W. (ed.), 1987. *The Image of London – Views by Travellers and Emigres 1550-1920.* Trefoil/Barbican Art Gallery.

Watney, J., 1914. *An Account of the History of Mercers of the City of London ... .* Blades, East & Blades.

Watson, B., 2004. *'Old London Bridge' Lost and Found.* MoLA.

Watson, B., Brigham, T. & Dyson, T., 2001. *London Bridge.* MoLA (Monograph 8).

Watson, I., 2002. *Westminster and Pimlico Past.* Historical Publications Ltd.

Way, T.R. & Chapman, T.R., 1902. *Ancient Royal Palaces in and near London.* John Lane.

Webb, E.A., 1921. *The Records of St Bartholomew's Priory and St Bartholomew the Great, West Smithfield.* Humphrey Milford/Oxford University Press.

Webb, S., 2011a. *Life in Roman London.* The History Press.

Webb, S., 2011b. *Unearthing London.* The History Press.

Weever, J., 1631. *Ancient Funerall Monuments within the United Monarchie of Great Britaine, Ireland, and the Islands Adiacent.*

Weinreb, B., Hibbert, C., Keay, J. & Keay, J., 2008. *The London Encyclopaedia. Third Edition.* MacMillan.

Weinstein, R., 1994. *Tudor London.* Her Majesty's Stationery Office/Museum of London.

Weir, A., 1999. *The Princes in the Tower.* The Folio Society.

Wellsman, J. (ed.), 1973. *London before the Fire – A Grand Panorama (From Original Seventeenth-Century Engravings by Visscher, Hollar and de Witt).* Sidgwick & Jackson.

West, C., 2014. *The Story of St Katharine's.* Cloister House.

Wheatley, H.B. & Cunningham, P., 1891. *London Past and Present.* (Reprinted by Cambridge University Press in 2011).

Wheeler, H., 1930. *The Wonderful Story of London.* Odhams.

Wheeler, R.E.M., 1935. *London and the Saxons.* Lancaster House.

Whinney, M., 1971. *Wren.* Thames & Hudson.

Whipp, D., 2006. *The Medieval Postern Gate by the Tower of London.* MoLA (Monograph 29).

White, J., 2010. *London – The Story of a Great City.* Andre Deutsch/Museum of London.

Whitfield, P., 2006. *London – A Life in Maps*. The British Library.

Wickham, D.E., 1989. *Clothworker's Hall … .* Clothworkers' Company and Jarrold Colour Publications.

Wilbur, M.E., 1965. *The East India Company and the British Empire in the Far East*. Stanford University Press.

Wilkinson, J., 2006. *Westminster Abbey – A Souvenir Guide*. Scala.

Wilkinson, J., 2007. *Henry VII's Lady Chapel*. Tudsbury.

Willan, T.S., 1953. *The Muscovy Merchants of 1555*. Manchester University Press.

Willan, T.S., 1956. *The Early History of the Russia Company*. Manchester University Press.

Willes, M., 2017. *The Curious World of Samuel Pepys and John Evelyn*. Yale University Press.

Williams, E., 1927. *Early Holborn and the Legal Quarter of London*. Sweet & Maxwell Limited.

Williams, G.A., 1970. *Medieval London – From Commune to Capital. Corrected Edition*. The Athlone Press.

Williams, W.P. (ed.), 1980. *Index to the Stationers' Register 1640-1708*. Lawrence McGilvey, La Jolla.

Willson, B., 1903. *Ledger and Sword, or The Honourable Company of Merchants of England Trading to the East Indies*. Longmans, Green & Co.

Wilson, A.N., 1983. *A Life of John Milton*. Oxford University Press.

Wilson, A.N., 2004. *London – A Short History*. Weidenfeld & Nicolson.

Wilson, D., 1978. *The Tower – 1078-1978*. Hamish Hamilton.

Wilson, F.P., 1925. *The Plague Pamphlets of Thomas Dekker*. Clarendon Press.

Wilson, F.P., 1927. *The Plague in Shakespeare's London*. Oxford University Press.

Wittich, J., 1996. *Discovering London Street Names. Third Edition*. Shire.

Wood, A.C., 1935. *A History of the Levant Company*. Oxford University Press.

Wood, A.C., 1964. *A History of the Levant Company*. Routledge.

Wood, M., 1986. *Domesday – A Search for the Roots of England. Revised Edition*. Book Club Associates.

Woodward, C.D., 2011. *A Miraculous Survival – The History of a Unique City within a City*. Phillimore.

Woodward, G.W.O., McIlwain, J. & Williams, B., 2014. *The Dissolution of the Monasteries. Revised Edition*. Pitkin.

Wright, J.D., 2017. *Bloody History of London … .* Amber Books.

Wright, L.B., 1943. *Religion and Empire – The Alliance between Piety and Commerce in English Expansion 1558-1625*. University of North Carolina Press.

Wright, S.M. (ed.), 2017. *Archaeology at Bloomberg*. MoLA.

Young, E. & Young, W., 1956. *Old London Churches*. Faber and Faber.

Zetterstein, L., 1926. *City Street Names … . Third Edition*. Selwyn & Blount Ltd.

OTHER RESOURCES

A Map of Tudor London – England's Greatest City in 1520. Town & City Historical Maps.

Four Very Detailed Maps – Medieval to Twentieth Century London (1520, 1666, 1843, 1902). Old House Books.

Londinium – A New Map and Guide to Roman London. MoLA.
William Shakespeare's London – A Commemorative Souvenir of Shakespearean London (featuring a reproduction of the Braun & Hogenberg map of 1572). Shakespeare's Globe.

Apps
Pepys's London app for iPhones and iPads (available for purchase through iTunes).
Shakespeare's London apps for iPhones and iPads (two separate versions, one available for free, the other for purchase through the App Store).
Streetmuseum and *Streetmuseum Londinium* app for iPhones and iPads (available for free through the Museum of London).

Websites
http://alpha.layersoflondon.org (includes an interactive map of the City of London and its environs in 1520).
british-history.ac.uk
britishmuseum.org.uk
cathedral.southwark.anglican.org (Southwark Cathedral)
cityandlivery.co.uk (City of London Livery Companies)
cityoflondon.gov.uk (links to the Billingsgate Roman House, the Guildhall Library and the London Metropolitan Archives).
colas.org.uk (City of London Archaeological Society)
archaeology.crossrail.co.uk
english-heritage.org.uk/visit/london
hrp.org.uk (Historic Royal Places, including the Tower of London, the Banqueting House, and Hampton Court Palace).
lamas.org.uk (London and Middlesex Archaeological Society)
archbishopofcanterbury.org/lambeth-palace
layersoflondon.org (selected time-slice maps)
london-city-churches.org.uk
londontopsoc.org (London Topographical Society)
museumoflondon.org.uk
mola.org.uk (Museum of London Archaeology)
nationalgallery.org.uk
npg.org.uk (National Portrait Gallery)
nationaltrust.org.uk/London
oldlondonbridge.com
pepysdiary.com
roseplayhouse.org.uk
rmg.co.uk (Royal Museums Greenwich, including the National Maritime Museum and the Queen's House)
royal.uk/royal-residences-st-jamess-palace
stpauls.co.uk
vam.ac.uk (Victoria and Albert Museum)
westminster-abbey.org
parliament.uk/about/living-heritage/building/palace/westminsterhall (Westminster Hall)

Index

Actes and Monuments 101
Act for the Dissolution of the Greater Monasteries 104
Act for the Dissolution of the Lesser Monasteries 104
Act for the Rebuilding of the City of London 190
Act forbidding Priests to Minister 144
Act of Supremacy 101
Acts of Apparel 74
Administration and Governance 18, 28, 63-9, 142-5
Aelfric, Bishop 30
Agas map 104, 171
Ague 60
Albemarle, Duke of 130
Alchemist, The 161
Aldermanbury 203
Aldermanbury Conduit 221
Aldermanbury Square 125, 236-6
Aldermen 29, 39, 52, 53, 59, 64, 73, 121, 142
Aldersgate, Ward 21, 150, 185
Aldgate, Ward 16, 21, 52, 119, 150, 213
Aldwych 25
Ale 58
Ale-houses 137
Alfred the Great 25, 29, 30

Aliens 62-3, 141
Allectus 16
Allegory of Reformation 106
Alleyn, Edward 156
All Hallows Barking 23, 30, 32, 81, 107, 184, 201, 206, 211, 228
All Hallows on the Wall 81
All Hallows Staining 78, 81, 213
Alms-Houses 150
Alsatia 105
Ambassadors, The 164
Ambresbury Banks 12, 15
Amen Corner 143
Americas 113, 114, 129, 148, 149
Amphitheatre 19, 21, 22, 23, 197
Anarchy, The 38
Ancient British London 11-4
Androgeus 13
Angel (Tavern) 130
Anglo-Spanish War 114, 134
Animal-baiting 72, 151
Animal bones 91
Anne of Bohemia 76
Anne of Cleves 102
Anne of Denmark 166
Apothecaries, Company, Hall 139, 140, 173, 239
Apprentices 74
Archaeological finds 22-3, 33-4, 91-2, 180

Ark, The 117
Artillery Lane, Passage, Yard 188
As You Like It 160
Askew, Anne 103-4, 144
Athelstan 29
Atys 20
Aubrey, John 84
Augustinan Order 54
Austin Friars Priory 51, 78, 216-7, 232-3

Bacon, Edmund 155
Bacon, Francis 143, 148, 159, 168, 170
Bagnall, Elizabeth 71
Ball, John 45
Banqueting House (Whitehall Palace) 124, 168-9, 173
Bankside 72, 151, 155
Barbon, Nicholas 170, 187
Barker family 141
Barnard's Inn, Hall 82
Barons' Wars 41-2
Baroque 194
Bartholomew Fair (event) 72, 151
Bartholomew Fair (play) 162
Barton, Elizabeth (Holy Maid of Kent) 102, 144
Basilica 16, 18, 19, 21, 23, 200
Basinghall Street 235
Basset, John 53
Battersea 14, 18
Battle of Barnet 50-2
Battle of Blackheath 97
Battle of Brentford 121-2
Battle of Deptford Bridge 97
Battle of St Albans 50
Battle of Turnham Green 122
Battle of Watling Street 15
Baynard, Ralph 76
Baynard's Castle 40, 50, 63, 76, 77, 78, 108, 182, 186, 223, 224, 239
Beaumont, Francis 159, 161
Becket, Thomas, Archbishop, Saint 55, 74
Bedlam: see St Mary of Bethlehem
Bedlam Burlial Ground 128, 130, 140

Behn, Aphra 168
Beer 58
Bell (Inn) 154, 233
Bell Inn Yard 233
Bell Savage (Inn) 137, 148, 154
Benedictine Order 54
Bermondsey 145
Bermondsey Abbey 55, 77, 82
Best, John 155
Bettes, John, the Younger 159
Billesdon, Robert, Billesdon Award 71
Billingsgate 18, 30, 70, 74, 80
Billingsgate Roman House 119, 130, 131, 170
Bircheston, Simon 43
Bishop's Book 102
Bishopsgate (gate, street, ward) 16, 21, 31, 62, 80, 139, 142, 168, 184, 185, 216, 232
Black Death 43-4, 61, 62, 79
Blackamores' Head 161
Blackfriars 20, 195
Blackfriars Lane 239
Blackfriars Priory 26, 77, 78, 82, 100, 105, 223
Blackfriars Theatre 154, 238-9
Blackheath 56, 98, 126
Blackman, Reasonable 141
Blackwall 145
Blagrave, William 155
Blanche of Lancaster 74
Blands, Mr. 139
Blank, John 141, 142
Bloodworth, Thomas 186
Bloody flux 58
Blome map 189
Boar's Head (playhouse) 154
Bocaccio 74
Bol 171
Boleyn, Anne 100, 101
Boleyn, George 101
Bolingbroke, Henry (future Henry IV) 46, 47
Bolton, William 168
Bona Esparanza 112
Bonner, Edmund, Bishop 108
Book of the Duchess, The 74

Borough Compter 68
Borough High Street 56
Boudicca, Boudiccan Revolt 15, 19, 23
Boudicca's Grave 11
Bow Church: see St Mary-le-Bow
Bowman, Christopher 131
Bradford, John 110, 111
Brandon, Charles, Duke of Suffolk 170
Braun and Hogenberg map 104, 171
Brayne, John 154
Bread Street, Ward 150, 161, 234-5
Brembre, Nicholas 46
Brent (river) 121
Brentford 14, 121
Brereton, William 101
Brid, John 68
Bridewell Palace 164, 239
Bridewell (Prison) 69
Bridges Street 155
Bridgettine Order 101
Briot 172
British Atlas of Historic Towns map 104, 171
British Library 66
British Museum 23
Broad Street, Ward 62, 150
Bronze Age 11
Brooke, Lord 121
Browne, Stephen 80
Bruges or Brydges, John 109
Building Works 19-21, 30-1, 76-81, 164-72
Bull, John 162
Bull (Inn) 154
Bunhill Fields 130
Bunyan, John 159
Burbage, Cuthbert 154
Burbage, James 154, 155
Burbage, Richard 155
Burleigh, Baron (see also Cecil, William) 115
Bury Street 200
Byrd, William 159
Byward Street 201, 206, 211, 228

Cade, Jack, Jack Cade's Rebellion 49
Caesar's Camp 12
Caire Lud 13
Campeggio, Lorenzo 100
Canary Wharf 9
Cannon Street 14, 22, 49, 183, 198, 218, 219
Canonbury Grove 135
Canonbury Tower 168, 172
Canterbury Tales, The 56, 74, 76, 162
Capital punishment 163
Carausius, Carausian Revolt 16
Carew, John 127
Carey, Henry, 1st Baron Brunsdon 118
Carey Street 137
Carleton, Dudley 96, 155
Carmelite Order (White Friars) 54
Carpenter, John 36, 65, 80
Carter Lane 223
Carthusian Order 54
Cassibelan [Cassivelaunus] 13
Castle Baynard, Ward 150
Catuvellauni 12, 13
Cathay Company 111
Catherine of Aragon 100
Catherine of Braganza 169
Catholicism 53, 101, 102, 103, 107, 108, 111, 114
Cavaliers 164
Cawarden, Thomas 105
Caxton, William 162
Cecil, Robert (1st Earl of Salisbury) 116, 117
Cecil, William (Baron Burleigh) 118
Cecil, William (2nd Earl of Salisbury) 117
Celtic London 11-4
Chamberlain, John 93, 95, 155, 158
Change, The 131, 191
Chantries 54
Chapman, William 171
Charles I 119, 120, 123, 124, 125, 136, 161, 163, 164, 168
Charles II 117, 126, 127, 128, 164, 169, 183, 184, 188

Charlton 24

Charterhouse 4, 78, 80, 82, 102, 105, 164, 168, 172, 173

Charing Cross 122, 127

Chatham 99

Chaucer, Geoffrey 74, 76

Cheap, Ward 150

Cheapside 18, 31, 49, 50, 57, 70, 72, 151, 162, 182, 184, 188, 203, 218, 222, 234, 235

Cheapside Conduit(s) 58, 220, 225, 238

Cheapside Cross 49, 108, 122, 222, 238

Cheapside Hoard 148

Chelsea 82

Cherabin 99

Chevalier de Bassompierre 153

Chocolate (hot), chocolate-houses 139

Christ Church Greyfriars, Newgate Street 64, 185

Christianity 17, 21, 39, 54, 57, 142

Christ's Hospital (School) 142

Chronicle of London 36, 52

Chronicle of the Grey Friars 106

Chronicles of the Mayors and Sheriffs of London 35, 42

Church of Paulesbyri 30

City of London School 64

City Wall 20, 21, 22

Civil War 119, 120, 122, 127

Clapham, Luke 169

Clarendon, Earl of 190

Claudius 15

Clay pipes 180

Clerkenwell 74, 152, 155, 158

Clerks' Well 74

Clink, Liberty of 159

Clink (Prison) 68

Clodius Albinus 16

Cloth Fair 170, 173

Clothworkers, Company, Hall 71

Cluniac Order 54

Cnut 26, 27, 31

Coat-hardie 75

Cobbie, Anne 142

Cock Lane 73

Cockpit Theatre 155

Cofee, coffee-houses 137, 138

Coffee House, The 138

Coleman Street 128

Colet, John, Dean 65

College Hill 64

College of Physicians 143

Commonwealth and Protectorate 124, 126, 132

Company of Merchant Adventurers to New Lands 147

Constables 66

Consumption 60, 140

Cook, John 127

Cooper's Row 201

Copper Plate map 104, 171

Cordwainer, Ward 150

Cornhill 15

Cornill (street) 31, 49, 70, 126, 137, 138, 188, 218, 233

Cornish Rebellion 98

Corporal punishment 67, 68, 144

Corporation 64, 65, 142

Councilmen, common 29, 64, 142

Counter-Reformation 108

Court of Augmentations 104, 105

Covent Garden 139, 169

Coverdale, Miles 101

Coverture 53

Crakows 76

Cranmer, Thomas, Archbishop 101, 102, 106

Creechurch Lane Synagogue 133, 134, 232

Crime 66, 67, 143

Cripplegate, Ward 21, 62, 133, 150, 155

Cripplegate Fort 20, 196-7

Cromwell, Oliver 120, 123, 125, 131, 144

Cromwell, Thomas 84, 101, 102, 104, 144

Crosby, John 52, 80

Crosby Hall 82, 215-6

Crosby Square 215

Cross Keys (Inn) 154

Crossbones Graveyard 130

Croxton(e), John 80

Crowmer, William 50
Crutched Friars 213
Culpeper, Nicholas 140
Culpeper, Thomas 144
Curtain (playhouse) 154, 159, 161
Custom House 70-1, 74, 186, 211, 228
Cymbeline 160

Dance of Death 79
Dark Age London 25-34
Davenant, William 159
Daye, John 144
De Briset, Jordan 55
De Farndone, Nicholas 73
De Flor, Henricus 72
De Jongh 171
De Montfichet, Richard 76
De Montfort, Simon 42
De Selve, Georges 164-5
De Vere, Edward, 17th Earl of Oxford 159
De Worde, Wynkyn 162
Deadman's Place 130
Decorated Gothic 82
Dee, John 111
Defensio pro Populo Anglico 161
Dekker, Thomas 118, 159
Deptford 56, 97, 112, 160
Devereux, Robert, Earl of Essex 110, 144
Dido, Queen of Carthage 160
Dissolution of the Monasteries 61-2, 82, 104
Divine Rights (of Kings) 119
Doctor Faustus 160
Domesday, survey, book 62, 63
Dominican Order (Black Friars) 119, 159
Doornick map 189
Dowgate, Ward 62, 70
Dowland, John 159
Drake, Francis 112, 115
Drapers 71
Dress, dress accessories 74-7, 162-4
Drury Lane 155
Dryden, John 159
Dunstan 31

Early English Gothic 81
East India Company 169
East Smithfield 44, 72, 151
Eastcheap 31, 70, 205, 210, 228
Economy, sectors of 147
Edict of Expulsion 56
Education 65, 142
Edward the Confessor 27, 31, 32, 55
Edward I 43, 57, 58
Edward II (King) 42, 43
Edward II (play) 160
Edward III 43, 47, 61, 74, 80
Edward III's manor house 77, 81
Edward IV 50, 51, 78
Edward V 50
Edward VI 106, 107, 140, 164
Edwards, Daniel 137, 138
Edwards, Tom 130
Egerton, Rafe 144
Eikon Basilike 161
Eikonoklastes 161
Eleanor Crosses 122
Eleanor of Castile 58
Elizabeth of York 167
Elizabeth I 99, 108, 109, 111, 112, 113, 114, 115, 116, 134, 149, 163, 165
Elsing Spital 62, 78, 221
Ely Court 173
Ely Palace 135
Emma of Normandy 27
Entertainment and culture 72-4, 151-62
Epping Forest 12, 32
Erkenwald, Bishop 30
Ermine Street 21, 199
Essex, Earl of, Essex House, Essex Steps, Essex's Rebellion 115, 116
Ethelred the Unready 26, 27
Ethered 26
Ethered's Hithe 30
Etherege, George 159
Evelyn, John 94, 96, 97, 122, 124, 125, 182, 184, 185, 189
Every Man in his Humour 161
Exchange Alley 138
Exports 70

Fabian, Fabian's Great Chronicle of London 51, 78
Fairfax, Mary 170
Fairfax, Thomas, Lord 170
Famine 42
Farrant, Richard 154
Farriner, Thomas 181, 186
Farringdon Ward 62, 150
Farthingale 163
Fauconberg, Bastard 52
Fawkes, Guy 118, 119
Femme covert 53 53
Fenchurch Street 18, 19, 31, 70, 130, 200, 213
Fiennes, James 58
Fifth Monarchists 128
Fillis, Mary 141
Finsbury Fields 158
Fire insurance, fire-marks 187
First Blackfriars Theatre 154
First Defence 161
First War of Scottish Independence 43
Fish Street Hill 181
Fisher, John 103, 144
Fishmongers 71
FitzAilwyn de Londonestone, Henry 39, 80
FitzOsbert or FitzRobert, William 39-40
FitzStephen, William 36, 57, 70, 72
FitzThedmar, Arnold 35
FitzWalter, Robert 40
Flamank, Thomas 97
Fleet Prison 69
Fleet (River) 59, 139
Fleet Street 137, 155, 162, 183, 185, 188
Fletcher, John 159
Folkmoot 28
Food and drink 18, 28, 57-9, 134-9
Forest, John 103, 144
Fortescue, John 67
Fortunata 19
Fortune (theatre) 155
Forty-Two Articles 42
Forum 16, 19, 21, 23, 200
Foster Lane 196

Foxe, John 102, 105, 110, 111
Franciscan Order (Grey Friars) 54, 103
Franciscus, Andreas 84, 85
Freedom of the City, Freemen 69
Friars 54
Frobisher, Martin 112
Froissart, Jean 36, 45, 46
Frost fairs 73

Gabriel (ship) 112
Galeys, Henry 65
Gaol fever 69
Gardiner, Stephen, Bishop 102
Garnet, Henry, Father 132
Geoffrey de Mandeville 41
Geoffrey of Monmouth 122
George, Duke of Clarence 50
George (Inn) 59
Gerard, John, Father 132
Gibbons, Grinling 137, 193
Gibbons, Orlando 159
Giltspur Street 196
Girard 77
Gisze, Georg 147
Giustiniani, Giovanni 120
Globe (coffee-house) 138
Globe (playhouse) 116, 154, 155, 159
Glyndwr, Catrin (ferch Owain) 48, 219
Glyndwr Owain 48
Goldsmiths 71, 146
Goffe 125
Golden Hind(e) 99, 112
Gothic 78
Governor's Palace 16, 18, 19, 21, 22, 23, 198-9
Gower, John 74
Gracechurch Street 22, 130, 233
Gray's Inn 66
Great Conduit 58
Great Fire of London 71, 77, 81, 82, 129, 131, 135, 142, 143, 147, 162, 164, 165, 172, 181-7, 188-93
Great matter, the King's 100
Great North Road 51

Great Plague 129-32
Great reckoning 160
Greenhalgh, Joseph 133
Greensted Church 32
Greenwich 114, 117, 180
Gregory, William 205
Grenade 84, 85
Gresham College 117, 142, 232
Gresham, Thomas 99, 142, 145
Gresham Ship 99
Gresham Street 18, 23, 197, 203
Grey, Henry 107, 108
Grey, Jane, Lady 107, 108
Greyfriars Priory 78, 107
Grim's Dyke 12
Grindal, Edmund, Bishop 157
Grocers 71
Guildhall 50, 64, 65, 70, 77, 80, 82,
    109, 186, 197, 203, 220, 235
Guildhall Art Gallery 182
Guildhall Library 36, 40
Gunnell, Richard 155
Gunning 126
Gunpowder Plot 118, 119, 132
Gwyn, John 122
Gwyn(ne), Nell 155

Haberdashers 71
Hackney 168, 173
Hackney Museum 33
Hackney Wells (henge) 10
Haiward & Gascoyne plan (Tower
    of London) 166
Hales, Robert 45
Hall, Edward, Hall's Annals 102
Hamlet 160
Hampden, John 119
Hampstead 10, 121
Hanseatic League 70, 147
Hardel(l), William 48
Hardicanute 27
Harold I (Harold Harefoot) 27, 30
Harold II (Harold Godwinson) 27
Harrison, Stephen 118
Harrison, Thomas 127, 144
Harrow Weald Common 12
Harvard, John 129
Haselrig, Arthur 119

Hawkins, John 148, 149
Hawksmoor, Nicholas 159
Helmet Tavern 128
Henrietta Maria (Queen) 167, 169
Henry, Philip 124
Henry I 38
Henry II 38, 55
Henry III 41, 42, 72, 80
Henry IV 47
Henry V 48, 49
Henry VI 43, 49, 50
Henry VII 84, 98, 100, 164, 165,
    167
Henry VII Lady Chapel
    (Westminster Abbey) 167, 172
Henry VIII (King) 55, 84, 98, 102,
    103, 105, 106, 162, 164, 165,
    166
Henry VIII (play) 155, 156
Henry VIII's wine cellar 172
Henry Grace a Dieu 99, 146
Henslowe, Philip 155
Herland, Hugh 80
Herman, Thomas 144
Hilliard, Nicholas 112, 159
Hoby, Edward 118
Hockley-in-the-Hole 152
Hodges, Nathaniel 131-2
Hodges, Thomas 138
Holbein, Hans 147, 159, 162, 164
Holbein Gate 172
Holinshed, Raphael, Holinshed's
    Chronicles 165
Holland, Aaron 155
Holland's Leaguer 153
Hollar, Wenceslaus 171, 189
Holles, Denzil 119, 122
Hollier, Thomas 140
Holy Trinity Minories 78
Holy Trinity Priory (Aldgate) 82,
    214
Holywell Mount 130
Holywell Priory 78, 105
Honey Lane 57
Honourable Artillery Company 99,
    121
Hooke, Robert 189, 191
Hoop and Grapes 82

Hope (playhouse) 155, 161
Horn, Andrew 36
Horsemonger Lane (Prison) 68
Hospitals 61-2
Houghton, John 102, 103, 144
Hounslow 10
Houppelande 75
House of Fame, The 74
Houses of Correction 150
Houses of Industry 150
Howard, Catherine 144
Howell, James 84
Hoxton 145
Hubert, Robert 186
Huggin Hill (bath-house) 18, 23
Husting 28, 39

Images, veneration of 102
Imports 19, 29, 67-70
Imprisonment 68-9
Indulgences 96
Ingelric 77
Inns 137
Inns of Chancery 67
Inns of Court 66, 67, 80, 82, 143,
    154, 168, 169, 172
Inter-Regnum 124-5, 127
Ireland Yard 159, 223, 238
Iron Age 11
Ironmonger Lane 204, 220
Ironmongers 71
Islam, Islamic World 134
Isle of Dogs, The (play) 155
Isleworth 102
Islington 135, 137, 168, 172

Jacob of Orleans 39
James I of England (James VI of
    Scotland) 114, 117, 118, 119,
    134, 149, 163, 166, 168
Jamestown 113, 148, 149
Janyns, Robert the Younger 167
Jerman, Edward 191
Jervas (wig-maker) 164
Jesuits 132
Jetons 91
Jew of Malta, The (play) 160
Jewel Tower 77, 81

Jews, Judaism 39, 40, 56-7, 132-4
John, King 40-1 45, 47, 74, 80
Jonathan's (coffee-house) 117, 159,
    168, 169
Jones, John 127
Jonson, Ben 118, 145, 155, 159,
    161
Jonson, Ben, Jr. 161
Jordemaine, Margery (The Witch of
    Eye) 68
Joseph, Michael (An Gof) 98
Judicia Civitatis Londoniae 29
Julius Alpinus Classicianus 15
Julius Caesar 13

Ketel, Cornelius 112
Killigrew, Thomas 155, 159
King Henry's Mound 10
King Lear 160
King's Bench (Prison) 50, 58
King's Book 102
King's Men, The 159
Kingsland 62
Kingston 109
Knightbridge 62
Knights Hospitaller 54, 55
Knights Templar 54
Knyvet(t), Thomas 118

Lambeth 82
Lambeth Palace 164, 165, 172
Lanfranc, Archbishop 77
Langbourn, Ward 62
Langland, John 193
Langley, Francis 154
Lanman, Henry 154
Laud, William, Archbishop 122
Law 29, 65, 142, 143-5
Lawes Resolutions of Women's
    Rights, The 132
Lazar(us) Houses 62
Le Sueur, Hubert 164
Lea (river) 25, 33
Leaden Hall, Leadenhall Market 64,
    80, 185
Leadenhall Street 31, 70, 126, 213,
    214
Leaf(e), John 110, 111

Leake survey 189
Legatine Court 100
Legend of Good Women, The 74
Leicester Square 14
Lely, Peter 159
Lenthall, William 120
Leprosy, lepers 60, 61, 62
Letter-Books of the City of London 35, 61
Levellers 123
Liber Albus 36
Liber de Antiquis Regibus 35
Liber Horn 35
Lidgate, John 80
Lilburne, John 122
Limehouse 145
Lincoln's Inn, Chapel, Gate-House, Old Buildings and Old Hall 66, 67, 172, 173
Lincoln's Inn Fields 158, 173
Lines of Communication 121
Lithgow, William 120
Little Conduit 58
Little Sanctuary 69
Livery Companies, Halls 64, 65, 69, 70, 72, 80, 82, 146, 150, 168, 169, 185, 186
Lloyd's (coffee-house) 137
Lodge, Thomas 149
Loimologia 132
Lollardy, Lollard Revolt 48, 54
Lombard Street 31, 218
Londinium 15, 18
London Bridge 19, 23, 26, 37, 48, 50, 56, 69, 80, 97, 109, 135, 183, 199, 204-5, 208-12, 227-8
London Metropolitan Archives 36, 38, 159
London Stone 48, 71, 218-9
London Wall 22, 197
Long Acre 139
Lord Chamberlain's Men, The 159
Lord Mayor's Show 64, 73
Lord Strange's Men 159
Loughton Camp 12
Lowonidonjon 12
Lud, King 13
Ludgate 21, 109, 195

Ludgate Hill 15, 20, 137, 139, 148, 163, 183, 184, 185
Ludgate Prison 132
Lundenburg 26, 31, 33
Lundenwic 25, 31, 33
Lyly, John 159

Machyn, Henry 94, 96, 108, 111, 140, 151
Magna Carta 40, 41, 64, 66
Maiden Lane 155
Main Plot (against James I) 114
Manningham, John 84, 117
Manny, Walter 105
Mansion House 64
Maritz, Pieter 135
Mark Lane 141, 213
Marlowe, Christopher or Kit 159, 160, 161
Marshall, Joshua 193
Marshall, William 41
Marshalsea (Prison) 41, 68, 155, 161
Martin Lane 137, 173
Marvell, Andrew 159, 161
Mary, Queen 100, 102, 107, 108, 109, 165, 170
Mary of Guise 107
Masons Avenue 235
Massacre at Paris, The (play) 157
Master Henry 80
Master of the Bears 72
Master of the Revels 105
Maurice, Bishop 77
May, Hugh 191
Mayor of London 29, 39, 45, 46, 52, 59, 64, 65, 73, 80, 108, 111, 121, 135, 142, 149, 150
Mayoral Charter 40
Medical Matters 28, 60-2, 139-41
Medieval London 25-93, 207-24
Mellitus, Bishop 27, 30
Menasseh ben Israel 133
Mercers 71
Merchant Adventurers 147
Merchant of Venice, The 160
Merchant Taylors, Company, Hall, School 71, 80, 82, 142, 217

Mermaid Tavern 161
Mesolithic 10
Mickell, Robert 131
Middle Temple Hall 143, 154, 172
Middleton, Thomas 118, 135, 159
Mile End 62
Milk Street 235
Mills, Peter 191
Milton, John 159, 161
Miracle plays 73
Mithras, Mithraism 17, 20
Monastic houses 54
Monks 54, 61
Montfichet, Richard, Montfichet's
    Tower 41, 62, 76
Monument 226
Monument Street 226
Moore map 171
Moorfields 16, 72, 187
Moorgate (gate, street) 197
Morality plays 73
Morat's 138
More, Thomas 80, 103, 144, 159
Morgan map 189
Munday, Anthony 159
Muscovy Company 147
Musaeum Tradescantianum 117
Museum of London 17, 20, 23, 32,
    33, 91, 126
Museum of London Docklands 180
Muslims (Mahometans) 134, 142
Myddelton or Myddleton, Hugh
    135, 136, 137
Myddelton, Thomas 135
Mystery plays 73

National Gallery 164
National Maritime Museum 180
National Portrait Gallery 96, 106,
    112, 114, 163
Navy Office 97, 98, 229
Neolithic 10
New Atlantis 148
New Bridge Street 239
New Model Army 121, 123, 128
New River, New River Company
    135-7
New World 113, 148

Newcourt and Faithorne map 171
Newgate 16, 21, 183
Newgate (Prison) 64, 69, 145
Newgate Street 70, 184, 196
Newington Butts 154
Newington Green Terrace 170
Noble Street 196, 221
Norden map, panorama 171
Norfolk, Duke of 102
Norman History 37-8
Norris, Henry 101
North, Edward 105, 164
North Woolwich 10
Norton Folgate, Liberty of 160
Nottingham, Earl of 116

Oak Room 137
Oath of Supremacy 101, 102, 103
Oath of Succession 101
Offa, King 30
Office of the Revels 105
Ogilby, John 126
Ogilby and Morgan map 189
Olaf, Olav or Olave, Olaf
    Haraldsson, Olaf II of Norway,
    Olaf Sagas 26
Old Bailey 128, 183, 196
Old Broad Street 216, 232
Old Jewry 56, 220
Old Kent Road 56
Old Poor Law 150
Old World 69
Oldcastle, John 48
Olde Cheshire Cheese 137
Olde Mitre 173
Olde Wine Shades 137, 173
Ordinance for the Regulation of
    Hackney-Coachmen in London
    and the places adjacent 172
Ordinance of Labourers 44
Ordinances for the Governance of
    the Stews 73
Orderic Vitalis 37
Orpington 23
Oteswich, John 75
Oteswich, Mary 75
Our Lady of Willesden 55
Oxlese 58

Oyster shells 92
Oystergate 70

Paige, John 149
Palace of Westminster 31, 42, 77,
    81, 118
Palaeolithic 10
Paradise Lost 161
Pardon Cloister 79
Parlement of Foules 74
Paris, Matthew 55, 60, 82
Parkinson, John 139
Parliament 29, 42, 46. 47, 117, 118,
    119, 120, 123, 124, 125, 126,
    132
Parliament Hill 11
Pasqua Rosee, Pasqua Rosee's Head
    (coffee-house) 137-8, 233
Paternoster Row 58
Paston, John 51
Patten 59
Patten, William 167
Paul's Whardf 184
Payne, Mr 130
Peacham, Henry 171
Peasants' Revolt 44-6, 64
Penn, William 183, 186
Pepys, Elizabeth 97
Pepys, Samuel 94, 96, 97-8, 127,
    130, 131, 134, 135, 138, 139,
    140, 141, 163, 164, 191
Pepys Street 21, 201
Perpendicular Gothic 79, 167
Persons of colour 17, 141
Pest-houses 129
Petrarch 74
Philpot, John 110
Phoenix (theatre) 155
Pilgrims, pilgrimages, pilgrim
    souvenirs 54, 55, 56
Pindar, Paul 168
Plague 43, 44, 60-1, 62, 129-32,
    140
Plantagenet History 38-47
Plantation Place 70, 200
Platter, Thomas 151
Playhouse Yard 238
Playhouses 105, 154-8

Plowman, Richard 169
Plowonida 12
Plumstead 11
Pocahontas 148
Poll Tax 44, 45
Pompeii of the North 23, 198
Poplar 145
Poplar Chapel 169, 173
Population 18, 28, 62-3, 141-2
Port of London 18-9, 69, 145, 199,
    204-5, 208-10, 226-7
Portsoken, Ward 62
Postern Gate 81
Pottery 91, 180
Poulaines 76
Poultry 15, 18, 23, 58, 70, 80, 198,
    219
Pratt, Roger 191
Pride, Thomas, Pride's Purge 124
Prince Royal 99
Princes in the Tower 50
Princes Street 18, 197
Proclamation as to Street Walkers by
    Night, and Women of Bad Repute
    73
Proclamation ... to Prohibit the
    Rebuilding ... after the Great
    Fire ... without Conforming to
    Regulations ... 188, 190
Protestantism 54, 97, 101, 102, 103,
    104, 106, 107, 108, 111
Provision for the Safe-Keeping of the
    City 65
Pudding Lane 18, 181
Publishing 161
Punishment 67-8, 143
Purcell, Henry 159
Purgatory 54, 102
Puritanism 121, 122, 132, 158, 163,
    169
Putney Debates 123
Pym, John 119

Queen Victoria Street 224, 239
Queenhithe 29, 30, 32, 70, 204
Queen's Chapel (St James's Palace)
    168, 173
Queen's Head Alley 139

Queen's Head Inn 129
Queen's House 114, 117, 169

Rainsborough, Thomas 123
Ralegh, Walter 80, 113-4
Ralph of Coggeshall 40
Ramsay, William 79
Ratcliff 15, 112, 145
Rawlinson 134
Recusancy Acts 111
Red Bull (theatre) 155, 158
Red Lion 154
Red Pale 162
Redcross Way 153
Reformation 55, 82, 97, 104, 132
Relics, veneration of 102
Religion 16-8, 27-8, 53-7, 132-4
Rembrandt 171
Renaissance 169
Reresby, John 93, 125
Restoration (of the Monarchy),
    Restoration London 125-32, 158
Restoration theatre 158
Restitutus 17
Reynolds, Richard 102
Rhys Ddu 48
Rich, Richard 103
Richard, Duke of Gloucester (future
    Richard III) 50
Richard I 39
Richard II (King) 45, 46, 47, 74,
    76, 80
Richard II (play) 116, 160
Richard III 50, 72, 78, 94
Richard of Devizes 36
Richmond Park 10
Robert of Avesbury 43
Roberts, John 144
Roe, Thomas 150
Roger of Howden 39
Roger of Wendover 39
Rogers, John 109, 110, 144
Roman London 15-24, 194-201
Romanesque 77, 81
Romeo and Juliet 160
Roper, Meg 103
Roper, William 103

Rose (maid-servant, burned to death
    in Great Fire) 159
Rose (playhouse) 154
Rotherhithe 77, 81, 145, 146
Royal African Company 148
Royal Arsenal 98
Royal Charles 98
Royal College of Arms 142
Royal Exchange 126, 145, 185, 186,
    233-4
Royal Exchange Avenue 217
Royal Naval Dockyards 98-9
Royal Oak 9
Royal Society 116-7
Royal Wardrobe 62, 77, 186, 187
Rubens 169
Ruffs 163
Russell, John, First Earl of Bedford
    106

St Alban Wood Street 81, 203
St Alphage Gardens 197, 221
St Alphage London Wall 81
St Andrew, Greensted 32
St Andrew Holborn 31
St Andrew Undershaft 78, 81, 85,
    214
St Andrew's Hill 223, 238
St Anthony's Fire (ergotism) 62
St Anthony's Hospital 55, 62, 217
St Bartholomew, Priory of 45, 105
St Bartholomew the Great 82, 105
St Bartholomew the Less 82
St Bartholomew's Hospital 62, 185
St Benet Fink 30, 217
St Botolph Billingsgate 171
St Bride Fleet Street 23, 32, 106
St Clement Danes 30, 170
St Dunstan and All Saints, Stepney
    32, 145
St Dunstan-in-the-East 81, 205-9
St Dunstan-in-the-West 163
St Dunstan's Hill 205
St Ethelburga Bishopsgate 78, 81,
    216
St Etheldreda Ely 78, 82, 170
St Faith 184, 185
St George the Martyr 69

St Giles Cripplegate 77, 78, 82, 112, 129, 161
St Giles-in-the-Fields 48, 62, 129, 171
St Helen Bishopsgate 52, 75, 78, 80, 81, 159, 169, 173, 215
St James Clerkenwell 110, 111
St James Duke's Place 81
St James's Palace 115, 164, 165, 168, 172
St John, Priory of (Clerkenwell) 45, 55, 77, 82
St John Wapping 123, 169
St Katharine by the Tower 77, 81
St Katharine Cree 78, 169, 173, 214
St Katherine Coleman 81
St Lawrence Jewry 30, 203
St leonard Shoreditch 78
St Magnus the Martyr 23, 102, 135, 199, 205, 208
St Margaret Fish Street Hill 181
St Margaret Westminster 82, 167, 170, 172
St Martin-in-the-Fields 129, 170
St Martin-le-Grand 65, 77, 107
St Martin Outwich 81
St Martin Ruislip 82
St Martin Vintry 64
St Mary Aldermanbury 193
St Mary Aldermary 78, 81
St Mary-at-Hill 78, 81
St Mary-at-Lambeth 77, 78, 117
St Mary Axe (church) 215
St Mary Axe (street) 214, 215
St Mary, Priory of (Clerkenwell) 77
St Mary Graces 44, 78
St Mary-le-Bow (also known as Bow Church) 40, 77, 221-2
St Mary-le-Strand 78, 107
St Mary of Bethlehem (also known as Bethlehem Hospital or Bedlam) 62, 78, 141
St Mary Putney 123
St Mary Rotherhithe 78
St Mary Savoy 170
St Mary Spital 42, 78, 82
St Mary Stoke Newington 167, 172
St Mary Magdalene Bermondsey 78

St Matthew Friday Street 137
St Michael Cornhill 81, 218
St Michael Paternoster Royal 64
St Michael's Alley 233
St Nicholas Deptford 160
St Nicholas Olave 26
St Nicholas Shambles 107
St Olave Broad Street 26
St Olave Hart Street 26, 78, 81, 209, 215, 232
St Olave Jewry 26, 204
St Olave Rotherhithe 26
St Olave Silver Street 26, 159, 236
St Olave Southwark 26
St Pancras Old Church 22, 32
St Paul Covent Garden 169, 170, 173
St Paul Shadwell 169, 173
St Paul's Cathedral 30, 44, 49, 51, 64, 65, 68, 73, 77, 78-9, 80, 85, 128, 167-8, 169, 170, 182, 183, 184, 185, 187, 191, 192, 193, 202-3, 222-3, 237-8
St Paul's Churchyard 138, 222
(St) Paul's Cross 144, 203, 222, 236-7
St paul's School 184
St Peter-le-Poer 82
St Peter-upon-Cornhill 21, 30
St Peter Westcheap 162
St Sepulchre Newgate Street 78, 109, 130, 145, 148
St Stephen Coleman Street 193
St Stephen Walbrook 132
St Swithin London Stone 48
St Swithun's Church Gardens 219
St Thomas's Hospital 62
St Vedast-alias-Foster 196
Salisbury Court 140
Salisbury Court (theatre) 155
Salters 71
Sandys, George 139
Sandwich, Lord 127
Sanitation 59-60, 139
Savage, Jerome 154
Savoy Chapel 172
Savoy Hospital 164, 172
Savoy Palace 45, 77, 164

Saxon and Viking London 25-34, 202-6
Sayes Court 96
Scales, Baron 52
Schaseck, Wenzel 36
Scot, Thomas 127
Scrip 75
Scroop, Adrian 127
Second Anglo-Dutch War 128
Second Blackfriars Theatre 154, 159, 160
Second Defence 161
Seething Lane 229
Sergeants 65
Seven Stars 137, 173
Seymour, Jane 106
Shadwell 15, 146
Shakespeare, William 50, 116, 143, 158, 159-60, 161
Shakespeare's House 238
Shambles 70
Sherborne Lane 5
Sheriff (Shire-Reeve) 52, 64, 110, 142
Shoe Lane 162
Shoes 76
Shooters Hill 11, 56
Shoreditch 154, 159
Shrewsbury Tumulus 11
Shrove Tuesday Riots 156
Sidney, Philip 159
Silk Route 69
Six Articles 102
Skinners 71
Slaves, slave trade 19, 29, 63, 148
Smeaton, Mark 101
Smith, John, Captain 148
Smith panorama 171
Social History 16-9, 27-9, 53-76, 132-64
Somerset, Duke of, Protector 80, 106, 165
Somerset House 114, 164, 165
Southampton, Earl of 116
Southwark 10, 14, 16, 17, 23, 30, 50, 56, 62, 68, 72, 109, 112, 116, 126, 129, 141, 151, 154, 155, 159, 182, 183

Southwark Cathedral 30, 74, 77, 78, 82, 104-5
Sovereign of the Seas 98
Spanish Armada 99, 112, 114-5
Spencer, Gabriel 145
Spenser, Edmund 159
Spert, Thomas 145
Spice Route 67
Spital Square 121
Spitalfields 16, 101, 121, 140, 187
Standard (Cheapside) 58
Standwich, John 45
Staple Inn Buildings 172
Star Inn 181
Stationers, Stationers' Company, Hall 162
Steelyard 62, 70, 147
Stephen, King 38
Stepney 129, 130
Stews (brothels) 73
Stocks Market 70
Stockton, John 52
Stone, Nicholas 173
Stoop, Dir(c)k 126
Stow, John 13, 80, 94, 95, 150
Strand 30, 137, 142, 173
Stratford 10
Straw, John 45
Street layout 21, 31, 81, 171
Strode, William 119
Strong, Edward 193
Strong, Thomas 193
Stuart History 116-32
Sudbury, Simon, Archbishop 45
Sumptuary Laws 75, 76
Sun (printing house) 162
Surgical operations 61, 140
Survay of London 96
Surviving structures 21-2, 31-3, 81-91, 172-8
Susan Constant 148
Sutton, Thomas 105, 168
Sutton House 168, 173
Swan (playhouse) 154
Swan Alley 128
Sweating Sickness 140
Synagogues 133, 134, 232
Syon Abbey 55, 102, 106, 139

Tabard (Inn) 58
Tabard Street 56
Tacitus 15
Tallis, Thomas 159
Tamburlaine the Great 160
Taswell, William 187
Taverner, John 159
Taverns 137
Taxatio Ecclesiastica 54
Taylor, William 48
Tea, teahouses 137, 138
Tempest, The 160
Temple 66, 74, 183, 184
Temple Church 41, 77, 78, 82, 170
Temple of Diana 20
Temple of Isis 20
Temple of Mithras (Mithraeum) 17, 20, 22, 23
Ten Articles 102
Tenure of Kings and Magistrates 161
Tetzel, Gabriel 36
Thames 9, 12, 13, 14, 16, 18, 20, 56, 57, 59, 70, 72, 73, 91, 99, 115, 135, 137, 180, 200
Thames Street 181, 199, 205, 208, 211, 228
Theatre, The (Shoreditch) 154, 159
Theatre Royal 155
Thedmar, Arnald 35
Theomantius 13
Thorney Island 31
Thornhill, James 193
Threadneedle Street 128, 217
Throckmorton, Elizabeth 114
Tilbury Fort 99, 115
Tillison, John 131
Tilney, Edmund 157
Timon of Athens 160
Titus Andronicus 160
Tobacco 114, 137, 140, 180
Torrigiano 16
Tothill Bridewell (Prison) 69, 151
Tothill Fields 137
Tower Hill 22, 68, 81, 102, 122, 127-8, 144, 186, 204, 214, 232
Tower Menagerie 72, 151

Tower of London 40, 41, 45, 47, 50, 52, 53, 56, 63, 72, 76, 77, 80, 81, 100, 103, 109, 114, 116, 130, 132, 151, 164, 166, 211-2, 229
Tower, Ward 62, 150
Trade and Commerce 18-9, 29, 69-79, 145-9
Tradescant, John, Jr. 117
Tradescant, John, Sr. 117
Trafalgar Square 9
Trained bands 100, 121
Treaty of Lambeth 41
Treaty of London 114
Treswell, Ralph 169
Trevelyan 125
Troilus and Criseyde 74
Troynovant 13
Tudor and Stuart London 93-180, 225-39
Tudor History 97-116
Tudor Street 59
Turner, Mr 139
Turner, Mrs 140
Turnham Green 122
Twelfth Night 143, 154
Tyburn (river) 58
Tyburn (site of execution) 48, 68, 69, 97, 102, 144, 145
Tyler, Wat 45
Tyranny, The 47

Ulster Plantation 146
Undershaft 72, 151
Ursewyk, Thomas 53
Utopia 103
Uxbridge 10

Valor Ecclestiacus 104
Van Dyck, Anthony 159
Vane, Harry 127, 144
Vauxhall 10, 14, 117
Vegetus 19
Venetians (breeches) 112
Venner, Thomas, Venner's Rebellion 128
Vertue, Robert 167
Vertue, William 167

Victoria and Albert Museum 23, 168
Vikings, Viking London 25-34
Villiers, George, 1st Duke of
  Buckingham 170
Villiers, George, Jr., 2nd Duke of
  Buckingham 170
Vintners 71
Vintry 70
Virginia 113, 146, 149
Virginia Company 148
Visscher panorama 171
Volpone (play) 161
Von Wesel 51

Waggoner 182
Walbrook (river) 15, 16, 18, 20, 23,
  59, 72
Walbrook (street) 20, 22, 23, 198,
  219
Walbrook (ward) 150
Waldstein, Baron 166
Walker, Edward 170
Walker, Robert 96
Wallace, William 43, 68
Walsingham, Francis 115
Walworth, William 45
Wapping 123, 145, 158
Warbeck, Perkin 144
Ward, John 52
Wardrobe Place 223
Warkworth's Chronicle 52
Wars of the Roses 50-3, 78
Warwick, Earl of 51, 52
Warwick Lane 183
Water supply 57-8, 64, 135-7
Waterloo 14
Watling Street 15, 21, 56, 183, 196
Wealth and Poverty 71-2, 150-1
Weaver, Hugh 144
Webster, John 118, 159
Welsh Revolt 47
Wentworth, Thomas, Earl of
  Strafford 119
West, Frances 131
West, Simon 162
West India Quay 180

West Smithfield 43, 44, 45, 48, 68,
  72, 103, 109, 110, 111, 144,
  151, 184
Westminster 14, 25, 30, 31, 62, 64,
  66, 69, 70, 77, 81, 82, 107, 117,
  122, 129, 130, 142, 151, 162,
  164, 170, 173
Westminster Abbey 31, 32, 37, 42,
  43, 49, 55, 58, 65, 74, 78, 80,
  82, 111, 126, 127, 143, 167
Westminster Hall 42, 47, 77, 80, 82
Westminster Palace Yard 114
Westminster School 65
Westminster Tournament Roll 142
Weston, Francis 101
Whalley 26
Whitechapel 154
Whitefriars 126
Whitefriars Priory 78, 82, 105
Whitefriars Theatre 155
Whitehall 120, 124, 126, 130, 142,
  183
Whitehall Palace 118, 142, 164,
  166, 168, 172
Whittington, Dick 64, 69
Wig and Pen 137, 173
Wildfire 52
William Charter 38
William Longbeard 39-40
William I 37, 38, 56
William II 38
Willoughby, Hugh 112
Wimbledon Common 12
Wimple 75
Winchester Palace 78
Wine 58
Winter's Tale, The 160
Wolsey, Thomas, Cardinal 100, 166
Women 27, 33, 68, 74, 76, 132
Wood Street 162
Woodford, Thomas 155
Woodford, Oliver 154
Woolwich 98
Wotton, Henry 155
Wren, Christopher 70, 159, 169,
  189, 191, 192, 193
Wriothesley, Charles 84

Wriothesley, Thomas 103
Wroth, Mary 159
Wyatt, Thomas the Elder 101
Wyatt, Thomas the Younger, Wyatt's
    Rebellion 108-9
Wyngaerde panorama 171

Yersinia pestis 44, 60
Yevele, Henry 80
York House 169, 173
York House Water-Gate 173
York Place 166

Zouch, Abraham 145